Flowers
When You
Want Them

Flowers When You Want Them

A GROWER'S GUIDE
TO OUT-OF-SEASON BLOOM

John James

Learn a lesson from the way
the wild flowers grow.

Matthew

HAWTHORN BOOKS, INC.
Publishers/New York

Line Drawings by the Author

In loving memory of

my wife, Harriet,

my sister, Ann,

and my father.

They loved flowers.

Contents

Preface

Who? What? When? Where? Why? And sometimes how?

Years ago, these questions were etched into the mind of every newspaper cub reporter. The opening of every news story had to answer these key questions. We still have that etching.

We will start with "what." Our subject is flower forcing. Forcing is a technique to cause a plant to bloom at a time other than its natural flowering period. Through the use of this technique, we can have poinsettias for Christmas, pussy willows in February, lilies for Easter, and chrysanthemums at any time.

Why write a book about forcing? Simply because a good thing is hard to keep. We florists want to share—and pleasure shared is pleasure doubled. God must have created the world for much the same reason. The sun shares its goodness in light and heat. A flower shares its perfume.

Forcing can be a fun project. It can be rewarding as a hobby, or it can be commercially profitable. It provides an opportunity for learning and creativity. It is both a science and an art. An exquisite, well-grown flower is in reality as much a creation as one on canvas. And the accomplishment of that creation requires information for the solution of complex problems.

Unlike so many changes made today, in forcing flowers there is no ecological change—no harm to the environment. We make no permanent change in Nature's laws or ways. She simply allows us temporarily to manipulate some growing factors. When we stop, everything reverts to normal.

The truth expressed in Ecclesiastes still applies: "To everything there is a season, and a time to every purpose under heaven: a time to be born, and a time to die; a time to plant, and a time to pluck up that which has been planted."

Forcing may be a mystery. Even though you are not an avid gardener, you may have wondered how florists get flowers to bloom at different times of the year. This is written for your curiosity, so that after reading you can say, "So that's how they do it."

But I address my attention chiefly to plant growers— amateur, professional, and commercial. I hope that the grower of a single plant will find as much of interest here as the greenhouse grower. For the difference between the small grower and the large is comparable to the difference between home cooking and cooking for a large institution. It lies in the amount more than in the ingredients. In the buttering one uses pounds while the other uses pats. But whether pound or pat, the ingredient must be mixed in at the right time and in the proper fashion to get the result desired.

I have striven to present information and suggestions in a basic nuts-and-bolts style, similar to instructions in a manual or recipes in a cookbook. Here and there, this may lead to choppy reading, but it should enable you to get the information you want fast.

Mostly we will deal in straight facts, but sprinkled among them will be opinions. This is especially true with plant variety recommendations. You may argue with them. They are given simply to provide you with a starting point. From where I take you here, you can branch off to other varieties that perform better for you.

I do not "think metric," and I suspect that most gardeners do not. So I have not used the metric scale. I have used "handfuls," "potfuls," "gallons," and "bushels." For those of you who do follow the metric system—and I envy you—there is a practical conversion table in the appendix.

Temperatures given will always be in Fahrenheit. Light readings will be in footcandles.

In plant lists or when referring to plant names, I use the most common name first, regardless of whether it is Latin or English. Very few know what a rose-moss is, but they recognize the name portulaca. However, the Latin name will always be given, and the authority is L. H. Bailey's *Manual of Cultivated Plants* (New York: Macmillan, Inc.; revised edition 1949).

The arrangement of material into chapters is purely arbitrary. One big chapter on forcing plants would be too unwieldy, so it seemed reasonable to group plants into smaller units based on their chief use. Actually, there are no sharp dividing lines; some of the plants in the chapter on cut flowers will also make good pot plants, and many plants recommended as pot flowers can be cut for vases and floral arrangements.

We have not gone into plant problems. That is not our realm. Chances are that if you keep things clean and sterilized—including the soil—you will not have many problems. Should some problem arise, the basic information provided in almost every standard book on houseplants will serve to enable you to deal with it or avoid it a second time around.

If you live in the Sun Belt rather than in the Snow Belt, you will need to make some adjustment to the dates given. Even in controlled conditions, it may be necessary to cut seven days from your growing time and, in some cases, to light or shade several days sooner or later. You will soon learn to judge the readiness of your plants and make allowances. The dates given refer to average conditions in the mid-Temperate Zone.

Because of wide variations in climate, location, and individual needs, I cannot be specific in recommending growing equipment or facilities. Most indoor gardeners already have a wide choice of equipment to help them—fluorescent lights, window bays, lighted plant shelves, and home greenhouses. Millions of persons have discovered that it is not difficult to grow plants around the house—indoors and out. The same equipment they now use for other gardening purposes can be used for forcing plants.

It is in about November that we start missing the flowers we had outdoors all summer. We begin to wish for some fresh cut flowers or some cheerful flowering plants. This yearning goes on all winter. It is a mark of culture, an innate desire for fine things as well as necessities. This is the gap that forcing flowers into bloom can fill. And since the need for flowers is acute in late fall, winter, and early spring—the normally flowerless periods—I will concentrate on this period with my forcing recommendations.

Although foliage plants are popular, instruction for growing them is beyond my scope. This is also the case for plants that are virtually everblooming. Plant hunters and hybridizers have given us some excellent everblooming tropical plants. They are beautiful. I am very fond of them and grow them. But since they are not forced, I exclude them from my discussion. I would love to tell you about my gesneriads and orchids, but that is not my purpose.

Besides, the exotic flowers cannot completely take the place of the familiar favorites—the spring, summer, and fall garden flowers. If only they would bloom in winter!

They can and they will. It may be a challenge in many cases, but it is my purpose to help you have these seasonal flowers out of season.

We are going to do uncommon things with common flowers—friendly flowers you know. You know them so well that you hardly notice them in the garden—until you miss them when they are gone. They are flowers that we term "ordinary"—marigolds, petunias, and zinnias, for example.

Have you ever seen a zinnia in bloom in wintertime? Thumbelina zinnias in a little pot on a kitchen windowsill cannot be matched by even the most exotic plants.

Have you ever had your bedroom brightened by a pot of sunny marigolds? Or had petunias in your sun-room—a showy mass of exquisite flowers spilling out of their containers and evoking comments from all who visit your home?

These are among the plants with which we will concern

ourselves—old friends in new surroundings. However, I will also treat many other plants, including some exotic varieties, that can be forced.

Some of the methods for growing and forcing plants in new surroundings and seasons are relatively new—many have been developed during my lifetime—and consequently we growers do not have the answers to all forcing questions. You will have to pioneer and be creative as well, adapting the general principles given here to your specific conditions.

As you do this, keep notes. In our greenhouses, we kept clipboards at each flower bed and recorded everything we did—fertilizing, watering, pinching, pruning, and cutting. Memory is a slippery thing and lets facts get away. Next year, should you want to duplicate a procedure, chances are you won't remember if you have provided yourself no memory aid.

I've given you some idea of *what* I am going to cover and *how* I am going to do it. I've talked about *where* and *when* we want the plants to bloom: in your home in winter. And as for *whom* this is written, obviously it is for you.

In our time, my wife and I spent many close and happy hours together working with plants. I sincerely hope that your time spent with them will be as pleasant.

May the time of your life with flowers be filled with gladness, and may you look back as I do now, filled with the excitement and wonder of it all. My sincere thanks for your interest.

I have many other people to thank, too—those who have touched my life and enriched it—many of whom are no longer with me.

I am most appreciative to friends and neighbors whose many kind deeds helped to save time for me when I was working late. A grateful nod goes to the United States Department of Agriculture for adding so much to our knowledge of forcing, to the Horticulture School of Ohio State University for their contributions and for their fine short summer courses for growers, and to flower and seed developers and suppliers—especially George Ball Company, Yoder's, Gloeckner's, and George Park Seed Company.

Finally, I was somewhat hesitant about writing this book. If it helps you in any way, I am pleased. My special thanks for the help I had with it go to Nancy Schneider for preparing the material and to Robert Oskam for his editorial judgment.

Truly, no man is an island. Nor does he reach alone for the stars, but stands firmly on the shoulders of others.

Avon, Ohio
September 1977

Flowers
When You
Want Them

Introduction

The flowers appear on the earth;
the time of the singing of birds is come. . .

The Song of Solomon

You can have flowers at will—flowers whenever you want them—by planning ahead and forcing plants into bloom. Forcing is a simple process—if you know *what* to do and *when* to do it. It's a matter of knowledge and timing—knowing a plant's flowering needs and then supplying these needs on schedule. For example, the poinsettia you carried over from last Christmas can be made to bloom during the coming Christmas season by controlling the light to which the plant is exposed in October. Or a garden lily, if properly cooled and stored in fall, can be made to bloom at Eastertime.

Do you want a specific flowering plant for a special birthday touch? Or for an anniversary? Chances are that whatever you want can be forced to bloom for the special time you want it.

Or perhaps you would like to have a year-round succession of cut flowers? You can. Because my wife loved cut flowers, I continually have fresh flowers in my home in her memory. This is made possible, especially in winter, through forcing.

Maybe you have a home greenhouse that you want to keep

bright with out-of-season blooms. Or you may want to grow some unusual types of pot flowers in your home. Forcing makes this possible.

Flowers fit in anywhere at any time. But a special flower for a special purpose at a special time carries an extra touch of warmth and meaning. Forcing allows you to express this sentiment.

And forcing can be fun. It provides an additional element of interest and skill to growing plants and flowers. It extends your horizons. It adds to your other green-thumb abilities.

Forcing is cooperating with nature. In this, there are three basic steps involved: getting plants, getting plants to grow, and getting plants to flower. We'll cover each step in detail for most of the popular flowers. And I'll keep my instructions simple and practical.

But before we get into the "how," we need to review our knowledge of plants—to develop an empathy with them.

It is almost unbelievable the number of stumbling blocks that nature can throw in our way. Seeds will refuse to sprout, plants will refuse to grow, flowers will refuse to form—until certain specific conditions are met. We need to know something about these conditions in order to cope with them—in order to cooperate with nature's requirements.

The first requisite for forcing is knowledge of what makes a flower flower. Most plants have amazing botanical time clocks. This in itself is a fascinating subject. The deeper we delve into it, the more we discover about this aspect of nature's processes, the more astonishing it becomes.

On the heels of the first spring thaw, the early wildflowers bloom. The maple trees and the witch hazel blossom, and they are followed by a succession of other flowering plants—the dusty roadside flowers of summer, the asters and goldenrod of fall, and finally, sometimes covered by the first snows of early winter, the hardy chrysanthemums end the flowering season. Each plant blooms in its time. Even tropical plants bloom in their season, wet or dry.

Suppose all plants bloomed at one time. How dull the remainder of the year would be! We even resent the lack of

bloom just in the wintertime, so we grow our tropical indoor plants and force other plants to bloom out of season.

Why does a flower flower when it does? What mysterious forces send the daffodils and the spring beauties into bloom, but not the daisies at the same time? We have developed some practical methods for growing flowers, and we have devised some techniques to bring them into bloom when we want them. But beyond that, our knowledge is sparse indeed. When we work with any part of the flowering process, we work with the unknown. We follow certain procedures that cause flowering, but more from observation than from understanding. We know that if we do this, something will happen. But for the most part, why it happens still eludes us.

Nature has endowed plants with a series of checks and counterchecks, reactions and balances, catalysts and regulators—all designed to keep the plant on a life schedule that will ensure its survival. We're still learning about this. Much of the process is still unknown. But we ought to be aware of what is known.

So we will try to venture a short way into the mysterious world of flowering, not only because it is interesting but also because it helps to have some basic knowledge whenever we run into problems or want to try something new. Our excursion may also point out how little we think about, and know about, many of the common occurrences around us. To a student, it may show how vast the frontiers of science still are. We tend to be complacent—especially with plants. Everything is known. Opportunity no longer exists, youth tells us. Yet the challenges to young people entering into research are many and varied. What makes a flower? If we knew that, we could feed the world. We could make flowers at will, seeds at will, grain at will.

Even though our understanding of the flowering process is limited, our practical knowledge is extensive. We know a great number of ways to make plants flower. Some of these techniques may be called "growers' secrets." But they are not, they are nature's secrets. We will share these together. I will go into some detail so that you can select the knowledge you can use and adapt to fit your interests. And regardless of whether you grow a lot of plants for profit or a few plants for fun, it is our hope that you will find a new idea on every page.

We repeat: Even though there are marvelous and intricate processes involved in forcing plants, forcing itself is simple. And I will keep it so. When I refer to a specific plant you may want to force into bloom, I will try to be clear and concise in my directions. And I will try to set up fairly accurate time schedules for you to follow.

This book can't include every plant suitable for forcing. But that will leave some room for you to experiment. I will cover the flowering plants my experience shows to be most popular. Plants are like people. You favor some persons and avoid others. In the same way, you undoubtedly have several flowering plants that you favor—some that you like and some that you don't. You select the ones in which you are especially interested. Chances are the species discussed here will include most of your favorites. And the information on forcing techniques should give you courage to experiment with plants not specifically covered.

On the other side of the coin, there are flowers that favor us and others that don't. While some flowering plants will so respond to your set of growing conditions that you can do nothing wrong with them, others will not respond.

My problem flowers are asters. My wife preferred them. Some of my friends can throw aster seeds on the ground and end up with a beautiful crop. But for me, growing them is a fight all the way. For me, even with the utmost care, the seedling will drop over with damp rot, the plants will be wasted by "yellows," and then the remaining greenery stripped bare by pests. But I still anticipate a day when, presto, beautiful asters!

The point is that you may have trouble with certain plants regardless of what you do. Be consoled that you are not alone. There's the guy who can't grow asters.

In regard to the many other plants that do respond, I've been asked whether I talk to them. When I ran a commercial greenhouse, I did, but what I said turned the air blue and should have stunted their growth. It didn't. I did pipe music into the greenhouses, and it helped. But I think it was because it put the high school boys who worked for me after school in a better mood. Consequently they handled the plants better.

Personally, I prefer silence. A quiet greenhouse, with its riot of eye-pleasing color and variety of nose-pleasing fragrances does not need sound. It is a peaceful and even awe-inspiring place. In the evening, when the day's activity is done, the feeling is somewhat akin to that of being in a cathedral.

I've always felt that the fact that a commercial grower has to make a living from his plants doesn't mean he can't enjoy them too. But then, I relate to plants. I can look at the beauty in a single flower and be fascinated. Even as a youngster, I would slough through wet snow in spring to search for the first hepaticas on the north-hill slope of our woodlot. And I choose to live with flowers indoors.

More and more people are coming to understand the decorative assets of flowers. The sight of a flowering pot plant on a window ledge is a joy. And fresh cut flowers in a room bring a touch of elegance that no expensive bric-a-brac can equal. A splash of vivid color in a bouquet can brighten a dreary room. Gracefully arranged plants can soften and im-

prove severe architectural lines. Even businesses are beginning to realize this. It is always a pleasure to enter a lobby
such as that of the Alcoa Building in Pittsburgh and see the
display of tropical and foliage plants growing there.

And there's a personal reward in growing, selecting, and arranging flowers for the home. So many of the things about us
are mass-produced. But when you arrange flowers yourself,
you alone have selected and placed them in a design that is
uniquely yours. You touch it with the magic of your personal-
ity and create new beauty. To my wife, such flower arranging
came naturally. My function was simply to enjoy them—
which I did and now sorely miss.

Flower arranging is not within the realm of forcing plants.
But the care and keeping of cut flowers and pot plants is. So I
will focus on the performance you can expect in your home
from your own forced potted flowering plants or those you
have bought or been given. This may help you to answer questions your friends may ask about the plants you give them. But
more important, it may help you to decide if you want to grow
and force a particular plant. Will its performance justify the
effort?

I will then go on to the cutting of flowers you may have
forced—or grown in your garden. The same cutting techniques
apply in both cases. Consequently, in any season, this book
can serve as a reference for when to cut and what to do.

In reviewing forcing techniques, I will start out with some
easy plants to force—dormant branches. Next, I will speak of
plants to grow and force, which means that I will be discussing
seeds and cuttings. And finally, I will tell you how forcing
itself is done—how to force flowers for any date or holiday
you want. In most cases, I will be able to give you only the
broad details; you will have to supply the creative ingenuity to
adapt the techniques to your own situation and method of
operation.

Forcing is not cut and dried. A lot of *you* has to go into it.

1
What Makes Flowers Flower?

Little flower—but if I could understand
What you are, root and all, and all in all,
I should know what God and man is.

Alfred Lord Tennyson

It is said that in creation, whenever God wanted to conceal something wonderful, he would make it commonplace. Sunlight is one of these wonders. And so are plants.

Consider the flowering plant you have on your windowsill. The sunlight streams in and touches it. It grows. This happens every day, and yet here, to paraphrase Shakespeare, are wonders undreamed of in your philosophy, Horatio!

Take photosynthesis, for example. We're all somewhat familiar with this process through which plants capture and convert the energy of sunlight into the energy of food. Yet, if we think about it, in this process the plants act as specialized organisms utilizing the radiation power of a millions-of-miles-distant star. The tremendous power carried by a beam of sunlight is harnessed by a tiny living plant cell and changed into energy-giving sugar. David has subdued Goliath and put him to work, to use a most inadequate metaphor.

Through photosynthesis, plants transform the sun's radiant energy into a form that is ultimately used to sustain all life on earth—plant and animal. All life depends upon this one process. It also is the source of all the energy we derive from coal, oil, and natural gas. You and I can be here only because that plant on your windowsill and billions of others like it have the capability of photosynthesis.

We know photosynthesis exists, and we know something of the process—we have a working model in every plant—and yet, with all our scientific and technical know-how, we have not yet been able to duplicate it.

Let's briefly review what is known of this intricate and fascinating process, that goes on within each of the plants with which we work. Whenever I think about it, I can't help but marvel at it, and experience renewed respect for this planet's other, nonanimal form of life.

In the process of photosynthesis, three separate systems are needed: a system to receive the light, another to transfer it, and still another to change it. The process is somewhat comparable to that by which raw material enters a manufacturing plant and is conveyed to a machine that will process it. Reception, transfer, change.

The *chlorophyll* molecule—the green stuff in a plant—is the receiving system. Light striking the molecule excites one of its electrons. This excitement is transferred along a chain of molecules to an ultimate recipient—a molecule that receives the accumulated energy. There are about five hundred chlorophyll molecules to one energy-trapping molecule. This last acts as a "sink," storing the energy until it is sufficient to split a water molecule into hydrogen and oxygen and thus form an electron-rich compound. In the process, oxygen is given off as a waste product.

It is mostly because of release of this waste product that the earth's atmosphere contains the oxygen essential for all animal life. Not only do we depend upon the plant for the bread of life but also for the breath of life.

A small amount of oxygen is reused by the plant. It also needs carbon dioxide, which we, and all animals, help to supply. Within the energy-rich compound of the "sink" cell, oxygen enters into a reaction with carbon dioxide and water to form a sugar. Solar energy has been converted into food.

It is only within recent years that scientists grasped this

broad outline of photosynthesis. There still is much to be learned.

As magnificent and essential as photosynthesis is, that beam of light striking your window plant is also involved in another amazing phenomenon—photoperiodism.

Photoperiodism is a sensitivity to periods of light and dark; the number of hours of daylight we have and the number of hours of darkness at night.

In the Northern Hemisphere, the farther south we go, that is, toward the southern latitudes of the United States or Europe, the more equal the length of the nights and days throughout the year. In the Southern Hemisphere, this tendency to equality between night and day occurs northward toward the equator. But in the northern areas of the Northern Hemisphere and in the southern areas of the Southern Hemisphere—the northern United States, Canada, and northern Europe; southern Australia, southern Africa, and southern South America—there are great variations in the proportion of hours of daylight to darkness during different seasons of the year. This is due to the variation in tilt of the earth as it travels around the sun.

While fishing in northern Minnesota during midsummer, I experienced nights when it never became totally dark; the night was so short that dusk merged into dawn. There were beautiful long, lingering sunsets, as if the daylight were reluctant to depart.

In her scheme of things, for temperate regions nature has fashioned plants that are attuned to a cycle of short nights and long days in spring and summer that give way to the long nights and short days of fall and winter. These plants have adapted their schedule of growth, flowering, and reproduction to the day-length/night-length cycle. Taken away from it, they will not flower or reproduce.

You may have experienced a side-effect of this phenomenon. As a gardener on tour, you may have been attracted to some beautiful flowering plant. You may have taken it home and planted it in your garden. To your disappointment, it never produced anything more than shoots and leaves. The day-night length may have been responsible.

We only learned about the effect of photoperiodism a few

years ago. Two scientists in the U.S. Department of Agriculture, W. W. Garner and H. A. Allard, ran into a problem with tobacco they were growing near Washington, D.C. It flowered so late in the season that its seed could not mature. They explored a number of possible causes for the late flowering before they hit upon day length. At the time the plants should have flowered to produce mature seeds before frost, the days were too long and the nights too short in Washington. They discovered that this variety of tobacco would begin to form flowers only when the days were between ten and twelve hours long. However, in Washington, that short a day didn't occur until late in summer. Even though the plant was ready to flower earlier, it would not bloom until it received a short-day stimulus.

The scientists then tested other plants to confirm their discovery. The results were amazing. They found that plants fell into three general catagories in their reactions to day length: short-day, long-day, and indeterminate. The indeterminate plants were not choosy as to the length of day.

The discovery of photoperiodism gave us many answers to botanical puzzles: why plants when planted at different times will flower at the same time; why plants flourish in some latitudes and are practically absent from others; why we do not have daffodils in July, asters in April, or goldenrod in May.

Further investigations into photoperiodism and its effect on flowering have resulted in some interesting discoveries. Spinach, to the delight of some youngsters, will not reproduce itself in the tropics because it must receive fourteen hours of light each day for two weeks in order to flower. Ragweed, hay fever sufferers should know, will not thrive in northern Maine. It normally starts its flowering process when the day is fourteen and a half hours long and blooms in the middle of August. In Maine the long summer days do not shorten to fourteen and a half hours until August. Buds started then cannot flower and produce mature seeds before a killing frost. On the other side of the coin, sedum (*Sedum Telephium*), which needs a day of sixteen hours or more, flowers beautifully in New England gardens but will not flower in Virginia or Tennessee or points south.

Plants are not alone in their reactions to photoperiodism.

Animals, too, have developed mechanisms that respond to the daily cycle of light and darkness. This sensitivity, photo-periodism, prompts the suspended animation of insects, the hibernation of mammals, and the nesting and migration of birds. Man's sensitivity to the day length shows in the unease he feels when his cycle of day and night is disrupted, as when he travels by jet a considerable distance in latitude. Since these cycles have predictable regularity, they have been termed *biological clocks* or, in the case of plants, *botanical clocks.*

The sensitivity of plants to variations in the length of day and night is put to practical use in forcing them to flower. A chrysanthemum, for example, responds to the increased length of night as fall approaches. Its botanical clock tells it to get ready to flower. And it does. However, if we provide ar-tificial light in order to extend the day and shrink the night, the plant will not flower. According to its botanical clock, long days and short nights are for summer growth, not for flowering. Based on this responsiveness, chrysanthemum growers have worked out complete programs that depend upon day–night lengths to force chrysanthemums to flower out of season.

Researchers have discovered that even a few minutes of illumination, interrupting a plant's nighttime period of darkness, affects the plant's flowering. When a short-day plant such as a chrysanthemum is illuminated in the middle of the night during its flower-forming season, it fails to bloom. On the other hand, a long-day plant such as pyrethrum can be made to flower in a short-day season by exposing it to light for a short time at night.

Obviously the critical factor in photoperiodism is not length of day but length of night. To be accurate, plants should be classified as *long-night* and *short-night* rather than *short-day* and *long-day.* But they are not. So now, whereas growers used to illuminate chrysanthemums from nearly dusk to almost midnight to get a long day, they now limit illumination to a few hours in the middle of the night. Evidently, whatever the process is that causes flowering within the plant goes on at night.

What is this master switch that changes the plant's activity from one of producing stems and leaves to one of making blooms, turning it from adolescent growth to adult reproduction? If we understood this mechanism that initiates plant flowering, through a wiser cooperation with nature, we could make great forward strides in our efforts to feed the world and to beautify it.

Home gardeners and greenhousemen were first to discover a range of techniques to force plants into bloom to meet deadlines. They did it without fanfare, through skillful manipulation not only of light but also of temperature, water, and nutrition. They discovered how, but not why. The biological process, the internal motivating factors that transform a plant from one that is foliage producing to one that is flower producing remained a mystery.

Scientists have also turned their attention to the second of two effective mechanisms that amateur gardeners and flower growers use to force plants into bloom—temperature. In the 1920s, noting the success that gardeners had with precooled bulbs, a German scientist, Gustav Gassner, discovered that he could influence the flowering of cereal plants by controlling the temperature of the germinating seeds. He experimented with winter rye. If planted in spring, winter rye will remain vegetative and will not flower throughout the growing season. However, if planted in fall, it will flower and produce grain. Gassner discovered that when the seeds are held at near freezing temperatures during germination, even though planted late in spring, the plants will flower and produce grain. He called the process *vernalization*. We call it simply *the cold requirement*. Hybridizers have used it for years. It is the only way to get rose seeds to grow, for example.

Further research has revealed these facts: that the process is reversible; that there is a critical period for effectiveness; and that substandard undernourished seeds cannot be vernalized—all of which we were aware of in our garden work.

There is now a theory that flowering depends upon the formation of a specific substance in the plant—a reproductive hormone or auxin-type stimulant.

What is this chemical basis for flowering? Why does a plant

start to flower? What changes a plant from producing vegetative growth to reproductive growth?

We know that with temperate-zone plants the main en-
vironmental factors that trigger or control flowering are
temperature and light. Day length is particularly important.
We know that some plants need long days and short nights to
start flowering, and others need short days and long nights.
We now suspect that the change-over to flowering is caused by
some substance produced by the plant's leaves, and that it is
then transported to the growing tips. This substance has not
been identified, but we have good evidence that it exists. And
we know that it is produced in the leaves because, when we
remove the leaves after the critical dark period for short-day
plants, the plants will not flower. Control plants with leaves
will.

We also know that the night length for short-day plants must
be continuous—if interrupted by a period of light at midnight,
the plants will not flower. So obviously light is involved, and
because light is involved we know that some pigment to absorb that light must be involved.

Through experiments, it has been discovered that light in
the orange-red part of the spectrum—particularly a wave-
length of 660 nanometers—is most effective in preventing
flowering. From this we deduce that the light-receiving
pigment within the plant is blue-green, the complementary
reflected color to the absorbed orange-red.

The exposure to orange-red light that stops flowering in
some plants is reversible. If shortly after exposure to light at
660 nanometers, the plants are exposed to light near the far
red (730 nanometers), they will flower. (The kalanchoe is
especially sensitive to this experiment.) From this we deduce
that the pigment involved reacts chemically in a different way
in absorbing orange-red light than in absorption of far-red
light. And that one reaction reverses the other.

Since sunlight has more orange-red than far-red light, we
suspect that the additional amount of orange-red absorbed
over the day length must be a factor. We also suspect that the
reaction to this absorption takes place at night and that the

night length controls this reaction. Experiments have indicated that this seems to happen. A cocklebur plant requires more than eight hours of night to flower. Given nine hours, it will flower, but slowly. However, when the dark period is extended, the bud develops more rapidly.

What can we deduce? One obvious conclusion is that the plant synthesizes the flowering hormone in the late stages of the dark period. The longer the darkness, the more hormone it can synthesize and the faster the bud will develop. But this happens only up to a point. We cannot prolong the darkness indefinitely. After twelve to fourteen hours, there is a reverse effect of diminishing returns, and after twenty hours the hormone is destroyed. Obviously, light is needed to stop the process in the leaves that destroys the hormone and to fix the molecule. And light is also needed to increase the flow of plant juices in the process of transporting the hormone from the leaves to the growing tip.

At the growing tip, the hormone acts upon the cells in some way to transform them from vegetative to flowering growth—instead of leaves a bud develops.

This is but a sketchy outline of the flowering process as we know it. It reveals the existence of an intricate and precise control system in part triggered by the cycle of light and darkness. There is a temperature-sensitive control system, and there are controls sensitive to moisture and/or its absence. We are slowly uncovering the workings of these mysterious forces. Just knowing that they exist is a big step forward.

Although we still have many missing pieces to the puzzle of the flowering process, we think we have an idea of what happens. But we still do not *know* what really happens. We still are far short of solving the mystery of what makes plants flower. Until we do solve it, until we truly know and understand the flowering process, we will have to continue with the practical methods we now use to force plants into bloom without always knowing exactly why they are effective.

2
Forcing Tools
and Techniques

What is needed to force flowers into bloom? What kind of equipment do you have to have? What are the tools and techniques for forcing?

All you need to force pussy willows is a vase and some water—simple equipment. If you are already growing flowers, for the most part what you already have will serve fine. To it you can add a sheet of black cloth. The other equipment you need depends upon what kind of plant, and how many of them, you want to grow.

None of the items mentioned below are specifically forcing equipment. They are standard for any type of gardening. So are the knives, cutters, trowels, pots, flats, and other "tools" you will need. Possibly the only different things you may want are thermometers, a string of lights or lights on stands, an electric-timer light switch, and the piece of black cloth for shading. And a hand mister if you do not have one. The rest of the materials discussed in this chapter may be considered optional. They add a further dimension to working with plants, but they are not requisite for indoor gardening or forcing.

It would be nice if we all had fully equipped greenhouses, but lacking that, there is nothing wrong with a sun-room, a window bay, a specially lighted area in the basement, a lighted flower cart, or windowsills.

BRACE

A window bay, home-built or prefabricated, is ideal for service as a greenhouse area for the indoor gardener.

A surprising number of Americans do have greenhouses, and you can do wonders in them, forcing all types of plants to bloom when you want them to do so. Home greenhouses have helped make many of us year-round gardeners. Where once they were exclusive to the wealthy, there are now several million home greenhouses across the land. They have been popular in Europe for years. They range from simple window bays to elaborate heated walk-ins. Some use traditional glass; others plastic.

One of the best home greenhouses costs less than the average car. Even with inflated utility prices, it can cost less to maintain than a car.

If you are handy with tools, home greenhouses are available as kits, and you can put them up yourself at considerable savings. A typical backyard size is 8 by 12 feet, although they start as small as 4 by 8 feet. The size to have depends upon the number of plants you intend to grow, the space you want to have, and what you can afford.

Greenhouses come in two basic types: lean-to and free-standing. The lean-to shares one of its sides with the home or garage. The freestanding unit may also be attached to a building, but more often it is off by itself. Supplying heat, water, and electricity to a lean-to or attached unit is usually easier and less costly than to a remote unit. In any case, the cost of operating a home greenhouse is surprisingly moderate, because the ideal growing temperature is usually much less than that maintained in the home. When shielded with a plastic covering in winter, additional economies result.

The equipment you do need with a greenhouse is a thermostat-controlled heater, a hose, and a plant bench or table. However, you may want to have a little more than that. You may want a good redwood plant bench, a sink, automatic watering system, automatic ventilating, and a humidifying and cooling system. These are refinements—luxuries, not necessities.

However, with fluorescent lights, any corner of the house can be a greenhouse of sorts—especially the basement. You can build growing shelves and hang light fixtures over them.

Or buy them ready-made. There are some excellent books available on growing plants under lights.

Inside the home, a flower cart is attractive and efficient. Or a reading lamp and a table can serve as a greenhouse for a few plants. The lights are important for growing flowering plants indoors away from windows. The average flowering plant needs well over 100 footcandles of light. The back of an average room in wintertime probably receives less than 40 footcandles. That may be all right for foliage plants, but keep flowering plants under lights or near windows. For the record, 250 to 500 footcandles is ideal.

You can check light intensity with a meter. Most photographers have them. A rule of thumb for light intensity with two 40-watt fluorescents in reflectors: plants 6 inches below get 500 footcandles, plants 12 inches below get 400 footcandles, and plants 18 inches below get 300 footcandles.

An increasingly popular sort of greenhouse is the bay—a window construction with shelves built out beyond an existing window frame. A variation consists of glass shelving installed across an existing window from the inside. Prefabricated models of either sort are available, or a handyman can easily construct one.

The type of greenhouse or growing conditions you have—windowsills, Grow Carts, or basement lights—is not too important. The difference is in the number of varieties and plants you can grow. You can adapt forcing techniques to one pot or to a hundred pots. However, there are two items that can be very helpful to the home gardener as well as to the commercial grower. They are the plant workroom and the cold frame.

The plant workroom can be a room or a corner, a part of the utility room or the basement, anywhere where you can do your plant work and be a little messy. Handling potting soil, transplanting, trimming, making cuttings, starting seeds aren't the neatest kinds of operations. It is less annoying to others if you can keep this clutter in one place. This work area should be warm and lighted so that you are comfortable. It should have a work table and storage bins for soil and peat and pots. There should be shelves for chemicals and racks for tools. And it ought to have a large, durable trash container.

I know a grower who has his potting bench on wheels. For his greenhouse, it is ideal. He can roll it to whatever area he is going to work. I liked it so well that I promised myself one— but never got it. Another acquaintance managed to get a discarded check-writing desk when a bank was being re- modeled. It is excellent for stand-up potting. But if you pot at kitchen-table height, get yourself a stool.

Along with the potting area or workroom a cold frame can be useful. Again, it is not exclusive to forcing, but a help to all gardening. Many serious gardeners already have one.

The cold frame can be as simple as a few uncemented concrete blocks stacked into a small rectangle and covered with an old storm window. Or it can be neatly made of wood, the sides cut on a slant from back to front to capture more light and to drain. The sash cover can be securely hinged. And at best, it can be heated with heating cables, when it becomes a hot bed.

If you are building a cold frame, the size to build is the size that will accommodate a sash you have or can get. That is usually about 3 by 5 feet. The top should slope toward the front with a drop of about 4 to 6 inches. Set the high side to the north to trap as much sun as possible from the south.

Locate the cold frame in back of a garage where it is out of sight. And if it is sheltered from the north and west, from where we in the Snow Belt get most of our blizzards, you gain an additional advantage. Add to your cold frame a mixture of rich loam with some peat or humus mixed in to keep it loose. Work this soil mixture up until it is about six inches deep. Bank the outside with straw or leaves and throw some soil on top to keep this insulation from blowing away.

In the spring, when the temperature gets warm—about 70 degrees—raise a corner of the sash. Or whitewash the panes of glass. This is necessary to keep the temperature inside the cold frame from building up too high from the heat of the sun.

Keep the soil moist but not wet. The need to water will be infrequent, since condensation on the glass will help retain moisture and humidity.

The purpose of a cold frame is to protect, hold, and carry plants over a season. It is not intended to be used for forcing

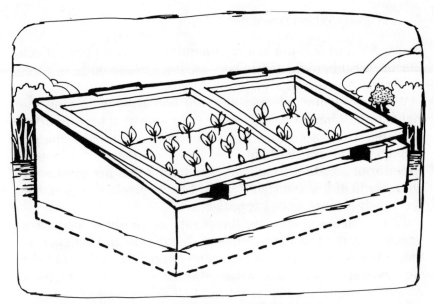

A simple cold frame.

plants. However, it is a big help in getting them ready for forcing. A hotbed may be used for forcing plants, even though it is not intended for this purpose. But it is more fun to move the plants indoors, where you can watch them develop and tend to them better.

One of the "tools" we use in forcing plants is *shade.* Sometimes this refers to the whitewash we spread over greenhouse or cold-frame glass or to the cheesecloth canopy we stretch over plants to cut down the heat intensity of sunlight. Usually we are indicating by the word *shade* the use of an opaque black sateen cloth to get short days in the control of plant blooming. It is this shade that is important in forcing plants to flower.

We define a *short day* as one with less than eleven hours of daylight. It is the type of day we get in fall when short-day plants set buds—chrysanthemums, for example.

To produce short days anytime, especially when normal days are long, we shade plants with the black cloth to cut out all light. In our experience a black sateen cloth with the black cloth of at least 64-by-104 mesh is best to use. Black canvas will work, but it is too heavy to handle and to support. Black plastic or rubber will not do because it is airtight and "sweats" underneath, setting up fungus problems.

When we were "pioneering," we had trouble finding the right cloth. It had to be light enough in weight to be supported by wires strung above the flower bed. Yet it had to be opaque enough to cut out the light. We finally contacted the mother superior of a Catholic convent. The habits that her nuns wore were made of just the right type of black sateen. Amused, she graciously steered us to a supplier.

To produce a short day, the plants in an entire bed, or a bench, or just a few pots are covered so that no daylight gets to them. Wires are stretched between supporting racks, and the cloth is draped over these wires. About 2 footcandles of light—which is very dark—is about all that is allowed. The usual practice is to cover the plants from 5:00 P.M. to 7 A.M. However, any combination to get a fourteen-hour night—for example, 6:00 P.M. to 8:00 A.M.—will do.

When draping the cloth, tape over any projections or sharp corners so that you will not tear the shading material. And holes must be patched if the shade is to be effective.

In December and January, when nights are naturally long, shading is unnecessary. The exception would be anywhere where artificial lights are being used. Then shade to keep that light from the short-day plants. After buds are initiated, shading is no longer necessary.

For shading in the home, instead of using a black cloth covering, a few plants can be moved into a dark closet every evening and be given twelve to fourteen hours of darkness. Should the closet door be accidentally opened and the plants be given a flash of light during the night, it would not affect most plants unless the light were prolonged—five to ten minutes. After all, in nature, brilliant flashes of lightning during a thunderstorm do not upset the bud formation for flowering. But for the best results, keep plants fully in the dark. A single plant can be shaded by placing a heavy paper bag over it.

Another important tool we use in forcing plants is lights. These are used in working with long-day or, more accurately,

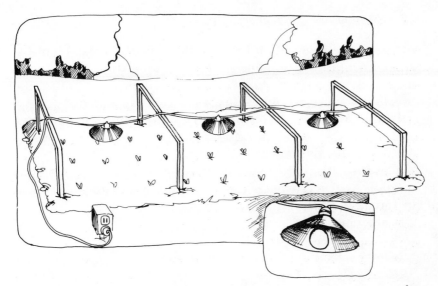

An easily set up arrangement such as this, outdoors or indoors, using regular incandescent lights, is sufficient for supplemental lighting on long-day plants.

short-night plants, which will not set buds unless the days are long and the nights are very short—under ten hours. The aster is one such plant.

To produce long days in fall and winter, supplemental lighting is needed. Fortunately, you do not have to imitate sunlight or daylight. The intensity of the additional light can be quite low, under 10 footcandles. Ordinary incandescent or fluorescent lamps are used. Because of the ease in putting up and taking down a string of light bulbs, most professional growers prefer to use incandescent lights rather than fluorescent tubes and fixtures.

As a rule of thumb, to produce short nights, use 60-watt bulbs about 2 feet over the top of the plants and spaced about 4 feet apart. Use reflectors to beam the lights down on the plants rather than letting light diffuse in every direction. We made reflectors out of aluminum pie plates by simply cutting a hole in the middle for the lamp stem to fit through.

In our pioneering days, we would light from sunset to about 10:00 P.M., giving the plants four to six hours of additional light. Then, when it was discovered that night length—a short night—is the trigger that initiates the flower buds, we cut the supplemental lighting time in half, lighting from 10:00 P.M. to midnight, or 10:00 P.M. to 1:00 A.M. The plants were fooled into reacting to two short nights in every twenty-four hours.

Lights can be turned on and off manually, but we are human and we forget. Automatic time switches are not expensive and are worth the investment.

The following are long-day plants that flower or set buds naturally when days are twelve or more hours long. They can be forced to flower earlier with lights.

Calceolaria	Gypsophila
Centaurea	Larkspur
China aster	Marigold
Clarkia	Pansy
Coreopsis	Salpiglossis
Cornflower	Scabiosa
Dahlia	Schizanthus
Feverfew	Shirley poppy
Gaillardia	Snapdragon
Gardenia	Stock

Some short-day plants that set buds when shade is used for twelve or more hours each day are:

Begonia socotrana	Gardenia
Bouvardia	Kalanchoe
Chrysanthemum	Poinsettia
Eupatorium	Stevia
Euphorbia	

There are flowering plants that are not affected by day length or night length. Among these are:

Anemone	Freesia
Aquilegia	Geranium
Calendula	Iberis
Cineraria	Ornithogalum
Cyclamen	Primula
Cynoglossum	Ranunculus
Delphinium	Rose
Dianthus	Zinnia

In our manipulation of plant flowering with lights, we discovered another interesting phenomenon. If we apply an additional light period to short-day plants such as the chrysanthemum while the plants are growing as seedlings, it delays bud setting. In this way we can allow the plant to grow tall and sturdy before we shade or expose it to short days.

The thermometer is an important tool because temperature is an important factor in forcing flowers. Temperature regulates the growth of almost all plants, and for some it governs the formation of flower buds. The temperature at which plants grow best is not the same for all. However, for most of our common flowering plants, the best growing temperature is between 50 and 65 degrees. In practice, this refers to night temperature, because day temperature is difficult to control with the variations in sunlight.

There is also a temperature at which plant growth slows and almost comes to a stop. We use this when we need to hold plants back. For many plants, that temperature is around 40 degrees. For others, it may be slightly higher or lower.

Maintaining the proper temperature depends upon the heating system in your home or greenhouse. It also depends upon where you are growing your plants. Obviously, you are not going to keep a living room where you sit and read or watch TV down to around 60 degrees. But you can keep a basement at that temperature when you are growing with fluorescent lights. Or a greenhouse, where you have full control of the heat.

Plants are flexible and will adapt a little to slightly higher temperatures than those at which they grow best, provided you keep the humidity up. Don't let them dry out. Grown at higher temperatures, they will be lacking somewhat in quality, which may not be too apparent unless you compare them with plants grown at proper temperatures.

On the subject of temperature, bottom heat helps in the development of roots in seedlings and plant cuttings. As a rule, an additional underneath temperature of 5 to 10 degrees over the temperature at the top is beneficial. (But not so for tulips; keep them on the ground.)

To apply bottom heat to seedling flats and pots, many

growers have racks built over heating pipes. But a warm-air register in a home just will not do. It causes undue dryness. It sets back the plants instead of aiding them. If you have no way to apply bottom heat, there is no need for concern. It helps, but it is not essential.

The effect of temperature on bud formation is still a mystery in flower forcing. Gardenias will not set buds if the night temperature is not kept down at 60 degrees. With the chrysanthemum, if the night temperature is kept too low—below 50 degrees—the plant will develop only blind shoots, no flowers. However, after buds are developed, temperatures may be dropped to hold the plants.

For an indication of the proper temperature for bud formation, when not known, look to nature. Maintain a somewhat similar temperature to that which exists when the plant is setting buds in its natural habitat. Is it on a warm summer evening or on a cool spring day?

Another important forcing tool is water. It is especially a factor in forcing bulbs, corms, and tubers. Most bulbs start growth when given water. Some, like the calla lily, go into dormancy when water is withheld.

Plants need water. It is as essential as light and air. Plants need water in the soil, and plants need water in the air. When the air is humid, less leaf transpiration takes place and less water is required by the roots. That is why we must keep up the humidity around new cuttings, since there are no roots to supply water. Misting helps reduce transpiration. Also, since transpiration is great during the summer when the air is dry, we must keep the soil moist.

Although water is important, too much water is harmful. The oxygen supply in the soil is reduced. Root hairs fail to function in soggy soil, and they may rot. Photosynthesis slows. The plant's growth suffers. Overwatering is probably the most common cause of pot plant failure.

How much water? It varies with the soil, the root system of the plant, the type and size of the plant, and the air temperature. After planting, while the root system is being established, one soaking may be enough for a week. After the roots are developed, the same plant may require water daily.

For plants in pots, you can tap the pot with the knuckle of your finger or with a wooden trowel handle. Dry soil will give a bright, hollow ring. Water it. A wet soil will sound dull—a dull clunk. No need to water. For plants in flats or beds, you can feel the soil. If a small sample of the soil crumbles easily, it can be watered. But if it becomes sticky and does not fall apart after squeezing, it does not need water. Another moisture check: Push a trowel into the soil and pull it out. If it grates going in and comes out clean, it is time to water.

Almost never use cold water. Nature doesn't splash icy water over her flowers. Keep water temperatures about the same as air temperatures.

When to water? For indoor plants, for greenhouse plants, and for garden plants, watering in the morning is a sound procedure to follow. Plants will have the water they need for photosynthesis and transpiration during the day.

Watering is important to forcing because only a well-grown plant can be forced into a beautiful cut flower or an attractive flowering plant.

Soil is important, too, for the same reason. Give your plants the type of soil they prefer—sandy for some, heavy for others, or a soft rich loam, or a coarse mixture. Know what your plant needs and supply it.

Especially know its pH requirements—neutral or acid soil. An inexpensive cardboard testing device for determining soil pH is available at most garden supply stores. To lower the pH, apply aluminum sulfate solution to the soil—not ammonium sulfate. (The two are sometimes confused.) Dissolve about one teaspoon of aluminum sulfate in a quart of water. To raise the pH, use lime or limestone. Mix about a cupful to a bushel of soil.*

In feeding plants, a balanced liquid fertilizer will be satisfactory for most. Or, to get the convenience of not having to feed plants regularly, you can mix a balanced slow-dissolving fertilizer into the potting soil.

However, some plants will have out-of-the-ordinary feeding

---

*For aid in working with smaller amounts, see the table of equivalents in Appendix C, pages 249–250.

requirements. Your Easter lily will need more nitrogen. For plants that need nitrogen, use ammonium sulfate, about a teaspoon to a gallon of water. Ammonium nitrate and urea can also be used—about ½ teaspoon in a gallon of water.

For phosphorous, apply superphosphate—about a cupful to a bushel of soil.

For potassium or potash, use potassium chloride or potassium sulfate—again about a cupful to a bushel of soil.

Many commercial growers are using air fertilization with CO_2 gas. Carbon dioxide gas is added to the air in a greenhouse to make more of this gas available to plants for photosynthesis. To accelerate the process, growing temperatures are raised. The effectiveness of this technique depends upon a delicate balance between the amount of light—sunny and cloudy days—and the growing temperature. For example, after a day of poor light in which the plant has produced little foodstuff, a high night temperature will cause elongation, or reaching. The additional CO_2 has thrown the plant off balance. Given increased light or lower temperatures, it grows normally.

Carbon dioxide as a fertilizer requires a closed greenhouse to retain the gas. Handled properly, it does increase plant quality and speed up flowering to some extent. However, it is not a technique that a small diversified grower can use efficiently—or needs to.

Plants are efficient food factories when they are young. If you give them enough of what they want at this stage, they will go on to make remarkable growth afterward, even though you do not continue to gorge them. Feed plants well during their growing stage and you can slight them somewhat later.*

Aside from fertilizers—and fungicides and insecticides—the chemical shelf has not contributed greatly in helping us to force flowers. However, a number of growth-controlling chemicals have been developed, some to induce root growth in cuttings, others to control weeds, and still others to make plants grow taller.

Also among them are some that are called growth retar-

*For further assistance in understanding fertilizers, see pages 251–253 in Appendix D.

dants. They only retard growth, not flowering. They keep plants shorter, dwarfing them. B-Nine, Phosfon-D, and Cycocel are examples. Through the use of these chemicals you can produce a tight, compact plant—an attractive smaller plant covered with flowers. These retardants can be incorporated into the potting soil, applied to the soil in solution, or sprayed onto the plant. The latter method is used most frequently.

Poinsettias and azaleas react favorably to Cycocel or CCC. When sprayed on azaleas, it stops the vegetative growth and increases reproductive growth. As a result, treated plants produce more flowers. In addition, most azalea varieties, when precooled and treated with CCC, can be made to flower for Christmas, which was previously possible for only a few varieties.

B-Nine sprayed on a pot of petunias reduces stretching and produces a plant that is a compact ball of flowers. Pot mums also react strongly to B-Nine, and treated plants can be forced to flower a week sooner than untreated plants.

Other pot plants that are noticeably dwarfed and improved by growth retardants are asters, marigolds, salvias, and zinnias.

Growth retardants are easy to apply. Briefly, the chemical—about 4 ounces to a quart of water—is sprayed on the foliage of plants from three to seven weeks after germination. For rapid growers, treat three weeks after sowing. For slow growers, treat seven weeks after sowing. Some plants may get a second spray—five weeks after sowing for fast plants and ten weeks after sowing for slow plants. Water plants before spraying. The foliage must be dry and the plants should not be watered for twenty-four hours afterward.

If the plants you grow for forcing respond to growth retardants, you can spray them and get more attractive plants and flowers. But this is a nicety, not a necessity.

Besides lights and shade, temperature, moisture, and chemicals to control plants, we have two other important forcing tools—timing and the pinch.

Plants that are indifferent to day length usually respond beautifully to scheduling, or timing. We know how long it takes for most plants to flower from a seedling naturally. We simply move that period around in the calendar—allowing for some extra growing days necessary in the dark of winter. We take a nasturtium that blossoms in sixty days from seed, and instead of planting it in the spring for summer flowers, we plant it in autumn for midwinter blooms. And by and large it works, except where there are other blocks, such as a cold requirement or dormancy. Timing and the scheduling of responsive varieties have made it possible to flower snapdragons all year around.

Closely allied to timing is the pinch—nipping off new growth. It is used to get bushier and more compact plants by causing side buds to send out stems. It is also used to delay flowering, because the plant has to regroup and start all over again. There are two types of pinches—soft and hard.

Rolling off or nipping off the tip of soft new growth, or new branching side buds, is termed a *soft pinch.* When the terminal bud is pinched, the buds at the axil or base of the leaves begin to develop and produce multiple flowering stems instead of one. Conversely, the side buds on some plants are pinched so

soft pinch   hard pinch

that there will be just one strong stem—one long-stemmed rose, for example.

A hard pinch is made later than the soft pinch, or takes off a greater portion of the stem, going down to just above a fully developed leaf. Shoots develop from the lead bud to which the pinch was made, and from several others directly below it. This new growth starts out at an angle, or "hook," from the original stem and is noticeable if a subsequent flower is cut below the pinch. Plant-show exhibitors lose points for it.

Both hard and soft pinches delay flowering and give the plant a chance to build itself. They also provide a definite starting point for new growth, and consequently the flowering date can be timed from the date of the pinch. An extra week is added for the plant to get going from a soft pinch. By way of example, with roses six weeks are required from the pinch to the flower. For Christmas flowering, the plants would be soft-pinched on November 1 and hard-pinched on November 7. Used by itself or with other forcing procedures, the pinch is a technique of major importance.

There are other techniques that we use to force plants into bloom, such as allowing a plant to become pot bound. But these are not common, and we will discuss them when we discuss the specific plant involved.

The techniques for forcing are simple. Most important for growing and forcing fine plants are controls on light, temperature, and water. Simple things. But the result is profound—a flower.

3
At Home with Pot Flowers— Selecting and Tending

Familiarity is hard on beauty alone, but gentle to hidden character in whatever form it may be uncovered. When we get to know a person's true values, some of the plainest people in the world become the most beautiful.

Plants are like that. Some of the most gorgeous flowering plants are of no use in the home. On the other hand, a simple, commonplace plant can bring with it the same bright warmth that is in the smile of a gap-toothed child.

Aside from beauty, we need to look at the performance of flowering pot plants at home. Do they wear well as part of our day-to-day home life, or are they temperamental? Do they require exacting care?

Many excellent books have been written about the care of flowering plants in the home. It is not my purpose to cover this familiar ground. I intend only to comment on their performance, along with providing a few suggestions about handling the plants you have forced into bloom when you are ready to bring them in and show them off. And I intend to be brief.

Maybe you've grown the plant in your basement under lights or in a back bay window or out in your home greenhouse. You've brought it through its youthful days, and now it is doing beautifully. Now you want to give it a place of prominence. Or you may want to use it as part of a holiday decoration. Or it is going to be a gift to a friend or relative, and you will be asked how to care for it. Then this is what you should know about your plant—and probably already do.

Plants should be kept in the coolest, most humid part of the house. Temperatures near 65 degrees are better than 75 degrees or more. If humidifiers are not used in the heating system, place the plant on shallow trays of wet pebbles or gravel and water. For plants that can stand misting, mist twice a day. For most plants, avoid soaking the blooms.

Improper watering is the greatest cause for loss of pot plants. You will be asked over and over, "How often should I water and how much?" I'm often puzzled about this myself.

There is no set rule that we can follow, because humidity and temperatures vary greatly. For this reason, no plant should be watered by any rule of thumb such as 2 cupfuls every second day. It may be fine in one situation but disastrous in another. You have to watch the plant for a few days and develop a feel for its needs—like a new husband or wife.

Overwatering is as harmful as underwatering. No plant should be watered when the potting soil feels moist to the fingers. Remember that an easy test to determine whether pot plants need water is to tap the side of a pot lightly with a butter knife or spoon. A clear ring means that the soil is dry, and a dull clunk means that water is not needed.

In no case should a plant be allowed to stand in water after its soil has become saturated. Yellow leaves that fall off easily are usually an indication of overwatering. So, too, are buds that droop and fail to open.

The temperature of the water used for watering should be around that of the room. In fact, if there is one rule that can be followed it is: Do not use cold water. Some plants, such as African-violets, like their water a little on the warm side.

Once a plant has been allowed to become too dry, pouring water on the soil is of little value. The water merely drains out of the pot through the cracked edges where the dry soil has pulled away from the pot wall. Instead, submerge the entire pot in a pail of water until the soil is completely saturated. Do

not submerge leaves or blossoms. Then, once no more air bubbles rise to the surface of the water, allow the pot to stand in a sink or elsewhere where excess water can drain off.

Some plants require much more water than others. Among these are: azaleas, chrysanthemums, cinerarias, cyclamens, hydrangeas, and primroses.

Plants are susceptible to change of temperature. Prolonged low temperatures or excessively high temperatures can be harmful. Direct drafts on plants should also be avoided. Poinsettias in particular are adversely affected by direct drafts.

Most plants like considerable light, although direct sunlight may not always be necessary. African-violets will do well in a north window. However, few flowering plants will blossom in a dark corner. This is a realm reserved for foliage plants.

A good yardstick to follow for the care and feeding of pot plants is to duplicate nature. When in doubt about a plant that you are growing, look up its background, and you will get a good idea of its cultural requirements.

The calla lily makes a good example. It makes a gorgeous, though somewhat large, houseplant. It is a native of areas of South Africa where it is extremely wet, except for two months when it is extremely dry. We duplicate this. We water copiously for ten months. Then, in July and August, none at all. After the plant dries back, we water again. We are rewarded with ten months of exquisite blooms.

In a nutshell, know the plant's native habitat—its requirements in its natural state—and duplicate it. This, of course, does not necessarily apply to plants that have long been cultivated. These, through breeding and selection, are acclimated to the conditions in our homes. They are usually not among the plants that may give us trouble.

With just a little care and under normal conditions, most flowering plants will do well. They bring their special charm and beauty into our lives in spite of what we often do to them.

Here are a few of the more popular plants and some suggestions for making them comfortable in your home.

AFRICAN-VIOLET *(Saintpaulia ionantha)*

Ideal houseplants. Thrive best in humid atmosphere—on bed of moist gravel. Water from bottom. Do not wet leaves. Avoid noonday sun. They will bloom almost the year around.

AGERATUM *(Ageratum Houstonianum)*

No problem. Good light and average watering are all they ask. Pick off wilted blooms. In spring, transplant to porch box or garden.

ASTILBE *(Astilbe sp.)*

Spirealike blooms. Fine houseplant. One of the few plants that does not resent overwatering. Set pot in a dish filled with water. After flowers have faded, move outdoors to wet location.

AZALEA *(Rhododendron sp.)*

Popular from Christmas through Easter. They do exceptionally well as houseplants. Keep soil moist at all times. Every week or so, put a few drops of vinegar in the water. May be watered from top or bottom. I prefer bottom watering in the saucer. Azalea plants are usually discarded after they have finished blooming because most azaleas are tender for outside planting in the North, and many people do not have facilities for carrying azaleas over the hot, dry summer. Nevertheless, if you want, they can be used again.

BEGONIA—Fibrous *(Begonia semperflorens)*

Excellent houseplant. Compatible. In bloom almost constantly. Keep soil damp but not wet. Mist leaves occasionally. Does well in sunshine or partly shaded area.

BEGONIA—Tuberous *(Begonia tuberhybrida)*

Not the best pot plant in the world. In fact, it will not do well in many homes. Likes high humidity and shade. After blooming, set outside in moist, shady spot.

BLEEDING-HEART *(Dicentra spectabilis* and *D. eximia)*

If you've forced plant to bloom for Saint Valentine's Day, it makes a suitable gift for that occasion and a satisfactory houseplant. Can be watered from top. Later in spring, transplant to garden.

BROWALLIA *(Browallia sp.)*

A pretty blue five-lobed flower. Blooms all winter. Nice compact plant; tends to spread and can be pruned. Ideal for indoor hanging basket. Tolerates warm temperatures in the home. Needs light. Must be grown in sunny window or under horticultural lights on dark winter days.

CALCEOLARIA *(Calceolaria sp.)*

Popular winter houseplant with unusual and interesting blooms. It does well in a window with a little morning sun and out of cold drafts. It likes moderate watering, a little on the dry side. May be watered from top, but keep water from leaves or they will spot.

CALLA LILY *(Zantedeschia aethiopica and Z. Elliottiana)*

A large plant. There are both yellow and white flowering varieties. Blooms repeat over long period. Likes average light, generous watering, and average temperature. Fine for average home. Is a bulb plant that can be dried back in summer and reused.

CAMELLIA *(Camellia sp.)*

Often sold by florists as a houseplant, but very difficult to grow under usual home conditions. The dry atmosphere causes buds to drop. Gorgeous flowers and foliage. The plant does well if the soil is kept moist at all times. In summer, set outdoors in light shade.

CHRISTMAS CACTUS *(Zygocactus truncatus)*

Sometimes called Thanksgiving cactus, according to the time it is in bloom, and classified in the genus *Schlumbergera*. This plant is temperamental for some growers, foolproof for others. Give it a dry-period rest in the fall. Move into a room or basement where it will get a long night of darkness for one month to set buds. Then grow in a sunny location. Water normally. One plant can last for years.

CHRISTMAS CHERRY *(Solanum Pseudo-Capsicum)*

These plants, also called Jerusalem-cherries, do splendidly in some homes but do nothing in others, where conditions may cause the berries to fall and the leaves to curl. Sudden chills and prolonged heat will have the same result. Where they grow, they do well in a fairly cool atmosphere away from drafts. The soil must be kept moist. The leaves should be misted from time to time.

CHRYSANTHEMUM *(Chrysanthemum morifolium)*

Pot mums are one of the most popular flowering plants. They keep well in average room temperatures with moderate light. Require lots of water. Blooms last a month. After blooming, cut back and plant in garden for bloom again in fall. Most forced mums are not hardy and will not winter over to next year.

CINERARIA *(Senecio cruentus)*

Bright, free blooming, and lasting, these are showy pot plants you force for late winter or spring. They are excellent houseplants, but must be kept in a cool spot away from direct sunlight. The soil should not be permitted to dry out. Use warm water. When cold water is used, the leaves wilt temporarily as if dry.

COLEUS *(Coleus Blumei)*

Asks very little and tolerates amost anything. Colors are brilliant when grown in sun or partial sun. Water moderately, feed lightly, and let roots get pot bound.

CROWN-OF-THORNS *(Euphorbia Milii)*

A thick, upright, thorny plant often called *Euphorbia Splendens*. Grows well on windowsill or under lights. Tends to be everblooming—tiny flowers in brick-red bracts. Tolerates temperature and humidity of a home. Water moderately. Lasts for years.

CYCLAMEN *(Cyclamen persicum)*

Beautiful and long blooming. Some people have the same plant for years. The trick seems to be plenty of bottom watering to keep soil moist and no drafts. Likes a cool north window. Yet florists no longer carry cyclamens, because customers find them difficult to grow. Most homes may be too warm.

EASTER CACTUS *(Schlumbergera Gaertneri or Rhipsalis sp.)*

Care is same as for Christmas cactus.

EASTER LILY *(Lilium longiflorum var. eximium)*

Traditional for Easter. Otherwise seldom used as a houseplant. Does well with average watering and average temperature. Remove pollen to prevent discoloration of flower. After blooming, hold until spring and transplant the bulb into the garden.

FUCHSIA *(Fuchsia sp.)*

Your forced fuchsia will do well indoors in spring. Moderate care and watering will do. Then, when the weather warms up, move it outside to a shady, wind-protected location.

GARDENIA *(Gardenia jasminoides)*

In the northern areas of our country, gardenias seldom develop well in the home. Because of sustained dry heat, the buds drop before opening. The plants require a moist, warm atmosphere and a bright location for flowering. In addition, the soil must never dry out or be kept too wet. Spray foliage with cool water daily.

GERANIUM *(Pelargonium sp.)*

Another popular houseplant that is easy to grow. Give it a sunny window, and whatever else you do to it is right. Will continue to bloom indoors until you're ready to put it outdoors in the garden, porch box, or patio.

GLOXINIA *(Sinningia speciosa)*

Splendid houseplants. But they will not tolerate too much direct sun, or water on their leaves and crowns. Water from the bottom by filling a saucer under the pot with water.

HYDRANGEA *(Hydrangea sp.)*

One of the best-selling flowering plants for Easter and Mother's Day. They need lots of water. Water daily. Plants wilt rapidly when they lack water. To revive, immerse the entire pot in a pail of water until the soil is soaked through. They do well in average sunlight. In spring, except in northernmost sections, transplant to your garden.

IMPATIENS *(Impatiens Holstii* and *I. Sultanii)*

Blooms with little attention. Simply water and feed moderately. Plants will get leggy if not given enough light and can be pruned to reshape. Move outdoors to shady garden in late spring.

KALANCHOE *(Kalanchoe Blossfeldiana)*

A fine winter houseplant. You can force it into bloom anytime from fall to spring. These plants must not be overwatered. Do not splash water on foliage. Water from the top or bottom. They thrive well in dry home atmosphere. After blooming indoors, some varieties can be used outdoors as a border plant.

LANTANA *(Lantana Camara)*

A well-shaped dwarf plant that is a delight. Nice for window gardens. Blooms off and on over a long period of time. Not fussy about humidity or temperature. Keep watered. Prune long branches and shape after each bloom.

LOBELIA *(Lobelia sp.)*

Masses of flowers throughout the winter. Does well in most homes. Grow in moderate light. Water and feed regularly. Can be used in a hanging basket.

MARIGOLD *(Tagetes sp.)*

A long-lasting houseplant when grown in the full sun. Water moderately. Fertilize occasionally. Then leave it alone. Should last six months before it gets woody. Pick off old blooms.

PETUNIA *(Petunia hybrida)*

This makes a fine spring houseplant by itself, or it can be used with other plants in combination plantings. Use with ageratums, coleuses, lantanas, dwarf marigolds, pansies, or salvias. Or petunias can be planted in porch boxes and gardens. They will withstand drought and heat.

POINSETTIA *(Euphorbia pulcherrima)*

Symbolic of Christmas. Lasts all year as foliage plant when properly handled. The red bracts last until Easter. The plants require good light, average watering, and warm temperature. Will not stand a sudden chill or overwatering, or leaves and bracts will fall prematurely. May be forced again next year.

PRIMROSE *(Primula sp.)*

Some persons are as allergic to the Obconica primrose as others are to poison ivy. Avoid them. Other primroses are excellent and beautiful. You can force primrose into bloom from January to April. Keep plants in a cool, shady spot. Water copiously. Keep water off leaves to prevent spotting.

ROSE *(Rosa sp.)*

Forced roses make fine houseplants. They require good light, average temperature, regular watering. Cut off old blooms. When weather permits, transplant to your garden.

SPRING BULBS: HYACINTH *(Hyacinthus sp.)*, IRIS *(Iris sp.)*, DAFFODIL *(Narcissus Pseudo-Narcissus)*, TULIP *(Tulipa sp.)*

These flowering bulb plants do not last long when brought into the warm home. But even for their short stay, the pleasure they bring makes it worthwhile. After flowering, the bulbs may be kept for planting outdoors.

THUNBERGIA *(Thunbergia alata)*

Large black-eyed-Susan type blooms. Likes warm temperature. Does well in a house. Feed and water generously. Grow on a sunny window ledge or under lights. In good light, it will bloom all winter. Needs trimming to keep it within bounds.

4
Cutting Flowers and Keeping Them

Cut flowers will look better and last longer if you treat them properly. Even though severed from the plant, they are living things. As with all living things, they relish a little tender loving care.

Suppose that you plan to use some of your own flowers to create a floral arrangement for your home or for a party or for a club meeting. How should you cut and handle your flowers? The question seems trite. To cut an armful of flowers is simple—and fun. You've done it for years.

It *is* simple and enjoyable to cut flowers. Nevertheless, cutting and handling the cut flowers is a rather critical operation. This is true whether you cut flowers that are in season in your garden or those you force into bloom in your home or commercial greenhouse.

Many a time I have stood before a bed of unusual trial flowers and wondered if they were ready to cut. I can sympathize with others in a similar situation. Uncertainty is frustrating. A flower grower must make decisions when cutting flowers. I hope I can help you to make them.

No doubt, you have bought or been given cut flowers that looked pretty in the box but didn't last the night. The petals fell. The buds drooped. You blamed yourself. And you may have been partly at fault. But the chances are that those

45

flowers were not handled properly after cutting or were not grown properly. That's why it pays to grow and cut your own—and it's a lot more fun.

I have some suggestions for cutting and handling. Whether you cut in the garden in season or in the home or commercial greenhouse off season, whether you buy flowers for your arrangements or grow and supply them yourself, there are techniques you can use to increase the vase life of cut flowers.

The whole thrust of these techniques is to get the flower to take water and sometimes food.

Because plants vary in structure and needs, we have to take these varied structures and needs into account. For example, plants have either woody stems, hairy stems, hollow stems or oozy stems. In general, we split the ends of woody stems, place the hairy stems in hot water, recut the hollow stems under water, and sear the oozy stems. In regard to plant needs, water is the most important consideration.

But let's start at the beginning. Suppose you are ready to go into the garden or greenhouse to cut flowers. Carry a small bucket of fresh, warm water with you. The temperature is important. It should be quite warm, or tepid, about 110 degrees. Never use cold water below air or room temperature. Cold water shocks flowers. Also, they are unable to absorb cold water as well as they can tepid water. By using warm water, you are cooperating with nature, because the plant fluids are warm.

Once flowers are cut, they need an adequate and continuing water supply to replace the life-giving food and fluids of the plant. This water must be clean and fresh—and immediate. Therefore, as soon as a flower is cut, get the stems in water. Carrying around armloads of cut flowers may be picturesque, but it's poor practice. Some flowers can stand a little withering; others never come back.

When we cut flowers commercially in the greenhouse, we have containers of fresh water ready and waiting before we start. After cutting, the flowers are kept out of water for as short a period as possible. A wilted flower may perk up again when given water, but it has one strike against it. It has lost some of its vitality and staying power.

Remove Lower Leaves

← split

Cutting a woody plant

cut on slant

cut hollow stem through node

Cut plant stems on a slant to expose more cut surface to the water. Cutting a hollow stem through a node further increases the amount of water-absorbing surface.

Use sharp knives and clippers. Dull tools crush the capillary tubes in the severed stems, making it difficult for the flowers to draw water. It is much like crinkling the end of a soda straw. Lacking water, the flower droops, and its vase life is shortened considerably.

Clean and sterilize clippers and other cutting tools on a regular basis. This helps to prevent the spread of harmful bacteria to the flower stem and the plant.

You should avoid cutting in the heat of the day. Morning or evening is a better time. Then the plant stems are filled with water and are in better condition to survive as a cut flower. This is not the case at high noon, when transpiration is at its peak. We growers prefer to cut in the late afternoon if possible. During the day, plants build up a food supply that helps to keep the cut flower longer lasting.

Avoid the tight bud or the mature flower. One may not open when cut; the other will soon drop its petals. Except for asters, chrysanthemums, marigolds, zinnias, and a few others that should be cut when almost fully opened, cut others when they are about half open. The buds should show petal color.

Cutting a woody plant

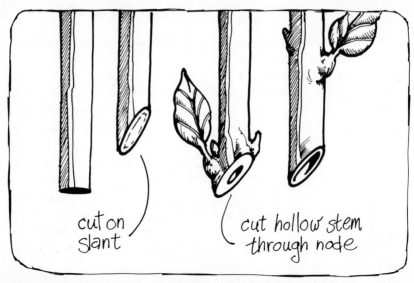

cut on slant

cut hollow stem through node

Cut plant stems on a slant to expose more cut surface to the water. Cutting a hollow stem through a node further increases the amount of water-absorbing surface.

Use sharp knives and clippers. Dull tools crush the capillary tubes in the severed stems, making it difficult for the flowers to draw water. It is much like crinkling the end of a soda straw. Lacking water, the flower droops, and its vase life is shortened considerably.

Clean and sterilize clippers and other cutting tools on a regular basis. This helps to prevent the spread of harmful bacteria to the flower stem and the plant.

You should avoid cutting in the heat of the day. Morning or evening is a better time. Then the plant stems are filled with water and are in better condition to survive as a cut flower. This is not the case at high noon, when transpiration is at its peak. We growers prefer to cut in the late afternoon if possible. During the day, plants build up a food supply that helps to keep the cut flower longer lasting.

Avoid the tight bud or the mature flower. One may not open when cut; the other will soon drop its petals. Except for asters, chrysanthemums, marigolds, zinnias, and a few others that should be cut when almost fully opened, cut others when they are about half open. The buds should show petal color.

MEXICAN FIRE-PLANT *(Euphorbia heterophylla)*

Cut when upper leaves are bright color and flower cluster has one to two opened flowers. Stems exude some milky fluid, but it is not necessary to sear the cut. Split stem ends and condition in cold water overnight. Lasts ten to fourteen days.

MIGNONETTE *(Reseda odorata)*

Cut when over one-quarter of the flowers on the spike are open. Condition in tepid water. Let stay overnight. Lasts one week or more.

PANSY *(Viola tricolor var. hortensis)*

When fully open, pull blossom off plant. Do not cut. Include foliage. Foliage on stem is important. Place stems in cold water and hold overnight. Lasts 4 or 5 days. Or, you can lift entire plant, wash soil from roots, and condition in cold water. Lasts about a week.

PETUNIA *(Petunia hybrida)*

For all types, cut flowers when almost or fully open. Flowers and leaves droop after cutting. Strip lower leaves. Place immediately in water. Dissolve sugar or flower conditioner in water, and hold flowers in this solution overnight. Flowers last almost a week.

PHLOX *(Phlox sp.)*

For all types, cut when clusters are over one-quarter open. Split stem ends. Condition in cold water overnight. Lasts ten to twelve days.

POPPY *(Papaver sp.)*

Cut as loose bud when flower is ready to unfold. Sear stem ends. Condition in cold water overnight. Some arrangers then drop candle wax on the petal base inside the flower. Lasts several days.

PRIMROSE *(Primula sp.)*

Cut when clusters are more than half open. Condition in warm water and hold overnight. Flowers last for a week.

ROSE *(Rosa sp.)*

In an arrangement, a rose is most attractive when three-quarters open. Cut before this stage. For hybrid teas, cut when outer petals are beginning to unfurl from the bud. For floribundas, cut when several blooms in a cluster are almost open and other buds show color. Cut stems so that two leaf nodes remain on the plant branch to develop new shoots. Cut just above this second node or eye. The rule of thumb is: Leave two five-leaflet leaves on the plant. Roses are best cut in the late afternoon, when the stem and flower are well nourished and watered. Recut stem just under a leaf node and split. Remove foliage from base of stem but retain as much foliage as possible. Submerge most of the stem in cold water and hold overnight. Roses will stand refrigeration and can be held for extended periods. In this case, recondition before using by recutting stems and submerging in fresh water. Lasts a week in an arrangement.

SALPIGLOSSIS or PAINTED-TONGUE *(Salpiglossis sinuata)*

Cut flowers just as they open. Submerge almost entire stem in cold water and hold overnight. Lasts about a week.

SALVIA or SCARLET SAGE *(Salvia sp.)*

For blue salvia, cut when lower half of spike is open. Condition in warm water and hold overnight. For scarlet and gentian sage, cut and handle the same, but split stem ends. Lasts a week.

SCABIOSA or PINCUSHION-FLOWER
(Scabiosa atropurpurea)

Cut when flowers are almost fully open. Split stem ends. Remove foliage. Condition overnight in cold water, which should cover most of stem. Lasts four to seven days.

SCABIOSA— PERENNIAL *(Scabiosa caucasica)*

Cut when almost fully open. Tight buds will not open in water. Thin out foliage. Submerge entire stem in cold water and condition overnight. Lasts ten days.

SCARLET PLUME *(Euphorbia fulgens)*

Cut when more than half the flowers on the stem are open. Split stem ends. Sear over flame. Condition in cold water overnight. Lasts about a week.

SNAPDRAGON or ANTIRRHINUM *(Antirrhinum majus)*

Cut when half of spike is in flower. Condition in tepid water. Let stay overnight. Adjust water for pH 4.0 with vinegar. Use commercial preservative. Lasts seven to ten days.

STATICE or EVERLASTING *(Limonium* sp.)

Cut when flowers are fully open. Condition in cold water for a few hours. They are "everlasting" in water or dried.

STEPHANOTIS or MADAGASCAR-JASMINE
(Stephanotis floribunda)

Cut when nearly open. Usually cut with very short stems. Stems exude a milky fluid, so sear and place in cold water. Hold overnight. Longer stems—a part of the vine—will be woody and should be split before searing. Condition in cold water. Lasts a week in an arrangement.

STOCK *(Matthiola incana)*

Cut when more than one-quarter of the flowers on the spike are open. Split woody stem ends. Condition in cold water acidified to pH 4.0 with vinegar. Lasts ten to twelve days.

SWEET PEA *(Lathyrus odoratus)*

For annual sweet pea, break off stem when almost completely in flower. For perennial sweet pea, cut when flower clusters are about half open. Condition in water at normal temperature overnight. Add sugar or flower conditioner to water. Lasts about a week.

TORENIA or WISHBONE FLOWER *(Torenia Fournieri)*

Cut, or lift entire plant, roots and all, when half in flower. Wash soil from roots of lifted plant. Condition in cold water. Lasts six to seven days.

TULIP *(Tulipa sp.)*

Cut when full bud. Cut above white portion on base of stem. Wrap a bunch of tulips in wet paper and submerge in cold water so that only the buds are not under water. Condition overnight. Lasts four to six days.

VERBENA *(Verbena hybrida)*

Cut when two or three of the outside rows of buds are open and others are just showing color. Split stem ends. Add sugar or plant conditioner to warm water and hold overnight. Flowers last one week.

VIOLA—HORNED VIOLET or TUFTED PANSY
(Viola cornuta)

Cut when fully open. Buds do not open in water. Submerge entire flower, stem and bloom, in a tub of cold water until flowers are crisp—about one hour. Remove, shake off water, tie in bunches, and immerse stems in cold water to condition overnight. Lasts about one week.

WALLFLOWER *(Cheiranthus Cheiri)*

Cut when nearly open. Does not keep well. Lasts only a few days.

YELLOW SPURGE or CUSHION SPURGE
(Euphorbia epithymoides)

Cut when half the flowers in a cluster are in full bloom. Sear the ends with a flame. Condition in tepid water. Hold overnight. Lasts about a week.

ZINNIA *(Zinnia sp.)*

Cut when flowers are fully open but centers are still tight. Strip almost all the leaves. Condition in cold water and hold overnight. Flowers should last ten to fourteen days.

5
Hastening Spring—
Forcing Branches

> For, lo! The winter is past,
> The rain is o'er and gone;
> The flowers appear. . .

> Solomon

Spring is pussy willows. And forsythias. And apple blossoms.

When you are bone weary of winter and can't wait for spring, that's the time to force these spring blossoms into bloom. That would be about a month or two before they would bloom normally. And that's about right for forcing.

When you force branches into bloom, you enjoy spring ahead of time. So bundle up. Go out in the yard. Cut some branches from your dormant flowering shrubs and trees. Select branches that will be pruned later anyway. Cut interesting shapes that will help make your arrangements unusual. Choose shoots with fat flower buds. The larger and fatter the buds, the better the blossoms will be.

A good rule of thumb is: After buds begin to swell a little in the late winter or early spring, the branches can be cut for forcing. Timing is a factor. On earlier cuts the flowers will not be as large. When you cut too early, there is also the possibility that the buds will shrivel up or drop off. On the other hand, nothing is gained by cutting too late. The plants will be in bloom outdoors about the same time as the forced branches. Therefore, stay between one and two months before normal blooming time.

If possible, cut branches during a thaw or on a mild day around noon. They are then filled with sap and in good condition for forcing.

Start during the January thaw. Get some pussy willow and witch hazel. Pussy willows are the easiest of all branches to force.

February will have some rain. After the rain is a good time to cut. Get some forsythia and cornelian cherry.

In March, don't miss the flowering crab. Its delicate pink should appear in the third week after you've brought the branches indoors.

Get a jump on spring. Let yourself go.

After cutting, slit and scrape cut ends to about 3 inches. Or split with a hammer—but do not mash. Submerge branches for about twenty-four hours in a tub of water at about 70 to 75 degrees, which is considerably warmer than the temperature outside. Then place the stems only in a container of cool water and put the container in a cool, semishady location—the garage, basement, or anywhere where the temperature is around 60 to 65 degrees. It's good practice to drop a few pieces of charcoal into the water.

After a few days, move to a lighter, warmer spot—but not a sunny window. A north window is fine. Or sunlight shining through a curtain. The addition of a commercial conditioner used for cut flowers seems to be helpful.

About once a week change the water and cut about 1 inch off the stem. Again add charcoal and conditioner. Once a day, or at least three times a week, mist the branches with tap water until they are wet. This takes the place of spring rain, adds humidity, and helps to keep the buds plump.

As blooms begin to appear, arrange the branches decoratively and move into bright sunshine. The sun puts color into the buds. Flowers opening in the shade will be a pale version of the real thing.

Are the blossoms too advanced for the date you want them?

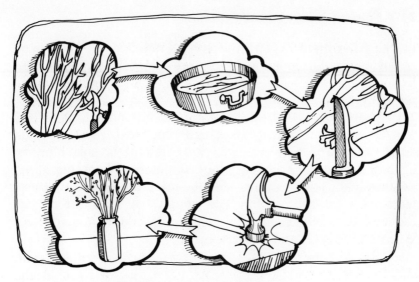

The basic steps in preparing branches for forcing.

You can retard them by moving them to a cool, shady spot with temperatures around 55 to 65 degrees.

Does it look like you are going to miss your date? Need to speed up the forcing process? Then put the branches in tepid water—100 to 110 degrees—each day, let the water cool, and let the branches remain in it until the next day. Misting with warm water will give them an additional boost.

Here are several more points of information to remember:

Shrubs that produce blossoms before leaves, such as the forsythia, force more readily than those whose leaves appear before the blossoms, such as deutzia and weigela.

The later the plant blooms outdoors, the longer it takes to force it indoors.

The closer you approach the blooming season when you cut, the less time is required for forcing.

Now it may be possible that it is not the early spring blossom that you want. You may want some later-blooming flower for some special reason. Maybe it is a May-blooming lilac that you want to bloom in late March or April. If the flower is still in its dormancy, it can be done.

But you cannot cut branches in the fall or early winter and expect them to bloom. Dormant branches have botanical clocks. They have a cold requirement, that is, there is a period of dormancy that must be met before they can start to flower. In our efforts to hasten spring and force branches into bloom, we can't skip winter entirely.

Here are some of the more common branches that can be forced and suggestions for forcing them. The forcing duration given will vary according to your area. It is based on an average of cutting six weeks before bloom and forcing at 65-degrees night temperature. The blooming date given will also vary with your location: Add roughly a month for New England and Minnesota and take away about a month for Washington, D.C., and Tennessee.

APPLE *(Malus sp.)*

Normal bloom in May. For blossoms in late February and early March, cut in late January and early February; blooms in four weeks. For blooms in late March and early April, cut in March; blooms in three weeks. Lasts one week.

AZALEA *(Rhododendron sp.)*

Normally flowers in May. For flowers in middle to late March, cut in late January and early February. Blooms in four to six weeks. Flowers last about a week.

BEACH PLUM *(Prunus maritima)*

Normal time of bloom is April–May. White flowers. For blooms early in March, cut in late January or early February. For blooms late in March, cut early in March. Lasts about a week.

BEAUTY-BUSH *(Kolkwitzia amabilis)*

Blooms naturally in June. Pink and orange flowers. For blooms May 1, cut March 15. Lasts two weeks.

BLADDER-NUT *(Staphylea trifolia)*

White flowers in clusters blossom naturally in April. For mid-March bloom, cut in late February. Forces in two weeks. Lasts five to seven days.

BRIDAL WREATH *(Spiraea prunifolia)*

Normally blooms in May. For blooms in mid-April, cut in mid-March. Lasts five to seven days.

CORNELIAN-CHERRY *(Cornus mas)*

May is natural bloom period. For mid-February bloom, cut in late January. Lasts seven to ten days.

DEUTZIA *(Deutzia sp.)*

Blooms normally in May and June. For blooms in late April, cut March 15. Lasts ten to fourteen days.

FLOWERING ALMOND *(Prunus Davidiana)*

Normal bloom: May–June. For blooms in February, cut a month earlier in January. For blooms in March, cut two to three weeks earlier. Lasts about one week.

FLOWERING CHERRY *(Prunus Sieboldii)*

Blooms normally in May. Pink flower. For late February blossoms, cut in late January. For mid-March blooms, cut in late February or early March. Lasts ten to fourteen days.

FLOWERING CRABAPPLE *(Malus sp.)*

Blooms naturally in May. For blossoms in late March, cut March 1. For blooms in early March, cut in early February. Lasts four to five days.

FLOWERING DOGWOOD *(Cornus florida* and *C. florida* var. *rubra)*

Normally blooms in May. For mid-April bloom, cut March 15. Lasts about a week.

FLOWERING PEACH *(Prunus Persica)*

May is normal blooming time. Red or pink flowers. For March 1 bloom, cut in late January. Lasts about a week.

FLOWERING PLUM *(Prunus triloba)*

Blooms normally in May. Pink blossoms. For middle to late February blossoms, cut in late January. For late March blooms, cut in early March. Lasts seven to ten days.

FLOWERING or JAPANESE QUINCE *(Chaenomeles lagenaria)*

Normally blooms in April. For flowers in mid-March, cut in late February. Forces in three weeks. Lasts ten days.

FORSYTHIA *(Forsythia sp.)*

Blooms normally in April. Yellow flowers. For bloom in early to mid-February, cut three weeks ahead. For bloom in late February to early March, cut two weeks ahead. For bloom in middle to late March, cut one week ahead. Lasts five to seven days.

FOTHERGILLA *(Fothergilla sp.)*

Blooms normally in April–May. White flower. For late March bloom, cut early in March. Lasts about a week.

HAWTHORN *(Crataegus sp.)*

Under normal conditions, blooms in May. For middle to late April bloom, cut in mid-March. Lasts one week.

HONEYSUCKLE *(Lonicera sp.)*

Winter honeysuckle blooms naturally in April. For early March blooms, cut in late February. For blooms late in March, cut early in March. Other honeysuckles that bloom in May may be cut for forced bloom in April. Blooms in one to two weeks. Lasts five to seven days.

JAPANESE BARBERRY *(Berberis Thunbergii)*

Small yellow flowers that bloom naturally in April. For early March bloom, cut in mid-February. Blooms in two weeks. Lasts two weeks.

LEUCOTHOE *(Leucothoe sp.)*

White flowers in April–May normally. For middle to late April bloom, cut in mid-March. Lasts ten to twelve days.

LILAC *(Syringa sp.)*

Normal bloom: May and June. For flowers in early to mid-April, cut in early March. Lasts five to seven days.

MOCK-ORANGE *(Philadelphus sp.)*

Blooms in June–July naturally. For flowers in mid to late April, cut in mid-March. Flowers last ten to twelve days.

MOUNTAIN-LAUREL *(Kalmia latifolia)*

Blooms May–June naturally. Pink or white flowers. For mid- to late April bloom, cut in mid-March. Lasts twelve to fourteen days.

PEAR *(Pyrus communis)*

Normally blooms in May. For blossoms March 1, cut in late January or early February. For blossoms in late March, cut in early March. Lasts ten to fourteen days.

PUSSY WILLOW *(Salix discolor)*

For February or March, cut seven to ten days before you want them. Remove bud scales to retard development of pollen. When fully developed, remove the water from the vase to extend usefulness. Lasts two weeks and longer.

RHODODENDRON *(Rhododendron sp.)*

Normal bloom in May and June. For late March bloom, cut in mid-February. For mid-April bloom, cut in mid-March. Lasts six to eight days.

SHADBUSH *(Amelanchier canadensis)*

Natural early April blooms. White flowers. For blooms in mid-February, cut in late January. Lasts one week.

SILVER-BELL *(Halesia sp.)*

White drooping clusters of flowers bloom naturally in April–May. For early March bloom, cut in mid-February. For late March flowers, cut in early March. Forces in three weeks. Lasts five to seven days.

SPIREA *(Spiraea sp.)*

Bridalwreath, Garland, Thunbergi, and Vanhouttei spireas normally bloom about April. For March flowers, cut in late February or early March. They force in two to three weeks and last a week or more.

WEIGELA *(Weigela florida)*

White, pink, and red flowers that bloom naturally in May–June. For blossoms in April, cut in late March. Branches are hairy and woody, so crush the ends and condition them first in warm water. Lasts ten to fourteen days.

WILD PLUM *(Prunus americana)*

Large flowers in small clusters in May. For late March bloom, cut in early March. Forces in two to three weeks. Lasts three days.

WITCH-HAZEL *(Hamamelis mollis)*

Yellow flowers may bloom naturally in December or January. If not, for blooms in December and January, cut one week ahead. Lasts almost a week.

6
Forcing Seeds and Plants to Grow

Plants—unlike the higher animals—can be propagated in two ways: sexually, by seeds, and vegetatively, by cuttings. The process of taking cuttings includes techniques of division, layering, and grafting. And we may stretch the word *division* to include bulbs, corms, tubers, and rhizomes. Some plants can be propagated through both methods, but others are limited strictly to one or the other. Name roses, such as Peace, can be propagated only through cuttings from which bud grafts are made. In this chapter we will concern ourselves with how to get seeds to sprout and cuttings to grow.

Voltaire, in a letter to Frederick the Great, wrote: "Madame du Chatelet is not yet delivered; it gives her more trouble to produce a child than a book." In somewhat the same way, it can sometimes be more trouble to get a seed to produce a plant than it is to write a book.

In seed germination, we have to learn to love obstinate and maverick seeds. There are many of them. The transformation of seed to seedling—the process we call germination—is such a common occurrence that we often take it for granted. Most of the seeds we plant begin to germinate as soon as they are embedded in moist material so that they can absorb water.

When the seeds we sow do not sprout, we blame the seeds. However, generally speaking, when we cannot get seeds to germinate, the fault usually is not that of the seeds, but ours.

Consider what would happen if all seeds germinated immediately upon contact with moisture. Since most seeds ripen in the fall, they would sprout about the time winter was at its worst, and the tender seedlings would be killed. Before long, the species would be extinct.

Thus, a reluctance to germinate is a condition for survival. In devious ways, nature must prevent seeds from sprouting until conditions are right for the subsequent growth of the plant. Within each seed is not only the spark of life but also an intricate mechanism to protect that life.

The essential part of the seed is the embryo it encloses. This embryo starts out as a single cell—the fertilized egg—and ends up becoming a tiny plant consisting of a miniature root and shoot. In the usual course of development, the growth of the embryo stops completely when the seed ripens. The ripe seed is detached from the mother plant, and the embryo begins an independent existence.

It is marvelously equipped. It has a food supply, a seed coat, and other appendages for its distribution and protection. The stored food nourishes the embryo until it becomes a self-sustaining seedling. The enveloping coat protects the food supply and the delicate body of the embryo. And there may be thorns for protection and wings for distribution. But not so obvious, there is usually an elaborate internal system to protect the seed from indiscriminate germination.

A seed is like a loaded pistol with a safety catch to prevent accidental discharge. The embryo "bullet" will not go off until the safety catch is released. Scientists call these ingenious safety devices blocks. Some of the more usual blocks are specific requirements of moisture, time, temperature, aeration, or light—or a combination of some of these requirements.

Moisture—or more accurately, the lack of moisture—is a common block. Seeds will not germinate when dry. But when the seeds are supplied with moisture, this block is removed, and where no further block exists, the germination process begins. This is true of the seeds of a large number of plant varieties, but especially those of our domesticated plants.

Most of our food plants and annual flowers fall into this group. They have only one block, and because of this we seldom see these plants growing wild. Their readiness to germinate when moisture is supplied makes them vulnerable to the vagaries of uncontrolled environment, thus endangering their survival. They continue to exist only because we have taken over their preservation. We withhold the moisture until conditions are right.

In order to survive, most seeds have more than one block to germination. For example, some seeds need time as well as moisture; they need a rest period known as afterripening, which may be several weeks or months in length. The forget-me-not is an example.

Temperature is a rather common block to germination. Most seeds will not germinate when the temperature is low. Some other seeds will not start to germinate at high temperatures. Larkspur and bells of Ireland are examples. And some seeds, even though they germinate under relatively high temperature conditions, first require exposure to near freezing before germination will begin. Rose and forget-me-not seeds are classic examples.

Aeration is another germination block. Some seeds will germinate under water, but most will not. They need air along with moisture—a damp, aerated seeding medium.

Then there is light. Most seeds are not influenced by light blocks as much as by the other blocks. But many, like begonia, columbine, cineraria, feverfew, and kalanchoe, need light to germinate. Such seeds should be planted on top of the soil, with little or no covering.

Research into starting seeds to grow has recently shown that the red portion of the visible spectrum stimulates germination. However, far-red light, on the boundary between red and infrared, is capable of reversing this stimulation of red light, and thereby inhibits germination. This reversal is itself reversed when followed by red light. It is always the color of the final light exposure that is decisive. We know this happens, but the reason remains a mystery.

There are still a lot of questions to be answered and problems to be solved in the entire area of seed germination. We
are only touching the hem of knowledge in this field.

We have mentioned only a few of the better known
germination-regulating mechanisms. It is important to know
that these exist. And it should also be remembered that
several of these mechanisms may be found in a single seed.

In general, most cultivated-flower seeds can be germinated
in the familiar "normal" manner described below. Where
there are exceptions, we will point them out.

All seeds should be sterilized with Semesan solution, used
full strength, or dusted with Arasan. The easiest way to dust is
to put the seeds into a little bag, add a pinch of Arasan, and
shake. Household chlorine bleach is also a good seed
sterilizer. Soak seeds about ten minutes in one part chlorine
bleach to ten parts water. The seeds are now ready for the
seeding medium.

The requirements of the seeding medium are different from
the growing mixture. Extreme friability and moisture retention
are of prime importance for germinating. The mixture should
not become so compact that seeds requiring months to a year
or more to germinate cannot break through.

Fertility of the seeding medium is not too important if you
follow the practice of transferring the seedlings to pots as soon
as they can be moved or else feeding them early with a
nutrient solution.

Here are some excellent germinating mixtures.

Use equal parts by bulk of:
- sand, vermiculite, and peat moss
- soil, vermiculite, and peat moss
- vermiculite and peat moss
- sand and peat moss
- sand and vermiculite
- sand, soil, and peat moss

I prefer the first and the fourth. But any of the above will
give comparable results. Seedlings will have no difficulty
breaking through and can be removed without injury to the
roots or adjacent seeds. However, if the seedling will not be

transplanted immediately, then the soil and peat moss plus either sand or vermiculite are the best mixtures to use. My wife liked vermiculite and peat moss or sand and vermiculite. But she preferred vermiculite alone. And because of its light, open texture, good aeration, and moisture retention, vermiculite is an excellent germinating medium with little damping-off problem. As damping-off—a fungus disease of seedlings—is an everpresent problem in seed germination, the soil and sand used for the seeding medium and the potting mixture should be sterilized.

Most soil-sterilizing directions will tell you to bake the soil in your oven. And this is fine—if you can stand the resulting unpleasant odor. For small amounts, it is much easier, and the results are perfectly satisfactory, to sterilize by scalding. Put the soil and sand mixture in flats or shallow pots and pour a generous quantity of boiling water through it. Then let it dry for a day or two before using. Just before use, sprinkle lightly with Semesan solution or Arasan.

I like to sow my seeds in flats or in aluminum containers about 4 by 6 inches and 1½ inches deep—the kind in which some frozen food is packaged—especially when there are only a limited number of seeds.

Small seeds are sown on the surface of the seeding medium or are barely covered. Larger seeds are sown deeper. The old rule for seed depth is a good one: "Sow to a depth equal to two to four times the diameter of the seed."

After sowing, I slip the flat or tray into a polyethylene plastic bag to keep the seeding medium from drying out. Thus, each seed tray becomes a miniature greenhouse with its own moisture control.

Moisture is important. The seeding medium must be kept moist, but never to the extent that a visible film of water surrounds the seeds. Excessive moisture can actually stop germination or cause abnormal development of the seedling.

Light is not necessary for the germination of most seeds. But it does have a stimulating effect on many and hinders only about twenty of several hundred common plants. With the exception of these few, I always expose my seed flats to light.

Plants for which this is not recommended practice are:

Calendula	Nemesia
Centaurea	Pansy—Viola
Cyclamen	Periwinkle
Cynoglossum	Phlox
Didiscus	Poppy
Forget-me-not	Portulaca
Gazania	Salpiglossis
Larkspur	Schizanthus
Myosotis	Sweet Pea
Nasturtium	Verbena

Most seeds germinate over a wide temperature range, but some will sprout only within narrow limits. The rule of thumb is: The temperature at which seeds will germinate is governed by the temperature existing at the plant's origin. Seeds of tropical or semitropical plants germinate best in warm temperature. Seeds of northern plants, in cool temperature. When in doubt, prechill for a while, or use alternate periods of low and high temperatures.

In broad terms, we can say that most seeds used for cultivated flowering plants are easy to germinate. There are exceptions, of course. Canna and morning-glory seeds are among them.

Hard-coated seeds, like those of canna and morning-glory, germinate faster when first soaked in hot water. Use water that is almost boiling, around 200 degrees. Let the seeds soak in this for about 10 hours as the water cools. The rule is: Soak until they swell. Some growers soak these seeds in alcohol for a day or two. The jokesters insist they pop themselves open when they hiccup.

For larger hard-coated seeds, such as sweet peas and acacia, you can remove the hard surface layer that forms the moisture barrier with sandpaper or emery cloth.

Treatment to break physiological cold blocks of some hard-to-germinate seeds is a process called stratification. By this we mean that seeds are placed in moist sand or peat and held at a temperature of around 40 degrees for a month or more. Seeds of bleeding-heart and rose are handled this way.

I stratify my seeds by placing them into small aluminum or plastic trays filled with my regular seeding medium. I plant the seeds to the proper depth, mist, and slip the tray into a plastic sandwich bag. I set this in the refrigerator, just above the fruit keeper. It is easy to check regularly. A glance tells you whether any seeds have sprouted. If you can't use the refrigerator, a cool fruit cellar will do nicely, or the cold frame outdoors.

If, after a month in the refrigerator or cold frame, the seeds have not sprouted, bring them into room temperature for a week or ten days. Then, if they still haven't germinated, move them back into the cool location for another month.

Under normal treatment, germination time varies with different plants. Some will germinate in a matter of days. Many annuals do. But others, such as roses and azaleas, may take years. For this reason, it is important to know the germination requirements of the seeds with which you work. If you do not and the seeds you plant require a long germinating period, you will be disappointed waiting for them to sprout. You might even discard them, thinking they are infertile.

After germination, the seedling is not fully independent. It must establish itself in soil before its reserve of food supplied by the endosperm is depleted. For this reason, and especially if you are using an inert seeding medium such as vermiculite or sand, transfer the seedling to soil as soon as possible. This early transfer avoids transplant shock and allows the seedling to get an early start in the manufacture of the food it needs.

The fertility of the growing mixture is important. I like a good friable mixture of two parts rich garden soil and one part peat moss. The soil should be sterilized to help prevent damping-off of the seedlings. And a little Arasan or Semesan added to the soil will help.

The temperature, moisture, and light requirements for the establishment of seedlings are generally the same as the requirements of the mature plant—with some reservations. If the mature plant likes warm humidity for growth, modify this in the seedling stage to keep damping-off from becoming a real problem. And even if the mature plant likes dry soil conditions, never let the seedling's soil get too dry. Also, as a general rule, the light need not be as intense as the mature plant will tolerate. It boils down to temperance. Temper all extremes.

If it is winter and the days are still short, additional artificial light will help the seedlings to get started and will accelerate growth. I built some wooden shelves for this purpose. Over each shelf are two 40-watt fluorescent lights, hung about 8 inches from the plants. Seedlings are exposed to this light for about fifteen hours a day.

To summarize the procedure for handling seeds and seedlings: Use a light, sterilized soil for your seed flats. Mix with peat, perlite, or vermiculite. If you use sand, perlite, peat, or vermiculite without soil, remove seedlings promptly or apply a weak fertilizer, as there are no nutrients in these materials. The soil should be moist when sowing seeds—but not wet. The row method is best; use a pencil to make a furrow. It is easier to remove the seedlings from rows than when they are scattered. To prevent the spread of damping-off, do not sow seedlings too thickly. Dust with Arasan. Do not cover fine seeds such as begonias and petunias. Instead water them with a fine spray. Place flats in plastic or cover with a pane of glass. For fine seeds sown on the surface, cover with newspaper. Promptly remove all covers when seeds germinate. Allow air to reach seedlings. The best germinating temperature for most seeds is between 65 and 75 degrees.

The manner in which tiny seedlings are handled has a great deal to do with later results.

When seedlings are transferred to pots or flats, poke holes into the receiving medium. Grasp the seedlings gently—avoid crushing them. Lower the seedling into the hole, using a pencil to guide the roots in if necessary; never jam or force the little plant into the soil. Should the roots become broken or the stem become crimped, throw the seedling away. The damage it has suffered will kill it anyhow. For extremely small seedlings, like those of begonias, use plant tweezers to handle them.

All seedlings can quickly become dehydrated. For that reason, transplant in a shaded spot. Do not remove tiny plants and leave them exposed to the air. Once out of the seeding medium, get them into the growing medium as fast as you can.

Do not plant seedlings too deep, just deep enough to cover the roots. After transplanting, feed immediately with complete liquid fertilizer—a 20–20–20 solution at about 1 tablespoon per gallon of water.

And now, let's look at propagation by cuttings.

Forcing often involves a sense of hurry. Flowers are wanted ahead of time. So growers look for short cuts. Propagation by cuttings is one. It usually takes less time than growing from seed. It also gets you an exact duplicate of your specimen plant. Seeds do not always produce uniform plants or flowers that run true to color. Cuttings are an assurance that you will get the color and form that you want.

The cuttings we make for the flowers that we normally force are either stem or leaf cuttings. We take a part of the stem or a leaf from a plant and root it. A proper balance in four areas is necessary for the severed stem or leaf to live and form roots—temperature, moisture, air, and light.

Each plant has a temperature at which it grows best when rooted. But most cuttings have a common characteristic in that they root better with bottom heat—around 70 degrees—with the top temperature about 10 degrees cooler. In greenhouse practice, cuttings are inserted into flats and placed over heat pipes—but not on them. Any source of bottom heat can be utilized as long as it does not overheat or dry out the medium in which the cuttings are being rooted. In any case, keep rooting flats off the ground. They will do better on benches.

For success in rooting cuttings, a heating cable with thermostat control is a big help. Place a 3-inch layer of sand on the bottom of a propagating bed or flat and bury the heating cable in 1 inch of sand. Place a sheet of glass over the sand surface, butting several sheets together over a large surface, and add about 3 inches of sand and vermiculite mix on top, or whatever rooting medium you use. Set the thermostat so that the bottom sand is kept 5 to 10 degrees warmer than the air on top.

The cuttings must not be allowed to dry out. Moisture is im-

Cross-section of a heated propagation tray.

portant. The rooting medium must be kept moist at all times.
And this need for moisture extends to the air around the cuttings. The air should be kept humid. Misting helps.

This does not mean that the rooting medium and plants
should be kept soggy wet. Nothing could be worse. Air is
needed within the rooting medium. It should be loose and
porous, never soggy. Even cuttings that will root directly in
water do not favor a water-saturated, airless rooting medium.

When frequent misting is used, drainage must be excellent.
The secret of success with misting is to have movement of air
around the base of the cuttings. Frequent misting also calls for
a weekly application of fertilizer—25–10–10 at the rate of ¼
ounce per 1 gallon of water, with ferbam added for fungus
disease protection. Cuttings not heavily misted should not be
fed.

Good air circulation over the cuttings is important, but
drafts should be avoided. Also avoid direct sunlight. The new
cuttings cannot provide the moisture required by accelerated
transpiration in sunlight and will wilt. If necessary, use a
cheesecloth canopy to shade the cuttings.

The procedure for making cuttings is less involved than the
explanation makes it sound. Use only strong cuttings from

strong, healthy plants. Sterilize beforehand everything that comes in contact with your cuttings—knife, rooting medium, and flats—and hands should be scrubbed. Cuttings are highly susceptible to diseases. Unclean conditions spell failure.

Clean, sharp sand is a favorite rooting medium among most growers. To the sand, some vermiculite, perlite, or peat is often added. The sand gives good heat conduction and firms the cuttings, the perlite brings improved aeration, and the vermiculite and peat give better moisture retention. For azaleas, camellias, gardenias, and other acid-loving plants, use peat alone or as the principal part of a mixture.

When preparing to take cuttings, first tape your thumb to protect it, because you need to use a sharp knife. Cut across a stem just about ½ inch below a node. The exception is a gardenia cutting, which should have a long stem from the cut end to the first node.

Let as much foliage as you can remain on the stem. For some plants, such as gardenias, no foliage should be removed. But for most, to avoid crowding in the rooting flat, some excess foliage may be removed. Also, the foliage should be removed

Propagating with stem cuttings.

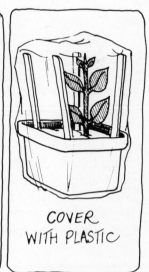

REMOVE LOWER LEAVES

PLANT

COVER WITH PLASTIC

from the portion of the cutting that is inserted in the rooting medium. Again, the gardenia is an exception—no foliage at all should be removed.

You can start your cuttings in flats or directly in 2½-inch pots. If started in pots in which they will be left to grow, use a rooting medium of soil, sand, and peat.

Before inserting your cutting into the rooting medium, dip or dust the cut end with hormone or rooting powder. Some growers dissolve the hormone powder in rubbing alcohol and dip the cut ends into this solution.

Poke a hole into the rooting medium with a pencil or knife, insert about one-third to one-half the cutting, and then firm the base with your fingers.

Water settles the rooting medium around the cutting. If peat is used, be careful not to overwater. Stop before you can squeeze out water drops when the peat is pressed between the fingers.

Light, of course, is essential for food production in the plant and for growth. But direct sunlight is too demanding, causing the plant to lose moisture that it cannot replace rapidly enough because of rootlessness. For this reason, cuttings should be kept in semishade or shaded with cheesecloth or other light material to provide open shade.

Success with cuttings starts with the proper selection of the stock plant. Only a strong, healthy plant should be used. From it, take cuttings of normal growth. Neither the most vigorous shoots nor those that are old and hardened make the best cuttings. Take stem cuttings anytime the plant is actively growing.

The type of stem cuttings to make will vary with different plants. In length, they may range from 2 to 5 inches. One exception would be gardenia cuttings, which are made 6 to 10 inches long in order to get large-sized plants sooner.

In summary, dip base end of cutting in hormone or rooting powder. Then insert in sand and peat, sand alone, or perlite. Give slight bottom heat if possible. Shade for the first few days. Check moisture. Mist occasionally. Cuttings will root in four to six weeks. Chrysanthemums, with frequent misting, will root in three weeks. Pot rooted cuttings in 2½-inch pots. Feed with liquid fertilizer. Handle so that there is no slowing down of growth.

Plants used for forcing that are often propagated by stem cuttings are:

Aster	Gaillardia
Campanula	Lupine
Centaurea	Phlox
Chrysanthemum	Pyrethrum
Dianthus	Salvia
Delphinium	Veronica

A leafbud cutting is a variation of the stem cutting. It is generally used only when cutting stock is scarce because one can use every available "eye."

First, you take a stem cutting. If the plant is alternate leaved, that is, the leaves are not directly opposite each other on the stem, cut a sliver of the stem with a leafbud and leaf. To do this, place the knife on the stem about ½ inch above the leafbud or eye. Cut one-third into the stem and then down to about three-quarters inch below the eye or bud. Cut off. Repeat this with the other buds on the stem.

If the plant has opposite leaves, cut the stem about ¼ inch above the leaves and ¾ inch below. Then split the stem in half lengthwise. You will have two leafbuds, and each has half of the stem.

Treat your leafbud cuttings with hormone or rooting powder. Then insert them into a rooting medium so that the bud is slightly below the surface. Firm so that your cuttings will not topple when watered. Pot in soil when well rooted, even if leafbuds have not started to grow. Once started, they will grow rapidly and catch up with full stem cuttings.

For some plants, root cuttings are the favored method of propagation. To get plants for forcing, root cuttings may be made from:

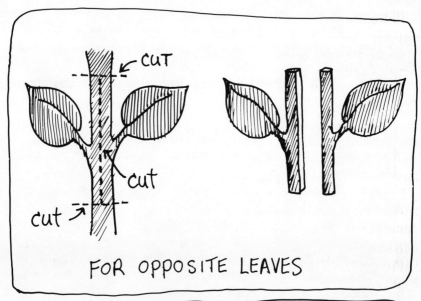

FOR OPPOSITE LEAVES

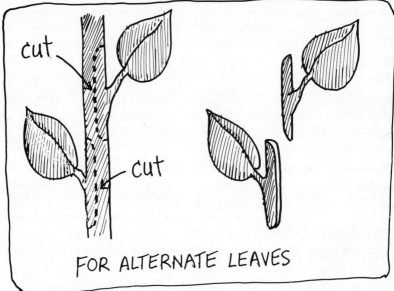

FOR ALTERNATE LEAVES

How to take leaf cuttings for propagation.

Anchusa	Poppy
Anemone	Phlox
Bouvardia	Stokesia
Gypsophila	

Select a medium fleshy root. Sever from plant and cut into 1- to 2-inch pieces. Place on soil—not in a rooting medium—in shallow flats. The root pieces may be closer together, but they should not touch. Cover with about ½ inch of soil. After roots have produced a small growing plant, move to pots or beds.

Finally, a number of indoor plants are easily propagated from leaves—not the leafbuds but the leaves themselves. Almost everyone is familiar with the leaf propagation of African-violets. Begonias and sansevierias can be handled in this way, as can most plants that have thick, fleshy leaves with pronounced veins.

By way of example, you may take a leaf from some of the fibrous-rooted begonias, cut the veins in several places, lay the leaf on top of a rooting medium, pin it down with toothpicks, and cover it lightly with peat, sand, or vermiculite. New plants will develop from the cuts across the veins.

Other plants need not have the veins cut. For bryophyllum, simply spread the leaf on the rooting medium, pin down, and cover lightly. A single sansevieria leaf can be cut into a number of pieces and each piece inserted upright into a rooting medium.

When a full leaf is used, as for African-violet, *Begonia heracleifolia*, gloxinia, and peperomia, and it is inserted upright into the rooting medium, cut so it has a part of the leaf stem on it. This will help to hold the leaf above the surface of the rooting medium.

Once leaf cuttings are rooted, transfer to pots and handle as small plants.

The last type of propagation that we will consider—that from bulbs, corms, tubers, and rhizomes—is well known and widely practiced. A single daffodil bulb will multiply into a clump that can be broken apart into a number of single daffodil bulbs.

Stem-layering a potted lily for propagation. The same technique can be used in the outdoor garden.

Lilies offer a variety of propagation methods. The thick outer scales can be broken off the bulb in midsummer. Placed in flats of sandy soil and peat, these scales will establish roots by October. Then, there are lily bulblets: The tiger lily and others will produce small aerial bulbs which can be picked off and planted as seed. Another lily propagation method is stem layering: After flowering, bend over the stem and fasten it upright and partially inserted into a pot of moist sandy soil. Small bulbs will form in the axils of the leaves. Remove and sow as seed.

When reproducing lilies by scale cuttings, dip the ends in hormone rooting powder mixed with Fermate, a fungicide. This will help them root easier and will help prevent rot.

Dahlias, when not grown from seed, are propagated by root divisions and cuttings. Old clumps are stored in dry sand or peat at 40 degrees. When it is time to start forcing them, the clumps are divided into several pieces, each containing a piece of the stem with two good eyes.

Dahlias may also be propagated by cuttings. The old clumps are placed in deep flats of moist sand, soil, or peat and brought into a warm growing area. They are given bottom heat, or at least kept off the ground. When new shoots are 6 or 8 inches long, they are cut and handled as cuttings. In making the cut, sever through or just above a node. This makes it possible for the plant to produce another crop of cuttings.

Gladiolus—not commonly forced—produces new corms and cormlets just above the old corm. The cormlets will grow into flowering size within two to three years.

Plant propagation—whatever its form—is an interesting and exciting part of plant forcing. Unless we buy our plants ready to force, forcing seeds to sprout and cuttings to grow is the beginning.

And now that we have our plants, let's start forcing them.

7
Forcing Bulbs, Corms, and Tubers

Bulbs are packages of beauty. They are nature's way of wrapping up a spring promise in a daffodil and summer sunshine in a lily. They are also complete growth packages for the immature flowers. They are amazing food storage organs that enclose stems and leaves and produce roots.

To a gardener, the word *bulb* often includes other bulblike organs that are not true bulbs. They include the solid, flat stem bases, called corms, such as those of gladiolus and crocus; the thickened ends of stems, called tubers, such as those for begonias; and the elongated, thick stems called rhizomes, as those for cannas and callas.

In the plants that grow from bulbs, corms, and tubers —especially bulbs—nature has given the gardener a head start over those that grow from seed. And there is almost a guarantee of success, since almost everything that is needed is packaged within the bulb. Hyacinths and narcissus can be brought into bloom without soil, if you want, using just a few pebbles to support the bulb in water.

Most bulbs will bloom in the home with little effort and will blossom within a few short weeks. They are carefree. They are fragrant. They are colorful. And they are beautiful in form and variety. No other group of plants can offer so much.

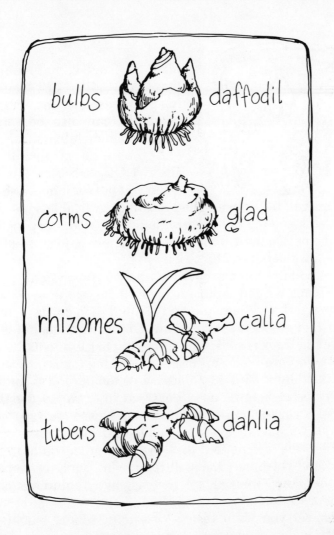

bulbs — daffodil

corms — glad

rhizomes — calla

tubers — dahlia

Bulbs, corms, and tubers can be forced into bloom through the bleakest part of winter, from November through April, bringing spring to the window garden, the sun-room, or the kitchen windowsill. And among them are some wonderful children's flowers. Most bulbs will grow for youngsters, displaying the miracle of growth before wondering eyes. One of my fondest memories is of the paper narcissus that I forced in a chipped sugar bowl many years ago.

The forcing procedure for bulbs is simple. In fall, plant the bulbs in pots or deep flats. Use good soil. Flats should be 4 or 5 inches deep, and pots 5 to 6 inches in diameter. In a 6-inch pot,

plant five or six tulip bulbs or three daffodils or hyacinths. Irises, crocuses, scillas, and grape hyacinths can also be forced—these in 5-inch bulb pans.

A good rule of thumb is to allow 1½ inches between bulbs when you pot for indoor use.

In general, bulbs need good drainage in friable soil—minus fertilizer, since the bulbs carry their own food. Bury the bulbs to their tips. Do not fill the pots completely with soil—allow ½ inch below the pot rim for water.

Bulbs will not force properly without a root system. To form roots, place potted bulbs—except irises—in a cold frame outdoors, or bury them, pot and all, and then cover them with sawdust, or woodchips and straw. On the average, bulbs need about eight weeks of this cold treatment to form roots.

When you are ready to force them, bring them into an area of subdued light with 45- to 50-degree temperatures for about two weeks. Hyacinths need darkness to draw up the flower stem, so cover the tops of the pots with newspapers. After two weeks they are ready to force at 60 to 65 degrees.

Besides the spring bulbs, there are other bulbs, corms, tubers, and rhizomes that will force well, such as cyclamen, anemones, and lilies. Each has its own requirements and forcing procedures.

Whenever you want results in forcing plants quickly and effortlessly, whenever you want the promise and color of spring to dispel the doldrums of winter, force some bulbs, corms, or tubers into bloom. One caution: They will capture your heart.

AMARYLLIS *(Amaryllis sp.)*

CONTROL: Dormancy. Temperature. Timing.

Amaryllis bulbs can be forced easily to produce their brilliant blooms for Christmas, or for late winter and spring. Although normally grown and propagated from bulbs, amaryllis can also be grown from seed. And since they lend themselves well to home cross-pollination to produce new hybrid strains, we'll start with seeds. Plant from these seeds will flower the third year after sowing. It takes patience.

Plant the seeds and grow the seedlings directly in 2½-inch pots. Do not disturb the roots. In the fall of the second year, move to a larger pot. Your plant is now a bulblet.

The usual method of propagating amaryllis is from bulblets. This is the only way to propagate a particularly desirable specimen that you have grown or may have developed.

After an amaryllis has flowered, small bulblets, or offsets, are formed during the summer growing season. When you are repotting the bulb in fall, remove these bulblets. Be sure each bulblet has roots. Pot each bulblet in an individual pot with a good soil and peat mixture. In growing these bulblets, do not disturb the roots. They will flower in the second year.

In forcing amaryllis to flower for Christmas, or anytime during the late winter, full-grown bulbs are usually used. They are grown in Holland and are specially prepared —precooled—for forcing. For early forcing, make sure the bulbs you get are precooled. They are usually available from suppliers from November on. (There is no other way to determine whether a bulb has been precooled than to rely on the supplier's word.)

Bulbs are sold by sizes that are based on the bulb's diameter in inches. Sizes range from 2½ to 4 inches. The larger the bulb, the greater the number of flowers it will produce.

Do not expose precooled bulbs to excessively high or low temperatures before potting. Pot immediately after you get them.

For Christmas flowers, start precooled bulbs early in November. For flowers anytime after Christmas, pot about eight weeks before the date that you want flowers. The rate of growth and flower timing can be controlled by temperature.

Use a large enough pot—probably 5 to 7 inches—to allow for 1 inch of soil between the bulb and the pot. Potting soil should be a mixture of soil, peat, and humus. For depth, pot the bulb so that the upper third is exposed above the soil line.

Water well when first potted. Then, water sparingly for ten days until root growth has started. Use lukewarm water. During the leaf-growing period that follows, water more frequently and feed with a diluted balanced fertilizer once a month.

For starting and growing amaryllis bulbs, keep temperatures around 60 to 70 degrees. If necessary to delay flowering, reduce temperatures to 45 or 50 degrees. When in bloom, growing the plant at 60 degrees helps to keep the flowers in good shape longer.

After your amaryllis has flowered, keep it in growing condition through the summer or as long as the leaves are green. A shady location outdoors is ideal. This rebuilds the bulb. In early fall, or after leaves dry, plants should be taken indoors and kept in a cool, dry, dark location until they begin to show signs of growth, usually in late fall or early winter.

Before you force them again, they should have a minimum of two months dormancy. Do not take them out of their pots. Just topdress, water, and feed.

Amaryllis bulbs are available in colors ranging from pure white through various oranges and reds—rose, scarlet, carmine, crimson—as well as variegated and striped flowers.

ANEMONE or WINDFLOWER (*Anemone coronaria*)

CONTROL: Timing.

You can grow anemones from seeds, root divisions, or tubers. Seeds and root divisions are started in shallow flats in April or May. Flats should have sandy loam with peat added. Grow in a sunny location until fall.

In fall—September or October—these tuberous roots you have grown—or tubers you have purchased for forcing—are potted in light soil. Water and move the pots to a moist, cool location—around 45 degrees. Hold them there for several days, covered with wet burlap. Then move to a 50-degree, light, and airy area. Water freely as plants develop. When flowering starts, feed occasionally with a dilute fertilizer.

Plants handled in this way should flower from January through March.

After flowering, dry off plants, cutting back on water until the leaves dry. Then clean the tubers and store them in a cool place. They can be used again in fall.

Excellent hybrids and strains are available, and they offer a great variety of brilliant colors—except orange and yellow. For double flowers, try St. Brigid, and for singles, try de Caen.

CALLA LILY *(Zantedeschia sp.)*

CONTROL: Timing. Water.

Calla lilies are native to areas of South Africa where growing conditions alternate between being extremely wet and extremely dry. To grow callas, we must duplicate these conditions.

Callas are produced from rhizomes—gnarled-appearing bulbs. They are generally grown in pots, either as large decorative pot plants or as cut flowers. They have a long blooming season, extending through winter and spring—and even into summer if desired. Callas can be forced for Easter, and are occasionally associated with this season. But they are not the Easter lilies of tradition.

Native to shady areas, callas will grow well in moist, semisunny locations. But they will also thrive in full sun in winter.

Callas are propagated by division of a rhizome or by offsets of a rhizome. These are usually available in late summer or fall.

Rhizomes are sold by sizes that express the diameter in inches. They usually range from 1 to 3 inches. Generally the larger sizes produce more and larger flowers.

In August or September, plant each rhizome in a 5- or 6-inch pot in loose peat–sandy-loam potting soil. The soil should be slightly on the acid side. Barely cover the top of the rhizome and leave space in the pot for soil to be added later. Topdress with soil when roots appear on the surface.

Water moderately until roots are established, then thoroughly and continuously. Feed weekly with liquid urea at 1 ounce to 7 gallons water or ammonium sulfate at 1 ounce to 2 gallons water. (Refer to Appendix C table of equivalents for aid in working with lesser amounts.) Keep night temperatures about 55 to 60 degrees. Grow in full sun during the winter and in partial shade during spring and summer.

When several pots are grown on a bench, allow plenty of space between them—up to 2 feet. Spray to prevent aphids and red spider mites. But especially watch for root rot. It spreads rapidly and will infest other callas. Remove and discard any diseased plant.

For cut flowers, you can expect to cut eight to ten blooming stems from a single plant during a season. Or as pot plants, you will have a continual succession of blooms.

For Easter flowering, the common yellow calla of the garden is often used. Plant the rhizome in late December in a rich peat and loam mixture. You can plant directly in 4- or 5-inch pots, or start in flats and move to pots when growth has started. Grow at 60 degrees. Water and fertilize regularly.

If summer blooms are not wanted, bring callas into dormancy in early June. In any case, flowering should be brought to an end by late summer.

Dormancy is induced by withholding water. Stop watering and let the plants gradually dry and be dry all summer. Store the pots with dry soil and rhizomes in a dry place. In August, take the spring-dormant pots out and start watering again. Rhizomes can be used over and over, and they get larger each year. During the dry period large rhizomes can be shifted to larger pots. Remove the offsets. These can be potted and grown into new plants.

Three species of callas are commonly grown. *Aethiopica* is a large white calla, usually used for cut flowers. The variety *Godfreyana,* called Godfrey, is shorter and more compact and is used for flowering pot plants. And the golden calla, *Elliottiana,* is grown for both uses—cut flowers and pot plants.

Florists also grow what they call black callas (*Arum pictum* is most used; *Arum palaestinum,* which is less hardy, is occasionally available), but these are no longer botanically classified among the true calla lilies. Care and forcing procedures, however, are the same.

Forcing callas is a classic example of cooperation with nature, for you will have to supply the same arid dormancy and wet growing conditions that the plant had in its native habitat.

DAFFODIL, NARCISSUS, JONQUIL *(Narcissus sp.)*

CONTROL: Temperature. Timing.

These hardy, early outdoor bulb plants with unusual floral forms and colors are harbingers of spring. They are happy plants, filled with cheer, and they left the heart out of winter doldrums. They can be easily forced indoors. They can even be forced as early as Christmas if you so desire.

For Christmas, King Alfred *(N. Pseudo-Narcissus)* is the variety we usually use. Only the largest precooled bulbs can be used for this early forcing. These are available in late September and early October. Plant immediately. Set the bulbs in deep flats or pots of light garden soil and peat. Bulbs may touch in flats. In pots space three in a 5-inch pot, and four or five in a 6-inch pot. The top of the bulb should be 1 inch below the surface of the soil. Water thoroughly.

Place the flats or pots in a dark, 45- to 50-degree location —in a storage cooler or a cellar or outdoors under wet straw.

On December 1, check growth of bulbs. If there is an inch of shoot showing, the bulbs can be forced for Christmas. Bring these into a 60-degree area. Water freely with water at room temperature. Shade with cheesecloth until the light sprouts turn green. Then give them full sunlight.

On December 5, bring in the bulbs with 1-inch growth for forcing for New Year's.

From December 10 on, bring in the remainder of the bulbs for January blooming.

For midwinter flowering, precooled bulbs are no longer necessary. A number of other varieties can be used besides King Alfred. Plant and handle these as you would the early precooled bulbs, potting in October and keeping the pots cool at 45- to 50-degree temperatures to allow them to set roots.

After December 15, these midwinter pots may be brought indoors anytime there is at least a 1-inch shoot. The rule is: For the flowering date you want, allow five to six weeks at 55-degree growing temperature. Allow four weeks if you are going to grow at 60 to 65 degrees.

Around March and April, Eastertime, the problem is not one of forcing but of holding the bulbs back. Almost any variety can be forced. Taken out of their cool 45- to 50-degree storage, they bloom in ten to fourteen days. Your efforts must be directed to keeping the storage bulbs as dark and as cool as you possibly can. Pot as late as you can. And make sure they are well covered with straw to prevent temperature variations. There is an exception in the *Narcissus* group to the need for cold storage to form roots. It is the paper white narcissus (*N. lotus albus*). Bulbs may be planted in soil or pebbles or water, and they flower easily for Christmas or any time from November to April. Plant bulbs six weeks prior to the time you want them to bloom in winter. In the spring, use bulbs that you have kept cool to prevent sprouting. These bulbs will set roots, grow leaves, and flower in three weeks. It is an excellent bulb for a child to grow, and it is also ideal for classroom demonstration.

All members of the *Narcissus* group, whether grown in pots or in flats for cut flowers, should be kept well watered. They may be given a light feeding of dilute fertilizer, but this is not essential.

After blooming, the bulbs can be planted outdoors for next-spring blooms. Keep watering as long as leaves stay green, or let the rain do it outdoors. When the leaves have dried, remove the bulbs and plant them in your garden, or hold them on a dry shelf and plant them in the fall. Do not use them again for forcing. Let them herald the arrival of spring outdoors.

DAHLIA *(Dahlia sp.)*

CONTROL: Timing.

As indoor flowering plants, dahlias seem to have regional popularity. In some areas, they are unknown. In others, they are widely used for cut flowers and pot plants.

The dahlias used for pot plants are dwarf varieties. They can be grown from cuttings, tubers, or seeds. Growing from seeds gives you a chance to see the flower in your garden and to make a selection of which tubers you want to force.

Seeds sown in February should produce fine flowering plants in fall. They should germinate in two to three weeks at 65- to 75-degree temperatures. Try the Unwin Dwarf mixture, which produces plants that grow to 18 inches tall with double blooms 3 inches across in a variety of colors. Or get some tubers of Single Dwarf dahlias for finishing in 6-inch pots. Only 16 inches high, they flower almost continuously if the faded blooms are picked off. Murillo and Snow White are strong favorites.

Inspect and tag your garden plants in the fall, selecting specimens you like either for propagation or for forcing as pot plants. After the first killing frost, carefully dig up the clumps with a fork, shake off loose soil, and store upside down in a cool dry place until needed. The specimens you choose can be propagated by dividing the tubers or by cuttings taken from the tubers. It is important that each cutting have a heel, or eye, at the base. These cuttings grow readily when planted in a cool spot at about 55-degree night temperature.

For flowering plants in 4-inch pots for Mother's Day, use either the tuber or cutting or grow from seed. Sow dahlia seeds in October and transplant seedlings to pots. Pot cuttings in November. Or pot divided tubers—not cuttings—in January. Use friable garden soil. No special care or temperatures are required. Give normal sun, warmth, food, and watering. After flowering in May, they can be moved to the garden, where they will bloom throughout the season.

FREESIA *(Freesia sp.)*

CONTROL: Timing.

Freesias are grown from small bulblike corms that you can grow from seed or buy ready to force. Although usually forced for cut flowers, they make unusual and fragrant pot plants.

Freesias thrive in warm temperatures and, because of this, are easy to grow in the home.

You can start with seeds. If you do, it takes about a year. You first grow to produce corms. The procedure is easy, and you'll find it satisfying—like baking a cake from scratch.

In spring, sow seeds in a flat of peat. First, give the seeds a good toweling, or rub them together briskly between the palms of your work-gloved hands to remove the outer coat. Then soak for twenty-four hours in warm water before planting. Sow in a soil-sand-peat mixture and set the flat in a warm area of about 70 degrees. Germination is slow and may take three weeks to one month at 65 to 75 degrees. After germination, move the flat with the seedlings, untransplanted, to a cold frame outdoors when danger of frost is past. Throughout the summer, water and feed with a balanced liquid fertilizer such as 4–12–4.

In early September, withhold the water and move the flat to a dry place. Let the soil and foliage dry. After a few weeks, remove the small corms—usually in late September or early October. Plant these corms—or ones you have bought—in pans, shallow pots, or flats of friable peat and soil mixture. Space about 2 inches apart. A 5-inch pan will hold ten to twelve corms.

Water, and hold at 60-degree night temperature, covered with newspaper, to set roots. Then bring into room temperature. This program should bring the plants into bloom in January and February. Use supports to get straight stems.

For March flowering, plant bulbs in November. Cut and handle like Dutch iris (see pages 110–112).

HYACINTH *(Hyacinthus orientalis)*

CONTROL: Timing.

Three separate forcing methods are used to force hyacinths in three different blooming periods. These periods are Christmas, January–February, and Easter.

For Christmas blooms, only the large bulbs can be used for forcing. These bulbs must be specially prepared by being stored at 80 degrees after digging. These prepared early-forcing bulbs are available in September and October, and they should be planted immediately.

Plant one bulb in a 4-inch pot, two in a 5-inch pot, or three in a 6-inch pot. Use porous, sandy loam. The top of the bulb should be about ½ inch below the surface of the soil. Water. Store outdoors in the coldest place you can find, and cover with straw. If a cold cellar or cold storage is available, store at 45 to 50 degrees.

About November 30, the pots should be moved to a dark, warm, 70-degree location. The plant will grow rapidly, but the leaves will be light colored. When leaves are 8 inches tall, the potted plants should be moved to a light area to darken the leaf color. The temperature should be reduced to 50 degrees to harden the plant and to retard the flowering until wanted.

For January–February flowering, it is not necessary to use prepared bulbs. Pot in the fall, water, and store outside in a cool location covered with straw. Bring the pots into a warm area on December 15 to 20—or twenty-five to twenty-eight days before you want them to bloom. Grow at 60 degrees. If flowers are slow to form, or if you want them to bloom sooner, increase the growing temperature. Decreasing the temperature will retard them.

For Easter, hyacinths force so easily that it is difficult to hold them if Easter is late. Slow-blooming varieties—Nimrod and Bismarck—are used for delayed bloom. Prepared bulbs are not necessary. Pot in late fall, and hold outdoors in the cold, keeping them well covered with straw. Bring in the plants as wanted—about three to four weeks before Easter or, for a succession of blooms, every two weeks starting January 15 and continuing through February 15. Grow at 60 degrees. When plants are in bud, a slightly higher temperature will speed them up, and a lower temperature will retard them.

For varieties that produce heavy spikes, staking and ties are usually necessary.

Hyacinths can also be forced in pebbles and water. Some gardeners hold out a bulb from fall garden planting to force in this way on the kitchen windowsill.

After forced blooming, it is usually best to discard the bulbs.

IRIS *(Iris sp.)*

CONTROL: Temperature. Timing.

The iris used for winter forcing is the Dutch iris. It is also called the German iris or Japanese iris. Since the summer

bearded iris and its 150 related species such as flag, mourning, Persian, orchid, and Tangerian irises are not used for forcing, we will not concern ourselves with them. We'll concentrate on the group which includes *Iris tingitana* (Wedgewood), *Iris Xiphium*, and *Iris reticulata*—the Dutch irises, as they are commonly known.

There are three broad flowering periods for forcing Dutch iris, as well as three variations in technique. For earliest flowering, field-grown bulbs must be heat cured and pre-cooled. This means that after the bulbs have been dug —usually in July—they are given a 10-day curing period at 90 degrees, and then six weeks at 45 to 48 degrees in a cooler. The bulbs must be planted immediately. If planted on September 25, then grown as cool as possible—45 to 55 degrees—they will flower for Thanksgiving.

For early flowering—the late December and Christmas flowering—the bulbs are dug from the growing field on September 1. They are cleaned and placed in a cooler until October 15. Only large-sized bulbs of the variety Wedgewood are used.

When these bulbs become available to you in mid-October, plant immediately, or the effect of the precooling may be lost. Plant in deep flats. Ordinary loose garden soil will do. Space bulbs 3 by 3 inches at a depth at which the tops of the bulbs are covered. Water moderately, but do not fertilize.

After planting, move the flats into a dark, cool area of about 50 degrees. A basement or covered cold frame may do. Hold the bulbs in this cool, dark location until the shoots are 1 to 2 inches long—usually about thirty days.

Around November 15, forcing can begin. Uncover the flats and bring them into a light, cool area. Give them ample water, air, and sunlight, and a night temperature of about 60 degrees. The daytime temperature can go to 65 or 70 degrees on bright days. Daily watering is essential. Flats must not be allowed to dry out or iris will not bloom. Once forcing has started, do not move the flats. For a succession of cut flowers over several weeks, bring the flats out of the dark, cool area at one-week intervals.

For January flowering, midwinter-forcing varieties are used, such as Blue Ribbon. The procedure for forcing is the same as for Wedgewood except that the bulb precooling period is only eight weeks long. Bulbs come out of precooling around November 1.

For iris blooms in February and March, you can get color variations from blue. Varieties such as Moonlight, Pacific Gold, and Snowdrift can be used. These need an eight-week precooling. Plan your precooling or buy bulbs that are ready to plant around the last of November or early in December. After the dark-cool treatment, they should be ready to force in a 55- to 60-degree area by January 1.

For spring forcing—for flowers in April and May—the smaller bulbs can be planted, and precooling is no longer necessary. Simply hold the Dutch iris bulbs dormant and dry at an 80-degree temperature until November. Plant and allow to sprout in a dark, cool location. Begin forcing at 50 to 55 degrees in late January. This forcing temperature varies because in this case the smaller the bulb used, the lower the forcing temperature. We force at 50 degrees for small spring culls and at 60 degrees for the larger winter bulbs.

For shipping or holding, iris should be cut in bud stage when color begins to show. For immediate use in the home, it may be cut when wide open.

IXIA or CORN LILY *(Ixia sp.)*

CONTROL: Timing.

Although ixias are seldom grown as house plants, they are easy to grow indoors in a sunny but cool location. They would be ideal for a sun-room.

The attractive, brilliantly colored flowers can be forced into bloom from December through April by making successive plantings. They are grown from corms.

For late December and early January bloom—about Christmas time—plant in August. For January and February flowering, plant in October. For March flowers, plant in November. For April blooms, plant in December.

Plant corms five or six to a 5-inch pot, and about 1-inch deep, in sandy loam. For early plantings, use only the large size—¾-inch corms. For later plantings, you can use the smaller sizes—even ½ inch.

For August planting, water and put pots in a shady, protected spot or cool basement, and cover them with wet burlap and keep burlap damp until young shoots appear. Then move them into the light. Grow at a night temperature of 50 to 55 degrees. Water generously.

For later plantings, water and bring directly into cool growing area. No period of darkness is necessary. Water moderately until rooted, and then generously.

Apply a weak liquid fertilizer when flower stems appear and again when buds are formed. Support the plants with a stake.

After flowering, reduce the watering until leaves turn yellow. Then stop watering. Store pots with corms in dry soil and reuse them again next season. Simply start watering. Or, remove the corms, store dry, and replant next season.

A number of excellent varieties are available in a wide range of colors.

LILY *(Lilium sp.)*

CONTROL: Temperature. Timing.

The indoor gardener will find the many new and colorful hybrid garden lilies to be a rich source for fine flowering pot plants. By forcing them to bloom indoors, you can advance the lily season by several months. And you do not need a greenhouse. The conditions in your kitchen or sun-room are ideal.

Commercial growers find lilies to be profitable plants for late winter and spring.

The control for forcing lily bulbs is their immediate response to cold treatment. The bulbs can be taken from your garden or from stock at a nursery supply store or garden shop in fall, then cold-treated. Or, you may be able to buy already treated bulbs. (Again, you have to rely on a dealer's word when looking for precooled bulbs.) When you buy pretreated bulbs, they should be potted immediately.

The bulbs from nursery stock or your garden will first have to be treated. This treatment is simply a matter of placing the bulbs into a plastic sandwich bag and storing them in your refrigerator for six weeks to two months. The storage temperature should be between 34 and 40 degrees. Then pot the bulbs, place them in a sun-room, and they will flower in seventy-five days.

By way of example, let's say it is late October or early November and you have just bought or dug some Harmony lily bulbs. Harmony is an orange red, upright-flowering Mid-Century hybrid type. You would like to have it bloom in a pot indoors? No problem. Cool bulbs in the refrigerator until January 1. Pot, and they will bloom on March 15. For flowering on February 15, cool from October 1 to December 1. By storing the bulbs and then varying the date when they go into the refrigerator, you can have lilies flowering over a long season.

After lily bulbs have been given their cold treatment, pot in 5- or 6-inch pots—one bulb to a pot. But first, place a handful of pebbles on the bottom of the pot for drainage. Then fill with good garden soil, peat, and perlite or coarse sand to which has been added 1 cup of superphosphate per bushel. Bury the bulb so that the tip shows. Water.

I cover my pots with newspapers for two or three days. It keeps the soil moist and gives the roots a chance to get started.

The bulbs start growing almost immediately. A 60-degree night temperature and 70 degrees during the day is ideal, but a few degrees one way or the other doesn't seem to bother the plants. Give the tiny shoots good light. And feed regularly with a balanced liquid fertilizer.

Hybrid lilies are classed as upward flowering, like tulips, and outward flowering, like daffodils. Some excellent upward-flowering varieties are the tall, red Enchantment; the medium-tall, red-flowering Cinnabar; the medium-tall, yellow Joan Evans; and the short, orange red Harmony.

Some fine outward-facing hybrids are the short, red Fireflame; the tall, red Paprika; and the short, yellow Prosperity.

I especially like Harmony, Fireflame, and Prosperity for pot plants. The taller lilies make better cut flowers than potted plants.

There are also species lilies that force well and make attractive pot plants. Among them are *L. japonicum, L. rubellum, L. cernuum, L. speciosum,* and *L. amabile.*

After forcing, do not discard your hybrid or species lily. Set it aside and continue moderate watering. Move outside after danger of frost is past. If the plant tries to flower again in late summer, pinch off the bud. This allows the bulb to regain its strength. In the fall, plant outdoors in the garden. It will flower normally next summer.

Hybrid and species lilies are commercially and aesthetically desirable plants. You probably have grown these colorful lilies in your garden for years. Now grow them indoors.

LILY-OF-THE-VALLEY *(Convallaria majalis)*

CONTROL: Timing. Temperature.

These tiny, fragrant white bells are grown from pips, or crowns. When forced indoors, they are useful as cut flowers and as pot plants.

Pips are generally imported from Holland, Germany, or France. For early forcing, they are dug in September and October and stored for two months at below freezing temperatures. About the first of December, or anytime thereafter, the pips are ready to be forced.

For flowers when you want them, simply plant the pips twenty days prior to the date you want them.

Take the pips out of their cold storage and thaw them at room temperature. Then plant immediately in 5-inch pots, eight to ten pips per pot, or in deep flats about 2 inches apart. Sand and peat is usually used as potting soil. Allow ½ inch of the crown to extend above the soil surface. Pack the soil firmly around each pip. Water thoroughly. Cover with canvas or cloth to maintain shade, humidity, and temperature.

Some growers set the flats or pots over heat pipes to get a temperature of about 80 degrees underneath and 75 degrees on top. But a warm closet or storage space at room temperature will do almost as well.

After two weeks, gradually expose pips to air and light.

For Mother's Day, plant on April 22. For Easter or weddings, plant twenty-one days ahead.

You can also force your own lily-of-the-valley for late winter and spring bloom. Lift clumps from your garden in fall. Pot in containers of light soil. Hold in a cold frame outdoors until January or February. They are alpine plants and need this cold treatment.

About the first of February, or thereafter, bring your plants indoors and place in a light, cool location with a night temperature around 60 degrees. Your plants will bloom in about five weeks.

When they are used as cut flowers, it may be of interest to know that lily-of-the-valley spikes are graded by the length of the stem and the number of bells per stem. The top grade, "Extra," have over twelve bells on stems over 12 inches long. In between, about ten bells on 9-inch stems, are "Selected." About seven bells on stems 7 inches or under are "Seconds" or "Shorts." Twenty-five stems surrounded by leaves is a bunch. The stage at which to cut is when the terminal bud has lost its green color.

Given its cold requirement and started in time for the date you want it, lily-of-the-valley is an easy plant to grow and does well in a warm home. This delightful, fragrant plant offers so much from so little.

ORNITHOGALUM or CHINCHERINCHEE
(Ornithogalum thyrsoides)

CONTROL: Moisture.

This is a rare beauty. It is seldom grown as a pot flowering plant, although it is easy to grow. It is more often used for cut flowers—and is one of the longest lasting among flowers. Cut flowers, which are shipped from South Africa to the United States and Europe, will bloom beautifully for three weeks in water in your home.

The attractive white flowers covering long spikes are usually grown from bulbs. The bulbs keep under any condition and may be handled under any condition. No special treatment is needed.

For Easter flowering, pot in November. Use sandy loam. Plant several bulbs about 1 inch deep in a 5-inch pan. Water moderately at first, then freely when actively growing. Feed with dilute fertilizer—any balanced formulation you have, at about a teaspoon to a gallon of water.

The plant likes a sunny location with a temperature of about 55 to 60 degrees at night. The white flowers are borne on spikes 4 to 6 inches long, and the flowering starts at the bottom. As a cut flower, the spike may be cut when the bottom flowers are open.

Several weeks after flowering, reduce the water and then stop entirely. Allow the pot and the bulb to dry, and keep dry all summer. Water and reuse in fall. Lasts indefinitely.

RANUNCULUS (*Ranunculus* sp.)

CONTROL: Timing. Temperature.

With magnificent camelliatype blooms, Ranunculus makes an excellent winter forcing plant. Yet, it is not commonly grown.

The roots are tuberous, like small dahlia roots. For indoor forcing, start in the fall. Place three or four tubers in a 6-inch shallow pot or pan. Use a mixture of sand, peat, and humus as potting soil. Plant the tubers vertically, about 2 inches deep. Water and move pots to a cool area or cold frame where temperatures are about 45 degrees.

For flowering in March and April, bring pots into warmer temperature—around 50 to 55 degrees—late in February. Shade from the direct sun. Water freely. Feed weekly with a dilute balanced fertilizer—a teaspoon of liquid 4–12–4 in a gallon of water.

Most of the outdoor garden types will force well. There is an excellent selection of colors—pink, white, red, yellow, and mixed.

TUBEROSE (*Polianthes tuberosa*)

CONTROL: Timing.

This is one of our most fragrant flowers, so fragrant, in fact, that many find it objectionable.

Being a tall plant, it is seldom used as a flowering pot plant.

It is used for cut flowers, being grown in a corner of a home greenhouse or on a raised bench in a commercial range.

Tuberoses are grown from bulb-shaped tubers in rich sandy loam. When planting in deep flats, space 6 inches apart. In pots, plant three in a 6-inch pot. Plant so that the top of the tuber is just above the surface of the soil.

For Easter bloom, plant in December and January. For April and May, plant in January and February. For Thanksgiving and November, retard tubers by holding them in a cool, dry place through the summer, and plant in late August.

Grow tuberoses at 65- to 70-degree night temperature. Water moderately. Mist plants on sunny days. Feed regularly with a balanced fertilizer after growth starts and until flowers open.

Although tuberoses are available only in white—a gorgeous waxy pure white bloom on long spikes—you do have a choice of single and double flowers.

TULIP *(Tulipa sp.)*

CONTROL: Temperature. Timing.

There was a time when a single tulip bulb was worth a fortune. The popularity of tulips was so great in Europe in 1634 that it caused "tulipomania" in the Netherlands. A tulip madness swept through the land as men and women in all walks of life bought and sold tulip bulbs at ever-increasing prices. Men trading in tulips became wealthy overnight and, as suddenly, became paupers again.

Tulips are still important to Holland, no longer as single priceless bulbs, but rather collectively, as an export crop. Many of the tulips we use for late forcing are Dutch grown. Early-forcing tulips are generally American grown—in California.

All tulips require a combination of a certain amount of winter cold and a definite degree of cold. It is this combination that triggers and sustains the growth and flowering process. To meet this cold requirement in a concentrated period, you first refrigerate the bulbs and then root them in outside winter cold.

Bulbs are dug in late summer and shipped east for precooling in lockers, where they are held at 40-degree temperatures for six weeks. In this way, precooled bulbs are available in early October.

For tulips to flower for Christmas and in January, precooling is essential. Plant the precooled bulbs on October 1. Expose to outdoor cold through October and November and bring inside on December 1.

When released from storage, the precooled bulbs should be planted immediately in a loose, sandy loam soil. Drainage is important. For pot tulips, cover the bottom of the pot with gravel.

For pot flowers place about five or six bulbs in a 6-inch tulip pan. Plant with the flat side of the bulb facing the outside of the pot. This is a matter of appearance. The leaves on the flat side droop. For cut flowers, place bulbs in a deep flat about 1 or 2 inches apart. Bulbs should be planted so that there is 1 inch of soil underneath and the tops are barely covered.

Water thoroughly. Move pots or flats to a dark, cool storage area—around 45 to 50 degrees. They may be placed in a cool cellar, or outside covered with sand and straw. Let the bulbs remain at this under-50-degree temperature for about six weeks. Keep them moist during this period.

At the end of six weeks, the roots should have formed, and a 2-inch shoot should have grown from the bulb. At this stage, the bulbs can be moved at any time to warmer temperatures—usually 60 degrees—for forcing. Shade from direct sun for a few days until the pale shoots turn green.

At the 60-degree forcing temperature, tulips should bloom in five to six weeks in midwinter, four weeks in February, three to four weeks in March, and three weeks in April.

Water freely. Feeding is not necessary.

For flowers after January, precooled bulbs are not necessary. Store the tulip bulbs at room temperature until you use them. In practice, they are planted in late fall and held in the under-50-degree storage—usually in outdoor straw-covered rooting beds—until needed for forcing. This period should be at least twelve to fourteen weeks. In areas where winters are mild, tulips should remain under cool rooting conditions even longer or be stored in food lockers.

During forcing, increasing temperatures will speed up flowering, and lowering temperatures will hold the blooms.

For early forcing, the choice of varieties is important. Only a few tulip varieties force readily in January. Among them are Albino, Bartigon, Golden Harvest, and William Pitt. After February 1 and for Valentine's Day, a number of Cottage, Darwin, Mendel, and Triumph tulips will force readily. Bring indoors and start forcing about January 7. For March, April, and Easter, avoid the Triumphs. They open fast and do not keep.

Flowering pot tulips should be staked and tied. After flowering, tulip bulbs are usually discarded. They do not do well when transplanted to the garden.

8
The Top Ten
Forcing Flowers

I remember, I remember
The roses, red and white,
The violets, and the lily-cups,
Those flowers made of light.

Thomas Hood

We seem to have a national passion for the "ten best." We make up lists of "The Ten Best Plays," "The Ten Best Movies," "The Ten Best-Dressed Women," and "The Ten Top Tunes." Whatever "ten best" they be, they are not necessarily the best, they are simply the most popular.

Not to be outdone, I have made up my own list of "The Ten Best Forcing Flowers." Again, they are not necessarily the best plants to force but merely the most popular. And I am limiting myself only to those plants that can be forced.

Heading the list are the chrysanthemums—standards and pompons as cut flowers and pot plants. There is more acreage devoted to growing them and more volume in production than for any other flower. They can be used for almost every occasion. They are available the year around. And in their many forms and colors they are beautiful.

Roses certainly should be on our list—possibly in second place. They, too, are grown extensively, are used as cut flowers and potted plants, and are very popular. In popularity alone, they may be first. A rose is a standard for loveliness in flowers.

Carnations may be next, although they have dropped somewhat in popularity in recent years. They are chiefly used as cut flowers. As such, they excel in fragrance.

Two other cut flowers that are produced in volume should possibly take fourth and fifth place on our list. They are stock and snapdragons. Both find frequent use in all kinds of floral arrangements.

The Easter lily, though seasonal, may be high on our list. It surely takes first place among the plants grown from bulbs, tubers, corms, or rhizomes. We'll give it sixth place.

Three shrubby pot plants vie for seventh, eighth, and ninth places—the poinsettia, the azalea, and the hydrangea. The poinsettia has become the symbolic Christmas flower. Azaleas are not limited to a single holiday and are used as decorative plants throughout the late winter and spring season. The hydrangea, for some unknown reason, is an important Mother's Day and Memorial Day plant.

There are many floral contenders for tenth place. I pick geraniums, because they are inexpensive, because youngsters like to buy them as gifts for Valentine's Day, Easter, and Mother's Day, and because oldsters use them for cemetery decorations on Memorial Day.

So there they are—"The Ten Best Forcing Flowers." In your mind's ear, supply some fanfare—a blare of trumpets.

And here are my suggestions on how you can force them.

CHRYSANTHEMUM—MUM or POMPON
(*Chrysanthemum* sp.)

CONTROL: Light. Shade. Timing.

Once, many years ago, we are told, a beautiful Chinese maiden walked in a garden. She stopped before each flower and carefully studied it. It was apparent that she was searching for something, and there was about her an aura of mixed joy and sadness.

The joy came from the words of her sweetheart. He had expressed his love and proposed that they marry soon so that they might have many years together. Out of feminine curiosity, she longed to know how many years that would be, so she begged an elf to tell her.

The elf said, "You will live together as many happy years as the flower you choose has petals."

When she thought of how few petals a violet has or a petunia or a lily, she became sad. Which flower should she choose? She searched diligently day after day. Then, in the autumn of the year, a beautiful flower of countless petals bloomed. She promptly chose it. It was the chrysanthemum.

This legend goes back to antiquity. So do chrysanthemums. They were grown in Chinese gardens over two thousand years ago. In honor of an ancient grower and breeder, a city was named Chu-hsien—"City of Chrysanthemums." Later, the Japanese adopted it as their national flower. The Order of the Chrysanthemum became the highest honor a Japanese emperor could bestow.

During the great era of exploration and trade, the chrysanthemum was brought to Europe. The French immediately took these flowers to heart and soon developed improved new forms. The pompon varieties took their name from the pompons French soldiers wore on their caps.

When mums reached America around 1800, they had immediate acceptance. And this welcome has not waned. Today, they exist in many new types and varieties, all beautiful—spider, anemone, incurve, single, spoon, reflex, quill, spindle—in pure colors and in blends and in sizes ranging from petite miniatures to immense "football mums."

The chrysanthemum is the major commercial flower. It can be completely manipulated. It is captivatingly beautiful. Its floral forms and colors—in both "mums" and "poms"—fit into any occasion. It can be grown in all parts of the country, and at any time. In California and Florida, it can be made to bloom the year around outdoors. It can be used in imaginative arrangements and lasts long even under adverse conditions. It is a magnificent plant.

Any loose, friable soil with some humus added will grow

chrysanthemums. Peat mixed into a new bed helps to keep the soil at a pH of 6.0 or 7.0, which is ideal for mums, although not absolutely necessary.

When growing mums indoors, the soil should be sterilized. And add some superphosphate to it—about a 3-inch potful to a 5-by-5-foot space—to help the plants get started. (For growing as pot plants, note the information here, then follow instructions given starting on page 125.)

Mums tend to be heavy feeders, particularly in summer and fall. Set up a regular feeding routine, feeding more at those times of greater need. Many growers use 10–4–6 liquid fertilizer. Others use a balanced 20–20–20.

Chrysanthemums use considerable water in hot weather, and daily watering is necessary. However, the soil may be allowed to dry on top and the leaves to droop a little—but not wilt—before watering. Then water thoroughly.

Of course, on the dark days of winter, feeding and watering should be reduced. Drop to about three-quarters of the amount you water and feed on summer days.

Most chrysanthemums are grown from rooted cuttings. Growers buy the plants already rooted. This is ideal, but if you are going to grow only a few pots or flats, you can root your own cuttings.

First, select your stock plants—from a florist's pot that has already bloomed or by lifting and potting some of the plants you have in your garden. Spray outdoor plants with insecticide and fungicide before bringing them indoors. Then if you hold them cool and on the dry side, you can keep them semidormant until you are ready to work with them.

To get stock plants going, bring them into 60- to 65-degree temperatures and water and feed them. Pinch new growth to get breaks, or branching. Light at night, to keep them from forming buds. Set a 40-watt bulb a couple of feet over the plant from 10:00 P.M. to 12:00 midnight.

When shoots are of sufficient length, take cuttings that have three or four leaves, or nodes. Make the cut just below a node and remove the leaf. Dip in rooting hormone and insert in a mixture of moist sand and peat. Cuttings root in two to four weeks.

You may find it easier to buy your cuttings. A nearby chrysanthemum grower usually has a few extra plants included in his shipment.

Cut Flowers

In growing chrysanthemums as cut flowers, there are five principal procedures that must be performed to force bloom at a specific date. These are plant, pinch, prune, light, and shade.

The commercial suppliers of rooted cuttings have worked out detailed schedules for these operations for the varieties they offer, and they publish these schedules in their catalogs. The suppliers also cooperate with large growers and set up tailor-made schedules keyed to the grower's specific locale and facilities.

These schedules are based upon how a variety functions under the temperatures in which it will be grown and the time of year. This information is also listed for the specific variety in the plant propagator's catalog.

Two typical forcing schedules may look like this:

Flowering Date	February 15	October 30
Plant	September 20	June 10
Pinch	October 10	June 30
Light	October 10	None
Prune	October 25–30	July 20
Discontinue light	December 5	
Shade	None	August 30
Discontinue shade		October 15

There is no secret about these schedules. They are a service of the propagator. You can make your own once you know the purpose of each operation. With this in mind, let's run through the plant-pinch-prune-light-shade procedures.

For cut flowers, plant your rooted cuttings directly into growing beds. The soil should be medium moist. Plant as shallow as possible—just over the root tops—and firm the plant into the soil with your fingers. After planting, mist or spray with water.

Space plants about 6 by 6 inches for pompons and 7 by 7 inches for standards. This spacing, along with a pinch, helps control spray size for poms and flower size for standards.

In the plant-pinch-prune-light-shade schedule, pinching is one of the key dates. It supplies a pivot point from which other operations are planned. It starts all plants growing at the same time.

Plant your cuttings about two weeks before the scheduled pinch date to allow them to become established. When you pinch, take only the top ½ inch. A slight push with your finger will snap off the new growth. The pinch will cause the plant to send out a number of new branches. After a few weeks, prune these new stems to two stems per plant on inside rows and three stems per plant on outside rows. This keeps the center of the bed open for better air circulation. These are the stems that will carry your flowers.

Through the procedure of pinching and pruning, you have more than doubled your output per rooted cutting. However, you need not pinch, if you so wish. You can grow your plant single-stem. For single-stem plants, plant your cuttings on the pinch date and space 5 by 5 inches.

In any case, mums grow tall, and your plants will need support. Use a wire-and-crossed-string support that can be raised as plants grow. Between each row of plants, stretch wires the length of the bed to a pipe at each end of the bed. The pipe extends across the width of the bed and is tied to two 4-foot poles that are driven into each corner of the bed. Then tie strings across the wires and between the plants in the width of the bed. As the plants grow, the end pipes are raised and tied higher on the end poles. When plants are actively growing, this support should be raised every seven to ten days.

To grow chrysanthemums the year around—or to force them at any time—it is important to remember that mums are "short-day" plants. More accurately, they are long-night plants. They will readily set buds when exposed to a night that

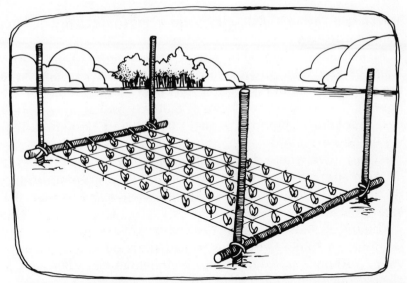

A simple wire-and-string support system for bedded plants that grow tall and will require support.

is longer than twelve hours. For this reason, outdoors they naturally flower in the fall, when the nights grow longer.

A cutting planted in spring will develop normally, growing through the short nights of summer and setting buds in fall. However, a cutting planted in fall or winter will immediately set buds, simply because the nights are long. Therefore, to postpone this bud setting, we must shorten the night with artificial lights. If we hold the darkness to seven hours, buds will not form.

To light a mum bed, hang a string of 60-watt bulbs with pie-pan reflectors, spaced about 4 feet apart on the string, about 3 or 4 feet above the plants. Technically, the light should be over 7 footcandles in the darker area between bulbs.

Years ago, we growers used to light our plants between sundown and 11:00 P.M. But now, to save power and cost, plants are lighted for a few hours in the middle of the night—usually 10:00 P.M. to 12:00 midnight—except for the period of

November through February, when they are lighted from 10:00 P.M. to 1:00 A.M.

At latitudes where day length varies from that of mid-America, the rule is to plan your artificial lighting so that there are only seven hours or less of darkness on either side of the lighting period. With sundown at 6:00 P.M. and sunrise at 5:00 A.M., one hour of light between 11:00 P.M. and 12:00 midnight would be sufficient.

At latitudes where day length does not vary greatly, lights are used during the growing period the year around. In northern latitudes, lights are used for growing between August 1 and May 30.

When the plants reach the desired height and you are ready for them to bud—a growing period planned in advance on your forcing schedule—the supplementary lighting is discontinued. Shading may begin if necessary.

Lighting prevented the plant from setting buds. Shading causes the plant to set buds. Chrysanthemums set buds when the night lasts twelve hours or longer.

In practice, black sateen cloth is spread over a wire frame so that it completely covers the plant bed from 6:00 P.M. to 7:00 A.M. In southern latitudes, shading is used to set buds during March 30 and October 1. In northern latitudes, we shade to set buds between March 25 and October 20.

Shading should not start until about forty days after the plants have been pinched. Shading can be discontinued for pompons when flowers begin to show color. For standards, discontinue shading when the buds are just under the size of a quarter.

To grow standard large-flowered mums, the plant must be disbudded. When a terminal bud appears—a large bud surrounded by a number of smaller ones—remove all the little side buds around the large bud by rolling or snapping them off. This takes care and practice. Let only the large center flower bud remain.

I used to fine myself 25 cents for every terminal bud I accidentally knocked off. That way I not only lost the flower but

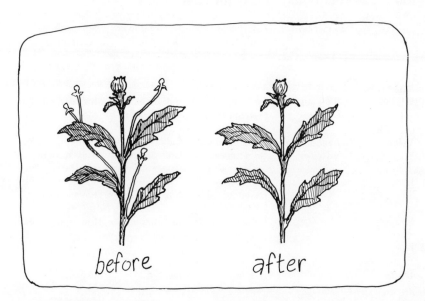

before   after

Disbudding.

a quarter too if I got careless. I dropped the coins into a coffee can to be contributed to the Red Cross, the Girl Scouts, or for high school band uniforms when the volunteers showed up to make their appeals. At first, these organizations fared quite well, but after a while I earned the reputation of being quite stingy, for I seldom knocked off a terminal bud.

There are some excellent varieties of both standards and poms. As a standard, you can't go wrong with Indianapolis— White, Yellow, Pink, and Bronze. The Indianapolis Pink and Bronze may "burn" in the hot summer sun and should be shaded with cheesecloth. Shoesmith and Mefo are also fine standard cut-flower varieties but require cooler growing temperatures. Among the poms, you can choose from a great number of varieties in many shapes, colors, and forms. Iceberg is a gem.

Some varieties perform better in one season of the year than in another. Here are some typical seasonal recommendations:

	Summer flower June–Sept.	Fall flower Sept.–Dec.	Winter flower Dec.–April	Spring flower April–June
Standards:				
White	Indianapolis Wh. Betsy Ross	Indianapolis Wh. Fred Shoesmith	Indianapolis Wh. Fred Shoesmith	Indianapolis Wh. Mefo
Yellow	Indianapolis Yel. Good News	Indianapolis Yel. Gold Shoesmith	Indianapolis Yel. Gold Shoesmith	Indianapolis Yel. Yellow Mefo
Pink		Indianapolis Pk. Lavender Queen	Indianapolis Pk. Lavender Queen	Indianapolis Pk. Lavender Queen
Bronze		Indianapolis Br.	Indianapolis Br.	Indianapolis Br.
Poms:				
White	Iceberg Shasta Pinocchio Ping Pong Igloo	Iceberg Shasta Pinocchio Ping Pong Igloo	Iceberg Snowcap Silversmith	Iceberg Shasta Snowdrift Pinocchio Ping Pong
Yellow	Yellow Iceberg Yel. Beauregard Yellow Shasta Yellow Igloo	Yellow Iceberg Yel. Beauregard Yellow Shasta Yellow Igloo	Corsair	Yellow Iceberg Yel. Beauregard Yellow Shasta Yellow Snowdrift
Pink	Bluechip	Bluechip Darkchip	Alvoda	Bluechip Masterpiece
Bronze		Beauregard Rubicon	Crackerjack Galaxy	Beauregard

Summer temperatures present a problem in growing mums the year around. Growing conditions must be kept as cool as possible. Should temperatures soar into the high 90s or hover around 100 degrees for a period of time, the buds may be damaged so that they will not bloom. High temperatures, even when they are not excessive, can retard blooming and cause you to miss your scheduled flowering date.

Winter temperatures much under 55 degrees are equally harmful. At low temperatures, mums will not set buds even with long-night shading.

Anytime you can maintain 60- to 65-degree night temperatures during summer and winter, with some moderate-plus degrees on bright days, you have ideal growing conditions.

That about covers the basics of forcing mums. Now a practical exercise. Suppose you want flowers in January, February, or March. Since the daylight is poor and growing conditions are not at the best, choose varieties that perform well in these months, varieties like Shoesmith in standards and Alvoda in poms.

Since the nights are long and the days are short, lighting is needed to keep buds from forming on the small cuttings. We need a period of growth that for chrysanthemums means short nights. Therefore, light on planting and continue until plants are tall enough to start flowering—usually in six weeks or about forty to forty-five days. Then discontinue lighting.

Since at this time of the year the natural day length is short enough to induce bud formation, there is no need for black cloth shade. Buds will form immediately, and plants will bloom, depending upon the variety, in nine or ten weeks.

Put it all together and your schedule might look like this:

Flowering Date:	January 15	February 15	March 15
Plant	September 10	September 20	November 5
Pinch	September 30	October 10	November 30
Light	September 10	September 20	November 5
Prune	October 15	October 25	December 15
Discontinue light	November 10	December 5	January 10
Shade	None	None	None

For Easter: plant December 1, pinch December 22, light December 1, and discontinue lighting February 1.

For May: plant January 1, pinch February 1, light January 1, discontinue lighting March 10. Shade in north not necessary, but in south start black cloth shade on March 10.

Here are several optional tips for an extra plus in flower quality: After you start shading, or discontinue lights for long nights, delete the ammonium forms of nitrogen fertilizers. I finish with potassium nitrate only, with excellent results. At the same time, taper off on water. Give only enough water to keep the plants from wilting. This helps harden the stems. But once the buds begin to swell, feed and water thoroughly again to encourage flower development.

Another option is interrupted lights. Instead of suddenly discontinuing the use of lights, there is a 9-off–12-on formula that works wonders. From the scheduled lights-out date, count back twelve days and stop lighting. Then after nine days, follow with twelve days of lights on. After the twelfth day, discontinue lighting. This will slow down flowering for about nine days, but the flower size and form improvement is spectacular.

In summer, some mums grow long necks, which detract from their appearance. B-Nine spray at 50 percent reduces the tendency to neckiness on summer standards.

Standards are usually graded by flower diameter, over 6 inches being the top grade. They are packed in boxes of twelve, or in special sleeves holding six, which are carefully wrapped in cellophane. Pompons are usually packed by weight, normally in 9-ounce bunches.

Pot Flowers

Potted chrysanthemums are grown and forced in much the same ways that standard mums and poms are grown for cut flowers. Grow at 65 degrees, give plenty of sunlight, water and feed generously, pinch on time, light and shade as needed, and give the plants ample growing room.

Pot mums are grown from rooted cuttings—either your own or purchased. Select equal-sized cuttings and plant five cuttings to a 6-inch shallow azalea pot. Although that is standard practice, smaller pots may also be used. Plant three cuttings in a 5-inch pot, and two in a 4-inch. Let plants develop about 4 inches of new growth before pinching. Then pinch back so that only about 2 inches of new growth remain, or two pairs of leaves. Feed with a nitrate and potash fertilizer every week, and give them plenty of sun.

Use a 3-to-1 soil and peat mixture to which has been added 1 cup of superphosphate per bushel of the potting mixture. Throw a handful of gravel into the bottom of the pot for drainage. Do not fill the pot with soil, but rather leave about 1 inch for watering.

Keep pots well watered—water at least once a day. Water twice a day when weather is hot and dry.

To keep pot mums from growing too tall, delay your pinch about one week. In addition, the use of a chemical dwarfing spray also helps. But the spray is optional. You can get full, compact pot mums by the delayed pinch alone—and then giving your plants space to grow. Obviously, crowding will cause spindly plants.

When standard mum varieties are used for pot mums, disbud to one flower per stem. When pom varieties are used, disbudding is not necessary.

For computing pot mum forcing schedules, varieties are classed under *short procedure* and *tall procedure* in the propagator's catalog.

A short procedure concerns a variety that is naturally short, such as Delaware. Give these varieties two to three weeks more light for winter flowering. Short-procedure mums may be grown without pinching if you use six or seven cuttings per pot, shade immediately at potting, and use a chemical growth retardant. Plants should bloom in ten weeks.

A tall procedure involves a variety such as Indianapolis that tends to be tall, especially in summer-fall flowering. These varieties must be shaded the same day as potted, and the pinch must be delayed.

For Christmas pot plants with no shading or extra lighting, use the variety Princess Anne. Pot cuttings on September 1. Use five in a 6-inch pot. Grow at 50 degrees during the night. Pinch ten days after potting.

Some excellent varieties for year-around pot mums are

Oregon in white, Yellow Delaware in yellow, Mermaid in pink, and Delaware or Red Star in bronze. There are also excellent bicolors available, such as Princess Anne.

A typical schedule for Delaware would be: Begin short days ten days after potting and continue until buds show color; pinch thirteen days after potting, or twenty days after potting on summer-flowering plants. Flowering takes place sixty-three days after short days begin—seventy-three days after potting.

Using Garden Mums

If you can get some rooted cuttings of garden chrysanthemums, you can easily force them into bloom for Easter, Mother's Day, or Memorial Day, and then have plants to set outdoors.

To set up your schedule for the flowering date you want, count back ten weeks for your planting date. Then schedule to light for one week from your planting date. Also schedule a pinch for three weeks from that planting date. Because the hours of daylight gradually increase with the earlier rising and later setting of the sun, to maintain night length start shade on March 15 and continue until buds show color.

For example: Mother's Day flowering—May 15; plant cuttings—February 25; light—February 25 to March 2; shade from March 15; pinch—March 17.

Some fine garden varieties for forcing are: Christopher Columbus, Silverplate, Lyria, and Horizon in white; King's Ransom, Pomponette, and Yellow Spoon in yellow; Alert and Spellbound in pink; and Remembrance and Lipstick in bronze and red.

Growing and forcing superior mums as flowering pot plants or as cut flowers is not difficult. It simply involves attention to a number of essential details—soil, moisture, drainage, and feeding; plant spacing and timing, pinching and pruning, shading and lighting; temperature and sunlight; planting shallow, supporting, disbudding, and controlling pests; and the proper selection of varieties. Forcing mums is nothing more than attention to commonsense growing practices to produce a plant that allows us complete manipulation, which means the ability to pinpoint blooming throughout the year to the exact day that we want the flower.

ROSE *(Rosa sp.)*

CONTROL: Timed pinches.

Every flower grower has a favorite plant. Mine are roses. Although I grow roses under all conditions, even indoors on a windowsill and under lights, I concede that, except for miniatures, they are not the kind of houseplants everyone will want to grow. But then, you may be an exception among window gardeners. You too may like roses.

Actually, roses, like orchids, are easy to grow. There is a mystique in vogue about growing both plants. People are impressed. "Oh, you grow orchids!" Or, "You grow roses!"

To begin, most growers buy dormant 2-year-old plants. In these, the flowering plant has been budded or grafted to vigorous rootstocks. They are ready to plant, force, and bloom. You save about a year's work. I prefer to lose the year and grow my plants on own-roots propagated from cuttings. I especially like own-root plants for forcing. Most varieties do better on own-roots than they do as grafted plants.

Cuttings are taken in October and November, although they can be taken at any time from indoor plants. Take a shoot from which the flower has just been removed. Cut off a section with two or three sets of leaves. Remove the lower leaves, but allow those on top to remain. Dip the cut end into hormone rooting powder and insert firmly in a sand, soil, and peat, or a vermiculite-perlite and peat rooting medium. Use a deep flat and build a plastic tent over it, or set wide-mouth glass jars over each cutting. Or you can insert the cutting to root directly in a pot, placing a glass jar over the cutting.

Keep the rooting medium moist but not soggy. Expect some leaves to drop. The cutting should be sufficiently rooted in four to six weeks, to be transferred from the flats to 3-inch pots. Use a soil and peat mixture. Feed with a balanced fertilizer.

When propagating own-root roses, an inverted glass jar over the prepared and planted cutting prevents excessive loss of moisture through transpiration while roots develop. Be careful not to allow direct exposure to the sun, or heat buildup inside the jar may kill the plant.

In about a month, all plants in the 3-inch pots can be moved to 4- or 5-inch pots. (Miniature roses are rooted in flats and moved first to 2½-inch pots and then to 3-inch pots.)

Rooted plants will bloom in the first season, but building the plant is more important than the blooms. Grow them outside in summer in the pots or in beds until the frost drops the leaves. Then move them to a cool storage area—about 40 degrees—until you want them. A garage or a shed will do nicely. Or, just before frost, bring the plants inside and let them continue growing. In either case, cut plants back to about 6 or 8 inches.

Growing roses for cut flowers is usually done on a large scale, but you may be able to make room in a corner of your home greenhouse for half a dozen plants.

The roses used for cut flowers are hybrid teas or floribundas. The classical florist rose is a hybrid tea. "Sweetheart" roses are floribundas. A few floribunda plants will give you a continuous supply of cut roses.

For cut flowers, get your roses started in January. From February 1 to June 1 indoor growing conditions are ideal. After June 1, your outdoor plants are in bloom. Indoors, the temperature soars. It is important to apply shading to glass in the summer.

In December or January, transfer your own-root roses from their pots to a bed, spacing about 14 by 14 inches. Or use grafted roses that you buy. Plant about ½ inch deeper than they were in the pot. Then each plant should be staked and tied.

In general, handle as you would an outdoor plant. Water. Feed sparingly every six weeks with a 4–12–4 fertilizer. Mulch to preserve soil moisture. (Ground-up corn cobs, peanut shells, or coconut husks make good mulches.) Allow air to circulate, using fans if necessary. Spray for red spider mites, black spot, and mildew.

Roses grow best at about 60-degree night temperature. They get spindly at higher temperatures and require considerable tieing.

Once the plants are in and new growth has started, you will need to pinch them. Pinch off the top part of the stem to remove the developing flower buds. This helps to build the plants. Later on, you will pinch to control the flowering date you want.

There are two types of pinches—soft and hard. The soft pinch is made when the flower bud emerges from the foliage around it. The stem is pinched just above the first five-leaflet leaf below the flower bud. The thumbnail and forefinger can be used. You take off the short, soft top section of the stem. After pinching, the terminal bud at the base of the leaf will grow and develop into a flower, which you will cut below the point of the soft pinch for that prized long-stem rose.

A hard pinch is made at a later point in the development of the shoot than is the soft pinch. The flower bud may be the size of a bean. A knife may be necessary. This pinch can be made at the first or second five-leaflet leaf below the flower bud.

From a soft pinch, only one shoot develops. With a hard pinch, several shoots may develop on the remaining stem.

Pinching is a good practice to build young plants. It also causes new shoots to start from the base of the plant. Hard-pinch these so that they develop into more than one stem.

Plants started in January will give you cut roses for Easter. You can cut a large crop if you want or pinch some buds back for flowers at a later date.

The timing for flowering is simple. From the time you cut a flower or make a hard pinch in winter, it takes eight weeks to produce a flower. In spring and summer, it takes six weeks. In fall, seven weeks. For a soft pinch, add four to seven more days. To get flowers for Christmas, for example, soft-pinch around October 20. Hard-pinch or cut, October 25. Grow at normal 60 degrees. After cuts have been made for Christmas, the plant, if let alone, should produce flowers again, in time for Valentine's Day.

Easter is a variable date, so you simply schedule back seven and a half weeks when it is early or seven weeks when it is later and make your pinch. Again, if let alone, plants from which cuts were made for Easter may again produce flowers in time for Memorial Day.

You can have roses when you want them by picking your date and counting back the necessary number of weeks to make your pinch.

If for any reason you must slow or hasten flowering, either lower or raise the night temperature from 5 to 10 degrees during the critical last two or three weeks.

The general rule for cutting is to allow two five-leaflet leaves to remain above the previous hard pinch or cut.

As the plants become established, to keep them from getting too tall, cut them back on a gradual basis. After some shoots have flowered, cut them back to 25 or 30 inches. But do not do it all at once. Let the others grow and flower. They can be cut later.

Every so often you will get a bullhead, a bud that has a flat undeveloped center and won't open. Every grower thinks he knows the cause—too much light, too little light, overwatering, too dry, too much heat, too little heat, nitrates, thrips. If you do not have thrips, just cut off and discard the bullhead. There are black sheep in the best of families.

Potted roses as houseplants can be grown from own-root or bare-root grafted plants. Again, I like my own-root plants.

For own-root plants, after their first summer outdoors bring the plant in and cut it back to shape it. This is the time to move it to a larger pot, usually 6 or 8 inches. When the plant gets established, it may be pinched for Christmas bloom on October 15.

Bare-root grafted plants will be stripped of their leaves by frost. Trim canes to about 8 inches and prune broken roots. Then force the roots into a 6- or 8-inch pot—which usually takes some doing. A twisting push seems to help. Tamp the soil firmly around the roots so that there are no air pockets.

Use fairly heavy potting soil with some peat and humus mixed in. Hold in a cool area, or cold frame, until ready to force. In December or January, bring in, water, and mist.

For Easter flowers, start a dormant plant on January 15 and grow at night temperatures of 45 to 50 degrees until February 5. Cover with wet burlap to keep moist. When shoots are started, you can expose the plant to sunlight. Grow at 55 to 60 degrees until March. In March, go slightly warmer if Easter is early, or slightly cooler if Easter is late. Buds should be developed by three weeks before Easter if the plant is on time.

For other flowering dates, the same pinching schedule used for cut flowers—eight weeks for winter, seven weeks for spring—can be used to bring potted roses into full bloom on the date that you want them. Or for continuous flowering, pinch at intervals, pinching off some shoots while you allow others to flower.

Potted plants, being portable, have one advantage over cut flowers in beds. You can move the pots into colder or warmer areas to hold them or speed them up.

Feed pot roses with balanced fertilizer every four to six weeks.

Hybrid teas are seldom used as pot plants. Use small floribundas, polyanthas, and miniatures for your potted roses. There are some excellent varieties available in solid colors and bicolors.

Among the smaller floribunda-type roses, there are many from which to choose. Pinocchio is an excellent salmon. For yellow, try Goldilocks. Jiminy Cricket is a bright orange. Garnette is a popular red. A sport of Garnette, Carol Amling, is a fine pink. Summer Snow is pure white.

Three polyantha roses, probably the pioneers among pot roses, are still outstanding—the salmon Margo Koster, the red Mother's Day, and the carmine old standby, Triumphe D'Orleans.

Miniature roses—scaled-down versions of the large hybrid teas and floribundas—are perfect in every detail. Miniature in bush and miniature in flower, the 6- to 12-inch plants with petite ½ inch blooms are charming as pot plants or for cut flower arrangements and corsages. They are not grown often enough. Pot dormant plants at any time, and grow at 60 degrees. They will bloom in six weeks.

Some of the older miniature varieties are still among the better ones. For red, there is Oakington Ruby and Tom Thumb. For pink, try *Rosa Roulettii* or Sweet Fairy, for white, Pixie; and Baby Gold Star is a fine yellow.

After blooming indoors, since pot roses are perfectly hardy, move them outdoors into the garden, where they will bloom for many enjoyable years.

CARNATION *(Dianthus Caryophyllus)*

CONTROL: Timed pinches.

Unless you have a fair-sized greenhouse, the delicate and fragrant cut carnation is not a very suitable flower to grow at home. In commercial trade, however, it is a major flower.

Where 50-degree night temperatures can be maintained, carnations are easy to grow. Once started and properly tended, you may cut the flowers over two seasons.

Carnations are usually grown indoors on raised benches from cuttings made in spring. If the home greenhouse can be kept cool enough during the summer, they can be handled indoors. Otherwise, they can be carried outdoors until fall and then moved to the growing bench. However, outdoor culture invites trouble since the soil cannot be sterilized. To be sure of disease-free plants, grow indoors, keeping the house as cool as you can.

Carnations are usually grown from cuttings. Most growers buy cuttings already rooted. However, cuttings can be made from the side shoots on flowering stems. Cuttings are usually taken in January and February. It is important to keep everything sterile—soil, tools, benches. Dip ends of cuttings in rooting hormone and insert in moist peat or perlite. Give bottom heat of 65 degrees if possible. Hold top temperature at 55 to 60 degrees. Cuttings should root in three weeks.

To grow cuttings—your own or purchased—use a loose soil with peat added—the mixture proportion should be about two to one. Have this rooting medium moist before transplanting. Rooted cuttings are usually ready to pot in April.

In any case, get cuttings into pots before mid-May to get them established before hot weather. Transfer cuttings to 3-inch peat pots. Set cuttings as high as possible in the pots. Place pots in deep flats. When plants are established in pots, pinch. Make a soft pinch of 2 to 3 inches of the new top growth—down to the first full curled leaves. Hold six to eight weeks after pinch. At this time the plant is full and ready to bench—usually in June.

When planting, plant shallow. Set 7 inches apart. Use sterilized sandy loam. Put the peat pot and all into the growing medium but keep the top of the pot's soil about ½ inch above the surface of the medium.

Ventilation and water are important. Water in the morning and, if in a greenhouse, with the vents open. Keep water off the plants. Water when needed—often in summer and less in winter. When soil crumbles between your fingers, water. And really soak them when you do.

Feed moderately. Usually nothing until fall. Then every two months apply a balanced liquid fertilizer such as 4–12–4.

Carnations like sunshine. Grow them in full sun.

Temperature is critical—50 degrees at night, 58 degrees on cloudy days, and 65 degrees on sunny days. In a greenhouse, balance temperatures by opening and closing vents gradually. Avoid sudden drops.

Pinching offers some control for flowering dates.

A support of wire and string mesh is needed.

Plants must be disbudded. All surplus flower buds on a stem should be removed.

For flowers at Christmas, pinch or cut in July. For early Easter, pinch or cut in August. For late Easter, in September. For Mother's Day, pinch or cut in October.

Flowers are cut the year around and plants are often carried into the second and third year.

The number of excellent varieties are almost astronomical. The Sim and Little types in white, pink, red, and yellow are usually outstanding. Apollo is a fine salmon pink, and Gayety an excellent red.

STOCK *(Matthiola incana)*

CONTROL: Temperature. Timing. Light.

Stock is an annual grown from seed. The need for ample growing space somewhat limits stock to larger home greenhouses or to commercial ranges. Where it can be grown, it is a commercially profitable cut flower, even though it faces stiff competition from California's field-grown crops.

To grow stock indoors, high temperatures are a major problem. When the temperature is too high during the period when buds should be forming—above 65 degrees for six hours— buds will not develop. As a result, you get blind, flowerless plants, a worthless crop.

Because of this problem of blindness at high temperatures, start stock between July 10 and February 10. This brings the bud-formation period into winter and early spring, when cool temperatures are easy to maintain.

Specifically:

For January flowering, sow seeds July 10 to 20.

For February flowering, sow seeds July 25 to August 5.

For March flowering, sow seeds August 10 to August 20.

For April and Easter flowers, sow seeds September 20 to 30.

For May and Mother's Day, sow seeds January 1 to 10.

For Memorial Day flowers, sow seeds February 1.

As a rule of thumb, for January, February, March, and April flowers, sow seeds about six months before the date you want them in flower. For May flowers, it takes about four and a half months, and for June flowers it takes about four months. Temperatures should be about 50 degrees nights. However, deduct one month from the growing time required from seeding to flowering if seeds are sown directly into deep flats or benches and not transplanted.

By using additional lights for one hour at midnight—60-watt bulbs spread 5 feet apart and 3 feet above the ground—the stock sown in August may be cut for Christmas.

The usual practice is to sow seeds in a sandy medium and transplant the seedlings. Seeds germinate in two weeks at 65 degrees in good light.

Stock requires porous, loose soil. Heavy, poorly aerated, clay-type soils just won't do. A mixture of loamy garden soil with a supply of organic matter plus gravelly sand will do fine. Then sterilize and pulverize this mixture.

Space stock about 4 by 4 inches and support the plants with a string grid. This grid consists of rows of wires set 4 inches apart running the length of the bed. The ends of the wires are fastened to cross supports, which can be raised on two corner posts as the plants grow. Then strings are tied to these wires to cross the width of the bed every 4 inches. The result is a 4-by-4-inch square in which an individual plant will grow and be supported.

Water on sunny days so that the lower foliage will dry before nightfall. This simple procedure will help considerably in keeping plants disease-free. Feed every ten to fourteen days with a liquid fertilizer high in potash rather than with a balanced formulation.

Stock grown at low temperatures—as low as 40 degrees—seldom has any disease problem. In fact, temperature is the big trick in growing stock. For large, heavy spikes and sturdy stems, grow stock cold—an average temperature of 45 degrees at night. From 35 to 45 degrees, you will get a superb bloom, but you extend your growing time to seven months in winter. Aim for an average of 45 degrees, with 55 degrees on cloudy days and 65 degrees on sunny days in winter. In spring, move up to 50 degrees at night, 60 degrees on cloudy days, and 65 degrees on sunny days. If you are running behind schedule to make a holiday cutting, allow the temperature to increase slightly in all three areas. But when you can, keep stock cool—and keep them dry at root level.

There is an excellent choice of colors available in the Column-type stock which is most often grown—white, rose, pink, lavender, and gold. Try these in Early Cascade.

Most seed will produce a small percentage of plants with blooms that are not double, or full. There are two ways you can keep these to a minimum. The first is to use seeds of the Trysomic type, which should produce about 90 percent doubles. The other method is to select the doubles from the seedlings. Here is how: Sow seeds in flats. When the seedlings appear, move flats to an area of 45 to 50 degrees night temperature. Within a week you will notice a mixture of light and dark green seedlings. The light green ones are the doubles. They will usually have indented leaves. Transplant them and discard the others.

There is also a dwarf Trysomic column stock available for use in large pots or window boxes, but it is not commonly grown.

SNAPDRAGON *(Antirrhinum majus)*

CONTROL: Variety scheduling.

Snapdragons make superb cut flowers. They are beautiful in form. They are colorful. They keep well. They are not limited to a single season. And they are easy to grow.

Snap varieties are classified into four response periods, or flowering groups. The classification is based on a variety's response to day-length, light intensity, and temperature throughout the year. This novel idea made year-around snaps a reality.

Group I flower December 10 to February 15 and produce quality flowers at low temperatures of around 50 degrees, under low light intensity, and with short days.

Group II flower February 15 to May 10, and October 25 to December 10.

Group III flower May 10 to June 30, and September 10 to October 15.

Group IV flower July 1 to September 10. These are summer varieties, which require long days and high light intensity and prefer high temperatures.

These are some of the varieties classed within the four groups:

Group I
White—Sierra, Ohio, Citation, White Knight, Pan American.
Yellow—Doubloon, Vermont.
Pink—Spanish Lady, Wintergreen.
Rose—Rosita, Wisconsin.
Red—Cherokee, Buccaneer, Apache.
Bronze—Coronado, Cavalcade, Eldorado.
Lavender—Senorita.

Group II
White—Snowman, Apollo, Twenty Grand.
Yellow—Golden Spike, Swaps.
Pink—Pink Ice, Native Dancer, Indiana.
Rose—Jackpot, Treasure Chest, Showgirl.
Red—Navajo.
Bronze—Gallant Fox, Martha.
Lavender—Lavender Lady.

Group III
White—Panama, Virginia, Delaware, Utah.
Yellow—Tampico, Colorado.
Pink—Florida.
Red—Tennessee.
Bronze—Kansas.

Group IV
White—Panama, June Bride, White Skies, Texas.
Yellow—Tampico, Dark Star, Spartan Yellow.
Pink—Florida, Miami, Kentucky, Spartan Pink.
Rose—Summer Jewel, Potomac Rose.
Red—Potomac Red.
Lavender—Arizona.

In the southern United States, only varieties in Groups II, III, and IV are used. Group II extends from December 1 through April. Group III extends from May 1 through June 15, and October 1 to December 1. Group IV extends from June 15 to October 1.

With variety scheduling, you can have snaps in flower all year around.

Desired Date for Cut Flowers	Variety to Use		Sow Seeds		Plant	
	North	*South*	*North*	*South*	*North*	*South*
Oct. 5–15	III	III	July 10	July 10	July 25	July 25
Oct. 20–30	II	III	July 25	July 20	Aug. 5	Aug. 5
Nov. 5–15	II	III	July 30	Aug. 1	Aug. 15	Aug. 15
Nov. 20–30	II	III	Aug. 5	Aug. 10	Aug. 20	Aug. 25
Dec. 5–15	I	II	Aug. 13	Aug. 20	Aug. 28	Sept. 5
Dec. 20–30	I	II	Aug. 18	Aug. 25	Sept. 3	Sept. 10
Jan. 5–15	I	II	Aug. 23	Aug. 30	Sept. 8	Sept. 15
Jan. 20–30	I	II	Aug. 28	Sept. 7	Sept. 13	Sept. 23
Feb. 5–15	I	II	Sept. 5	Sept. 15	Sept. 25	Oct. 5
Feb. 20–28	II	II	Sept. 15	Sept. 25	Oct. 5	Oct. 15
Mar. 5–15	II	II	Sept. 25	Oct. 10	Oct. 20	Nov. 1
Mar. 20–30	II	II	Oct. 10	Oct. 27	Nov. 10	Nov. 20
Apr. 5–15	II	II	Oct. 25	Nov. 20	Nov. 25	Dec. 15
Apr. 20–30	II	II	Nov. 5	Dec. 17	Dec. 5	Jan. 15
May 5–15	II	III	Nov. 30	Jan. 15	Dec. 30	Feb. 10
May 20–30	III	III	Jan. 5	Feb. 12	Feb. 5	Mar. 7
June 5–15	III	III	Feb. 15	Mar. 5	Mar. 15	Mar. 25
June 20–30	III	IV	Mar. 15	Mar. 25	Apr. 10	Apr. 15
July 5–15	IV	IV	Apr. 1	Apr. 10	Apr. 20	Apr. 25
July 20–30	IV	IV	Apr. 25	Apr. 25	May 15	May 10
Aug. 5–15	IV	IV	May 10	May 10	May 25	May 25
Aug. 20–30	IV	IV	May 25	May 25	June 10	June 10
Sept. 5–15	IV	IV	June 15	June 10	June 25	June 25
Sept. 20–30	III	IV	June 30	June 25	July 15	July 10

This schedule is based on the use of raised benches, 50-degree nights, single-stem culture, and the correct variety for the time of year.

Snapdragons are grown from seed. Prepare a flat of potting soil, vermiculite, and peat. Dampen with Pano-drench solution. The seeds are very small; they must be sown in rows on the surface. Slip the flat into a plastic bag for ten days to conserve moisture. Seeds germinate in one to two weeks at 65 to

75 degrees—70 degrees is ideal. After ten days, remove the plastic cover and drop temperature to 60 degrees. Do not allow seedlings to dry out. Keep medium moist and have air circulating over it. Mist on bright days. Transplant seedlings as soon as one pair of true leaves has developed. This procedure should prevent damping-off, a common problem with snap seedlings.

Grow snaps in three parts loose garden soil to one part peat. To this add ½ cup of superphosphate to each bushel. Transplant on schedule to raised benches. Space about 4 by 4 inches. Set seedlings shallow to avoid stem rot. They may topple during the first watering when set high. Check the bed and gently set them upright again.

Water when the soil feels crumbly. It is better to be a little on the dry side in winter than soggy. Water more frequently in warm weather.

Also, feed sparingly during the winter months, increasing as the weather warms. Use a 25–5–30 fertilizer.

Grow snaps at 50 degrees. This is a long-standing rule. The flowering schedules are based on this night temperature. A good daytime range is 55 to 65 degrees—around 55 degrees for dull days and 65 degrees for bright ones.

Snaps like sunlight. Be sure they get it. Sunlight improves the quality of the blooms. During the hottest months, glass may be shaded lightly to keep the temperatures down.

Provide a wire and string support.

For summer snaps, keep growing area as cool as possible and use summer varieties such as June Bride, Dark Star, and Miami, which are heat-resistant varieties in Group IV.

Most commercial snaps are grown single-stemmed, and the schedule is arranged on this basis. However, small growers may prefer a pinched crop, which yields fewer flowers at one time but over a longer period. For home growers, pinching is a good practice.

For a pinched crop, when transplanting seedlings, space them about 8 by 8 inches in a bench or deep flat. Let plants get well established. When they are about 8 inches high, pinch the top down to leave three sets of leaves. Plants will need supports. Use a support made of wire with crossed strings. Fasten this to corner posts on which the support can be raised as the plants grow.

To set up a flowering schedule for a pinched crop, first select the flowering date you want. Consult the schedule for growing single-stem plants for the dates to sow seeds and transplant the seedlings. Then add thirty days to both of these dates. This will give you the sowing and planting dates for pinched crops. Finally, pinch on the planting date given for single-stem culture.

For example, for flowers on January 1:

	Sow on:	Plant on:	Pinch on:
Single Stem:	August 18	September 3	(No Pinch)
Pinched Crop:	July 18	August 3	September 3

What this does is to give the pinched and single-stem plants an equal period of growing time.

Pinching is not recommended for summer flowering. Grow June to September blooms on single stems. Due to the rapid development of the flowers at this period, the stems on pinched plants would be too short.

After cutting, you can grow a second crop from the same planting. Thin new bottom shoots to four or five per plant. Water and feed. Plants will flower in about three months.

Dwarf snaps can also be grown as unusually attractive flowering pot plants. Culture and timing is similar to that of pinched cut flowers. Grow in 4- or 5-inch pots. When established, pinch 1 inch off to increase bottom breaks.

During winter months use lights to start plants flowering. Snaps are long-day plants. Use 60-watt incandescent bulbs 3 feet high and 4 feet apart for two hours at midnight.

There are some excellent dwarf varieties available, which do not need staking. Little Darling will form a husky, well-branched plant 12 inches tall in all colors. Floral Carpet and Tom Thumb do not need pinching and grow bushy plants 8 inches tall.

EASTER LILY *(Lilium longiflorum)*

CONTROL: Temperature. Timing.

Almost any of the many cultivated lilies can be forced to bloom indoors. However, some are more easily forced than others. Among them is the white *L. longiflorum,* closely associated with Easter. It and its varieties are the ones that are usually forced.

There was a time when the Japanese Giganteum was popular. Strains such as Creole and Estate have also been used. But now the two strains of lilies that have been found best suited to force for Easter are Croft and Ace.

Croft and Ace both make excellent Easter plants. Ace grows into a more compact plant and is a little slower growing. Consequently, it is more often used when Easter falls late in spring. However, most commercial growers favor Croft. Croft lilies are easy to care for, easy to force, and make excellent plants.

You'll find that you can get outstanding results forcing Croft or Ace in your home, especially if you can get precooled bulbs early in winter. This may present a problem to the home grower who wants just a few bulbs, however, your local greenhouse grower, who buys them in quantity, may sell you several.

If you are unable to buy precooled bulbs, you can precool and condition bulbs yourself. The procedure is not too involved. The first step is to get your untreated bulbs early— September or October if possible.

Or if you prefer not to buy your bulbs and you have Easter lilies from previous years growing in your garden, you can lift the bulbs in the fall and remove the bulblets. Commercial bulb growers do this. The bulblets, of course, are the tiny walnut-sized bulbs on the underground part of the stems, between the top of the bulb and the ground. For future lilies or forcing stock, these bulblets are planted outdoors and grown for a second year as "yearlings." In the far north, they should be protected from any hard freeze. In severe climates, some commercial growers dig and store them indoors for the winter.

The yearlings—either left in the soil or replanted—are grown a third year to make forcing stock. By then they should be good-sized bulbs—2 to 3 inches in diameter, or 7 to 10 inches in circumference. Commercially, forcing bulbs are graded by circumference in inches. Grade 9/10, for example, is bulbs 9 to 10 inches around. The bulb size is a good indicator of the number of flowers it will produce—about one flower per 2 inches of circumference. A 9/10 grade, for example, should have at least five flowers.

In September, if you have bought noncooled bulbs or have dug bulbs from your garden, remove the soil, bulblets, and top growth, plus some of the fleshy root growth.

To precool, first place your bulbs in semimoist peat moss in a plastic sandwich bag. Then store in the fruit-storage section of your refrigerator for about two months. Six weeks is sufficient at controlled 34-degree temperature. This is a minimum time. In practice, hold bulbs in your refrigerator until you are ready to pot them. This precooling brings bulbs into flower more uniformly.

There is an alternate procedure to take the place of the precooling. Bulbs may be potted immediately in the fall *if* the potted bulbs can then be stored in a uniform temperature of 50 degrees or less. In far northern climates, a cold frame covered with straw to minimize temperature variations may fill the bill.

Try both methods. But for most, a refrigerator is readily available for precooling a few bulbs.

There is considerable difference in opinion among growers about when to pot precooled bulbs. How long does the forcing take? It may vary from 100 to 130 days before Easter. In my case, growing Croft lilies, I find four months to be a good working period. Then, if the potting date falls around the Christmas holidays, I add a week.

So, if you've bought precooled bulbs or if you precooled them yourself, about four months before Easter get some 5- and 6-inch pots ready. Place about 1 inch of crushed stones or pebbles on the bottom of each pot for good drainage. Then start preparing your potting soil.

The potting soil should have a pH of above 6.5 but not more

than 7.0 and should have an ample supply of humus material along with some not-too-available plant food. I use ⅓ peat, ⅓ coarse sand, and ⅓ sterilized garden soil. To this I add a 3-inch potful of dehydrated manure and a 1-inch potful of ammonium sulphate per bushel of soil mix. The pH of the soil is fairly important. Use a pH tester. Potting soil far under pH 6.5 should have some lime or calcium nitrate added in place of the ammonium sulphate.

It must be remembered that Croft and Ace lilies are "stem rooting." They produce roots from the stem plant a few inches above the bulb as well as from the bottom. Therefore, the bulbs should be potted so that the top of the bulb is about 2 inches below the soil level. Potted in this way, the stem roots can help the bulb roots to supply the plant with food and moisture.

Water thoroughly after potting. Then, until active roots are formed, keep pots a little on the dry side. A waterlogged pot at this time prevents the development of roots so necessary for successful forcing.

For Croft lilies, if potted four or more months before Easter, first place the potted bulbs in a cool spot—around 50 to 55 degrees—for ten days. This helps the roots to set and seems to increase the bud count. For Ace—a slower growing bulb—move the pots directly to a 60-degree growing area.

In any case, around 105 to 110 days before Easter, all bulbs should be moved to the 60-degree growing area. This is the start of the forcing period. Your temperatures should be at 60 degrees during the night and 70 to 75 degrees during the day. Grow in full light. Water and feed regularly. By this time—105 days before flowering—the bulb should have a good root system.

At ninety-five days before Easter, the shoot should be showing above the soil line of the pot.

At eighty-seven days before Easter, the shoot should be 2 to 3 inches tall. It is at this time that the buds are actually initiated within the plant. Plants should be given full sunlight.

As the plants develop, the pots should be turned from time to time to prevent leaning. Pots should be spaced so that the leaves barely touch one another.

It is time to begin chemical feeding. Use a soluble balanced fertilizer low in phosphate or a straight nitrogen fertilizer, such as calcium nitrate or ammonium sulphate. Apply when watering. Feed every two weeks. A starved plant will tend to stretch. To keep from upsetting the pH of the soil, use 2 ounces of calcium nitrate to 5 gallons of water for one feeding and the same amount of ammonium sulphate for the next.

About 75 days before Easter is the time to assess growth progress and start manipulating. The slower-growing, shorter plants should be moved to a warmer area of night temperature—about 65 to 70 degrees. Plants developing faster than normal—tall, with a tendency to bud—should be put into cooler night temperatures—about 55 degrees. The laggards and the sprinters will be easy to detect.

Fifty days before Easter, buds should be visible in the growing tip. If not, move plants to a warmer area.

The last two to three weeks before Easter is the critical time. Weather can make a difference in speeding or slowing growth.

Sixteen days before Easter, the largest bud, which should now be about 2 to 3 inches long, should begin to point down. The other buds may still be erect, but they will soon follow.

Four to five days before Easter, the first flowers should begin to open. Plants should be given their last feeding.

Throughout the forcing period, slow plants should be moved to a warmer spot at night, and advanced plants held back by colder night temperatures. Such temperature manipulation is the best way to regulate growth.

Suppose your plant starts blooming two weeks before Easter. It may be put in a dark and refrigerated area for ten days or two weeks without adverse effects.

Suppose your plant is greatly retarded. Move to a warm place. Water with lukewarm water, spraying the entire plant. And, as a last resort, lights may be used. Light for about four or five hours during the night with about 35 footcandles. However, when using lights, temperatures must be held below 65 degrees to keep down the height and minimize legginess.

All this may sound involved. But in reality, lilies are easy to force. They respond readily to manipulation, and you can do so much with them. You'll find lilies to be exciting and satisfying plants.

POINSETTIA *(Euphorbia pulcherrima)*

CONTROL: Timing. Light. Shade.

Saint Louis Church on New Caledonia Island in the South Pacific may now be in the center of a congested city, for all I know. However, I recall the tiny church in 1942, set amid a small cluster of thatched native houses in a dense jungle, almost hidden under the teak and eucalyptus trees. On Easter morning, the church and homes were surrounded by hundreds of poinsettias in bloom. They were everywhere, and the entire scene resembled an immense ruby set in green jade.

Why not poinsettias for Easter here in America? Because the plants would seem to be out of season in our homes. We associate their red bracts and deep green leaves with Christmas. They are as much a part of Christmas as a choir singing "Silent Night."

This important Christmas plant responds to day length, so day length becomes our control mechanism to force bloom.

You can elect to grow your poinsettias from cuttings that you make or from cuttings that you buy, or to buy plants ready for forcing.

Poinsettias are somewhat persnickety plants, and frankly they are a challenge to grow from the beginning. Many growers avoid this by buying finished plants. But somebody has to start them, and here's how.

Start with a stock plant that has finished blooming. It may be the poinsettia you had for Christmas. After it has bloomed, set your plant somewhere out of the way—the basement is fine—and let it get quite dry. But not so dry that the stems wrinkle. Hold at 60 degrees until late March. Repot, water, and raise the temperature to 65 or 70 degrees. Give the plant good light. To speed up growth, temperatures may be increased to 75 degrees.

Feed weekly with a 20–20–20 liquid fertilizer. A good-sized

plant growing in a 12-inch pot will give you about twenty to twenty-five cuttings.

If the growth on the stock plant approaches 10 inches in length before mid-June, soft-pinch the tip. This will cause branching.

Take cuttings, starting in July. They should be at least 4 inches long and may be longer. Make the cut just above the second node on the branch. This gives your cutting a stem before its first leaf and lets two buds remain on the stock plant to grow future cuttings.

Do not remove any leaves from the cutting. Dip the cut end into rooting hormone and stick it into a deep flat of coarse sand or perlite. Space 3 inches apart in rows 5 inches apart. Shade cuttings from the direct sun. Use a cheesecloth canopy to let the air circulate. Give the flats bottom heat if possible—around 65 degrees—in any case, keep them off the cold ground. Water and mist regularly to keep the humidity up and the sand wet.

Cuttings may root in three weeks. As soon as roots show at the base, transplant the cuttings to 3-inch pots. Use two parts sterilized sandy loam to one part acid peat. To a bushel of this potting soil add a 2½-inch potful of superphosphate. (See the table of equivalents in Appendix C for working with lesser amounts of soil.) Poinsettias like an acid soil with a pH of about 4.5.

Poinsettia cuttings are often transferred directly from the rooting medium to 5- or 6-inch azalea pans in order to eliminate the move from the 3-inch pots. But it is not good practice and should be followed only with your late August cuttings.

After plants are established, feed moderately every two or three weeks with a liquid 20–10–10 fertilizer. Keep plants well watered.

To prevent poinsettias from getting tall and lanky, chemical regulators such as Cycocel are often applied at this point. The treated plants finish shorter, the stems are stiffer, and the foliage and bract colors are more intense. Cycocel is applied as a soil drench and is absorbed through the roots. Obviously, a good root system is necessary. It is usually applied two weeks after the rooted cuttings are potted in 3-inch pots. To 2 fluid ounces of Cycocel add water to make 1 gallon. Use ½ cup of this solution for each 3-inch pot. This treatment should be given before October 15 in the north, and before November 1 in the south. For full effect, delay shifting from 3-inch pots to larger pans until around September 30.

In mid-August the July-propagated cuttings may have an 8-inch growth and may be topped. This initiates branching and also gives you another cutting. Cuttings propagated after July should be soft-pinched—nip off the growing tip—to produce branches.

The last day to make cuttings is August 15. The last day for a pinch is September 5. The last day for replanting in the final pan is October 15.

The smaller late-propagated plants are not pinched but grouped together—three single-stemmed plants to a 6-inch pan.

During October and November, watering may be moderated somewhat, but feeding should be increased to every week or ten days.

Poinsettias respond to day length. To force them into bud, follow procedures similar to those for chrysanthemums. To delay bud formation, expose plants to light from September 20 to October 10, using 60-watt bulbs 5 feet apart and 5 feet high for one hour during the middle of the night. An intensity of 10 footcandles is sufficient.

Immediately after the lighting is stopped on October 10, the buds form. The plants respond to short days and low temperatures. Some growers shade to protect plants from errant light. Once the buds have formed, shading is no longer necessary.

Some growers bypass the lighting period and instead grow their plants at cooler temperatures—below 60 degrees. They run the chance of having plants that are not uniform and are in color too soon.

During the bud formation, grow plants at 60 to 65 degrees nights, and slightly higher during the day.

Your plants are on time if the top leaves darken around November 1 and if the red coloring is quite apparent around November 25.

Poinsettia varieties are constantly being improved. Barbara Ecke Supreme is still a fine red, vigorous, free-branching plant. For a pink, there is Ecke Pink, and for a white, Ecke White. Indianapolis Red and Mrs. Paul Ecke will do well in the south. The Mikkelsen hybrids—especially Paul Mikkelsen—are "tougher" poinsettias and withstand adverse conditions better than other varieties. They are also superior as cut flowers.

After the red bracts on your Christmas poinsettia fade and fall, usually in February or March, you can treat your poinsettia as a stock plant or you can let it grow as an attractive spring and summer foliage plant in your home. Pinch to shape it and keep it watered and fed. Then, forty days before Christmas, give it long nights with *no lights* at all and grow it cool—below 60 degrees. You will be able to enjoy your poinsettia again for the second Christmas.

AZALEA *(Rhododendron sp.)*

CONTROL: Timing. Temperature.

Colorful azaleas are among our most popular outdoor shrubs. Used indoors, azaleas can certainly be classed among our most beautiful flowering plants. And since they keep well in the home, they make excellent gift plants.

To force azaleas, you can turn to two sources for material—buy already rooted or grafted plants, or root them yourself and later graft them if necessary. A few varieties grow better grafted to another stock plant. For most purposes, however, rooted cuttings are very satisfactory and are widely used. They produce the kind of compact, bushy plants you want.

Rooting azaleas is very much like rooting any other woody plant, except that azaleas like their rooting and growing medium to be slightly acid. Cuttings are taken from May until early summer. Take new growth, 6 to 8 inches long, and remove lower leaves. Also remove any flower buds. Dip the cutting in rooting hormone. Insert into a mixture of sand and acid peat in flats. Use 65-degree bottom heat if possible. If not, hold at 55- to 60-degree night temperatures. Constant moisture in the air and rooting medium is important. Azaleas will root even under a continual mist or spray. For a few plants, rooting under jars often helps. Be patient. It may take them two to three months to root.

When rooted, usually in August or September, transplant to flats or pots. Flats are preferred because they hold moisture longer. Use a half and half mixture of loose soil and acid peat—sometimes called German peat. The growing mixture should test to a pH of 4.5 or 5.5. Water. Keep misted. Feed periodically with 4-12-4 fertilizer with iron sulfate added— about ½ teaspoon to 1 gallon of water. Grow at 60 degrees.

After the plants are established, in the fall, pinch off terminal shoots to encourage branching. Soft-pinch again the following March. By spring, these plants will be from 3 to 5 inches across at the top and are called liners.

In summer, they can be moved outside. Grow in semishade. Keep fertilizing. Prune wild growth. By fall, these liners will have grown to be 5 or 6 inches across. They should be moved indoors before frost.

Most growers bypass the rooting step and buy small liners in spring or larger ones in fall.

Either way, grow at 60 to 65 degrees. Fertilize every month, alternating between a balanced fertilizer and ammonium sulfate. Every second month, add iron sulfate to the watering—½ teaspoon to 1 gallon. Give frequent overhead watering and misting to maintain humidity.

Allow the plants to have plenty of space while growing. Crowding will result in poor plant shape. To maintain shape, keep pinching, pruning, and trimming back wild growth. Also cut off any early-formed flower buds.

Move outdoors again for the second summer. Keep in semishade. Water and feed. Make the last soft pinch on June 20. In August, expose to full sun. On August 15, shift to finishing pots. Plants should be a nice 8 inches across at the top and ready to force.

Temperature control is the most important single factor in controlling azaleas. Temperatures will need to be above 65 degrees to set buds, below 60 degrees for precooling, and around 45 degrees to hold plants back.

Buds are started by holding temperatures above 65 degrees for at least eight hours daily during a two-month period. At temperatures below 65 degrees, the plants will not set buds. Plants normally get this required high temperature during the summer, and they should be well budded by September 1.

There is an optional procedure you can use to ensure bud formation. About two weeks after the June 20 soft pinch— around July 5—many growers use growth retardants. Cycocel or B-Nine sprayed on azaleas checks plant growth to give you a better shaped plant, and causes buds to form. The usual time to spray with the growth retardant is about six months before flowering. Use 2 ounces of Cycocel to 1 gallon of water and spray plants twice, seven days apart. Or use B-Nine—6 ounces to 1 gallon of water—and apply twice with a seven-day interval. Thoroughly wet the leaves.

After spraying, start shading for a twelve- to fourteen-hour night to get about two months of short days at temperatures above 60 degrees.

Whether treated or not, around September 1 plants need precooling. Get the plants into cool temperatures at night— under 60 degrees—for from four to six weeks. Move them to a cold frame, covering them or moving them indoors if there is a danger of heavy frost. Try to protect plants from wide temperature variations during the cooling period, or plants will not force evenly. After the cooling period, move plants indoors to a light, 60- to 65-degree growing area.

For precooling, some growers, especially in the south, move their plants into refrigerated storage and use artificial light during the day. About 150 watts held 2 feet over the plants for twelve hours does the job. But be careful about overwatering. Under cool conditions, plants require less water. Other growers buy azalea plants precooled in the fall. In this case, plant immediately. Move into an area with 60- to 65-degree temperature. Water and mist.

During the forcing period, new shoots that grow around the flower cluster should be removed.

To force for Thanksgiving, use only the variety Coral Bells. Precool at around 50 degrees for four weeks—September 10 to

October 10—then force at 65 degrees. It will flower before November 20.

For Christmas forcing, there are a number of early varieties you can use besides Coral Bells—Alaska, Hexe, Mme. Petrick, Paul Schame, and Salmon Beauty. Precool for four weeks starting in early October at temperatures of around 50 degrees. Then grow at 65 degrees for seven weeks. Plants will be in bloom by Christmas.

For Valentine's Day, use varieties such as Jean Haerens, Red Wing, Mrs. Fred Sanders, and Albert Elizabeth. Precool and hold at low temperature until five or six weeks before Valentine's Day. Then grow at 60 to 65 degrees.

For Easter and later, all varieties can be forced. A few excellent ones are Chas. Encke, Empress of India, and Polar Bear. The problem at this time is not to force plants but to hold them. Store at around 45 degrees. Then, for early Easter, start forcing at 65 degrees three weeks before the holiday. For late Easter, start forcing two weeks before.

After blooming, repot the plant in fresh peat and soil mixture. Trim off some of the soft top growth. Grow at 60 degrees until the plant can be moved outdoors. Treat the same way as unforced azaleas.

Four types of azaleas are usually used for forcing.

The *indica* varieties are the large-flowered azaleas. Among them are Jean Haerens, Mme. Petrick, Triomphe, and Paul Schame.

The *Kurume* type are small flowered, dense, shapely plants. They are the hardiest of the forcing azaleas. Some fine ones are Coral Bells, Hexe, Snow, and Salmon Beauty.

Between these two species are two intermediate variations. The Rutherfords are crosses between *indica* and the *Kurume* and the blooms have superior keeping quality. Alaska, Dorothy Gish, and Snow Queen are typical Rutherfords. The other group, the Pericat, have medium-sized flowers and plants. They perform well as late Easter forcing plants. Marjory Ann and Rose Pericat are examples.

To recap: The formula for forcing azaleas—and they can be forced all year long with the exception of June and July—

involves four stages: growth, bud set, cold treatment, and forcing.

For growth, give warm temperatures of around 60 degrees and long days.

For bud set, continue warm temperatures of at least 60 degrees. Use growth-retardant spray about five or six months before flowering date. Then start short days by utilizing shade and continue for two months.

For cold treatment, store in below-55-degree night temperature, starting about two months after using spray. Hold for two months if plants get a constant 55 degrees or for three months if day temperature is higher. In the cold frame, reduce light intensity. In a dark commercial or floral refrigerator, give ten hours of artificial light to prevent leaf drop.

For forcing, bring into 60 degrees for four to six weeks, with natural daylight.

Using this formula, you can force azaleas to bloom within one year. Here is a schedule for Christmas blooms:

February 1—pot four rooted cuttings, instead of one, directly into a 6-inch azalea pan. Light for four hours each night— 10:00 P.M. to 2:00 A.M.—with 20 footcandles of incandescent light. Grow at 60 degrees. The light prevents bud formation and encourages growth.

May—soft-pinch main branches and side shoots when they are about 1½ to 2 inches long.

June 1—stop lighting.

July 1—apply Cycocel retardant—3 ounces per gallon.

July 7—give second application of retardant.

August 1—start shade for eight hours maximum daylight—5:00 P.M. to 9:00 A.M.

September 15—move to 55-degree night temperature. Store in cold, dark shed or refrigerator and give plants 20 footcandles of artificial light for ten hours a day. The cool temperature will develop the buds.

November 1 or 15—move plants to 60 degrees and natural daylight. For Hexe, move November 1, and for Alaska, move November 15.

HYDRANGEA *(Hydrangea macrophylla)*

CONTROL: Timing.

Hydrangeas, traditional for Easter, Mother's Day, and Memorial Day, are easily forced into bloom for these holidays. They are a major and profitable crop for most commercial growers. For the home or the home greenhouse, it is easy to grow and force hydrangeas into bloom. The procedure is the same for one plant as it is for a hundred.

First, it should be remembered that hydrangeas are deciduous, woody shrubs and should be handled as such. In their native China and Japan, flower buds are formed in the fall when temperatures drop below 65 degrees. The plants then go through a period of dormancy and cold exposure throughout the winter. In the spring, after a month or more of temperatures above 60, the hydrangeas bloom.

Our technique to force hydrangeas, then, is to simulate these conditions, handling the plant as a shrub with a dormant cold requirement. We take cuttings in the spring, root them, and let them grow through the summer. In the fall, when temperatures drop below 65 degrees, we let buds form for about six weeks. The plant is then subjected to a dormant period of about six weeks at temperatures between freezing and 50 degrees. At the end of this cold treatment, the plant forces readily at 60 degrees.

Commercial growers can, and often do, purchase cuttings already rooted, and then carry them through the summer growth and the fall bud formation and dormancy. Other growers buy dormant plants ready for forcing in winter. You can do the same for plants at home. Or you can make your own cuttings. Whatever your choice, we'll run through the complete procedure.

Hydrangea cuttings may be taken from late February through March and April. For smaller plants, they can even be taken as late as early July. Cuttings may be taken from a stock plant that you bought or raised for this purpose. Any healthy plant will do. Look for blind shoots on your flowering plants, that is, shoots that do not bear flowers. These are an excellent source for cutting wood.

There are three types of cuttings you can make.

There's the stub cutting, which consists of a 2- or 3-inch section of the stem with one set of leaves. This cutting, when grown into a plant, will produce two stems—one from each leaf axil. If these are later pinched, the resulting plant will have at least four large flowering stems. Several stub cuttings can be made from one stem. Cut it into sections so that each section has one set of leaves.

The second type of cuttings are the terminal cuttings. These are made by cutting off the top 4 inches of a branch that includes its terminal growing tip. Only one terminal cutting can be made from a stem, although several stub cuttings may also be made at the same time. These terminal cuttings grow faster than the other type of cuttings.

The third type of cutting is the single eye. Single-eye cuttings are obtained by slitting the stem of a stub cutting down its length so that each half has a single leaf and leaf axil. A single branch will result. Single-eye cuttings are best suited for early propagation, since there will be enough time to develop a multibranched plant through successive pinchings.

Cuttings taken in early March can be pinched twice and will develop plants with four to eight flower heads. These will be finished in 6-inch pots. May cuttings can be pinched once and will develop two to four heads. These plants will be finished in 5-inch pots. June and July cuttings are suitable only for single-stem plants, to be finished in 3- or 4-inch pots.

Only terminal cuttings should be made in June or July. Incidentally, these can also be made by topping the plants grown from February cuttings.

Cuttings can be rooted either in sand or in a sand and peat mixture. A flat will work fine for just a few cuttings. Do not allow the rooting mixture to dry. Temperature and humidity are important during the rooting period. Maintain a temperature around 60 to 65 degrees. Give bottom heat, if possible. Keep the humidity high with frequent misting. Or slip the flat under a plastic tent, with openings to allow for air circulation. An ample root system should have formed in three or four weeks. The cuttings can then be potted.

The potting soil should be loose and slightly acid. I prefer a mixture of good soil and peat—half and half. To a bushel of this mixture, I add 2 full handfuls of superphosphate and ½ handful of potash. In addition to this, when the plants are established in the pots, I give them a feeding of complete liquid fertilizer such as 4–12–4 every three weeks.

To save space, I first plant in 3-inch pots, then, in about two months, shift into 5- or 6-inch pots, in which the plants will flower. After potting, cover with newspaper or cloth for a few days until the plants become established. Grow at 60 degrees.

Now feeding becomes important. The ultimate color of the flower you want—pink or blue—dictates the fertilizer to be used. Although some varieties produce a better pink or a better blue than others, it is the pH of the soil and the presence or absence of aluminum that influence the color of the flowers.

The best pink color is obtained by the absence of aluminum in the soil and a pH of 5.5. A high-phosphate fertilizer should be used. It will tie up what aluminum is in the soil, making it unavailable to the plant. Feed every two weeks through September with a 4–12–4 or 10–52–17 liquid fertilizer.

To produce good blue hydrangeas, maintain the soil pH at 5.5 and use fertilizers containing only nitrogen and potassium, such as 15–3–15. Without phosphorous, the aluminum in the soil is available to the plant. In addition, three or four applications of aluminum sulphate—about a handful per gallon of water—during August and September will improve the formation of blue hues.

Be sure you label your plants *pink* or *blue*.

We've mentioned pinching—nipping off the terminal growth with the thumbnail and forefinger or with a small shears. Pinching of early propagated plants should be done twice—in April or May and again in June or July. Later propagated plants should be pinched only once, with the last pinch usually made not later than July 15. Pinching should be done in such a way that you leave at least two sets of healthy leaves on the branch.

Hydrangeas in 5- or 6-inch pots may be moved outdoors to partial shade during the summer. They should be watered and fed regularly. Add ½ teaspoon iron sulfate per gallon of water to the fertilizer. In August, they should be given full sun and sprayed occasionally on very hot days. In September, in the north, temperatures drop below 65 degrees, and buds start forming. Farther south, this may take place in October. The development of flowering buds requires about six weeks of temperatures below 65 degrees. You may move plants to a cold frame to have them handy, out of harm's way, and easy to protect, if necessary. Continue to give full sun.

Hydrangeas can stand light frost and temperatures as low as 15 or 20 degrees if they have become gradually conditioned to cold.

After about six weeks of bud formation at below 65-degree temperatures, or early in November, the plants should be moved to a dark storage room, with temperatures below 50 degrees. Near freezing would be better. You need an unheated shed or a fruit storage cellar where you can maintain a cold temperature. In the north in winter, the back of a garage may do. In the south, a local food or fruit locker may hold a few plants for you. The plants should get occasional watering, that is, should neither be allowed to dry out nor be kept soaking wet. Hold for about five weeks in cold storage, or longer if necessary for your scheduling purpose. During this storage, the leaves will fall off. That's normal. To prevent mold formation at this time, I usually give plants a spray with some fruit fungicide, such as Captan.

And now for the forcing. Ninety days before you want hydrangeas in full flower, take them out of cold storage. Grow them at about 60 degrees in semishade. That's all.

Suppose you want them for Easter. Date back three months. Take plants out of storage at that date. Grow at around 60 degrees. Flower buds should be the size of a pea at eight weeks before Easter. About six weeks before Easter, the buds should be the size of a lima bean. If they are not, increase the temperature slightly.

Varieties vary somewhat in their growth. Adjustments in temperatures can speed them up or retard them. Temperatures of 70 degrees with ample light will hasten development considerably. Cooler forcing makes plants taller. Warmer forcing tends to produce shorter finished plants. After you become familiar with varieties and growth rate, you are in complete control.

As mentioned earlier, feeding during the forcing period controls the color. Work 1 teaspoon of superphosphate into each pot. Follow the feeding program used for summer growth. A pH of 6.5 and the absence of aluminum produce a good pink color. Use liquid 10-52-17 every two weeks. For blue, a plentiful supply of aluminum and a soil pH of 5.5 bring out a good clear hue. Apply aluminum sulfate every two weeks with a high nitrogen-potassium fertilizer and add a pinch of iron sulfate. Plants should get four to six applications of the correct fertilizer during the blossom-forcing period.

Hydrangeas have large leaves, from which considerable moisture is evaporated. The plants require more water than small-leafed plants. The pot soil should be kept uniformly moist, but not soggy.

The most serious trouble in forcing hydrangeas is blind shoots, or branches that fail to bloom. Two conditions may cause this. The plants may not have had the required six weeks of temperatures below 65 degrees in the fall for bud formation. With less time, the buds may not be completely formed. And a higher temperature—above 65 degrees—promotes vegetative growth rather than bud formation.

Sparse and unhealthy leaves may also cause blindness. When the process of photosynthesis is impaired through summer leaf drop due to overcrowding, insects, or disease, blindness may result. Too-late pinching that prevented the plant from having enough leaves or too-late potting that caused the leaves to wilt are factors. Ample sunlight from August through October is another important requirement for healthy leaves and healthy bud formation. To avoid blindness, grow sturdy plants and give them the time and temperature needed for bud formation.

Which varieties should you grow? Some varieties do better for some growers than others. It's almost a matter of trial and error. Nevertheless, here are a few dependable standbys:

Alpengluhn—deep pink; makes a nice small plant.

Engel's White—standard white; grow and handle like pink.

Europa—blue or pink; an excellent early forcer.

Flamboyant—medium pink; a vigorous grower.

Kuhnert—an excellent blue; a tall plant.

Merveille—an excellent dark pink.

Merritt's Beauty—another good blue.

Rosabelle—deep blue or pink; a strong grower.

Rose Supreme—light pink; has a large flower head.

Sister Therese—an excellent white; has even larger flower heads, though it's a short plant.

Todi—deep pink; has large heads and excellent flowers.

GERANIUM *(Pelargonium sp.)*

CONTROL: Pinch. Timing.

Geraniums deserve a special award for stamina if for nothing else. They can be overwatered or underwatered in the home, they can tolerate full sun or full shade, they can be overfed or underfed, and they can be exposed to hot, dry indoor heat or to a cool, moist streamside location. They withstand all this abuse and still grow remarkably beautiful flowers.

Geraniums are simple to grow from cuttings, which is their usual form of propagation. Throughout the summer, cast a critical eye on the geraniums you have in your garden. Select several that are exceptional plants in growth and flowers. Early in fall, lift these, pot them, and bring them indoors as stock plants. They can be the source of hundreds of plants by spring.

From these stock plants, take cuttings from September on. Then, as the new plants are rooted and start to grow in pots, take cuttings from these, too. In this way, you increase the number of your cuttings by using two sources.

When making cuttings, first tape your thumb to protect it. Then, using a sharp, sterilized knife, nip off the tips of the new growth on your stock plants, making these cuttings about 3 to 4 inches long. Take several leaves on the stem. Strip the leaves

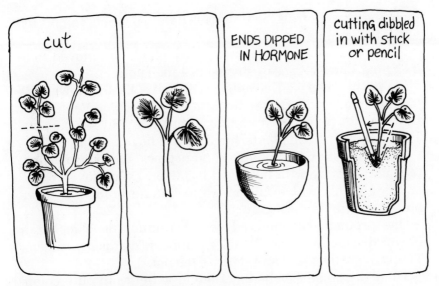

The basic steps in propagating geraniums.

off the bottom part of the stem, but allow at least two full leaves to remain at the top. Dip cut ends in rooting hormone and insert them into moist coarse sand or perlite. Space the cuttings 2 inches apart in rows 4 inches apart. Water sparingly, if at all, during the first ten days, but mist or spray frequently with water on bright days to prevent wilting. Shading the cuttings from direct sun for these ten days is helpful. Hold temperatures at around 60 degrees.

After ten to fourteen days, a callous will have formed on the end of the cuttings. Some growers pot at this point, but I prefer to leave the cuttings in the rooting medium and begin watering them so that they will set roots. In three or four weeks roots will have formed, and the cuttings may be potted.

Pot in 2½-inch pots. Use loose garden loam with some peat added—plus superphosphate, about 1 cup to 1 bushel. Grow at 60 degrees. Give plants full sunlight.

The plants that grow from cuttings taken in September can have terminal cuttings taken in December. If cuttings are not wanted, these plants must be pinched to encourage branching.

Pinching also controls the flowering date. To pinch, roll off the top of the terminal growth.

At the time of the first pinch, early plants are moved to 5-inch pots. Later plants are moved to 4-inch pots.

Plants pinched in December will make Easter flowers. A January pinch will flower for Mother's Day. For Valentine's Day, do not pinch early cuttings, and plant in 4-inch pots. They may not be full plants, but they will be in flower.

In a nutshell: Grow plants at 60 degrees, water as needed, feed periodically with balanced fertilizer. Do not overcrowd, or leggy plants will result. Pinch to initiate branching. Give plants sunlight for best growth.

One problem encountered with geraniums is blackleg, a fungus disease in which a black rot appears on the lower stem. Throw away the plant and sterilize the pot.

There are some excellent geranium varieties in pure colors and bicolors. Pink, Salmon, and Red Irene were outstanding performers for me. Better Times was also an excellent red. Salmon Supreme and Pink Champagne were fine flowers. However, I never found a white that matched any of these in plant, flower size, or performance.

In our greenhouses, we had created, through hybridization, a red and white bicolor that we called Danish Flag. It performed as well as the Irenes and was extremely popular. We marketed thousands. However, when we stopped propagating it, the strain was lost. Nevertheless, there are some other fine bicolors available for you to try.

Some geraniums may be grown from seed. Nittany Lion seed will produce plants that are true in color and form. The All-American winner Carefree may also be grown from seed. It produces seven or eight color variations and develops into strong, compact plants for summer pots or gardens. Seeds take about a month to germinate. Handle the seedlings as you would rooted cuttings.

Pelargoniums other than those termed zonal geraniums (*P. zonale*) differ only in the time it takes to produce flowers from a pinch. For Easter, pinch in December. For Mother's Day, pinch in February. Some typical alternate pelargonium types are ivy geraniums, Martha Washingtons, and lemon geraniums. Martha Washington *(P. domesticum)* is the plant that great-grandma used to have in her parlor. It is one of fourteen beautiful old species that we are neglecting, many of them scented, colorful, and unusual. Except for the popular zonal, geraniums are sorely in need of a press agent.

9
Forcing . . . Mostly Cut Flowers

According to a Chinese proverb, "customs and habits may differ, but the love of flowers is common to all people." However, the kinds of flowers we love often change as our customs and habits change. It shows in our floral arrangements.

Flower arranging, a recognized art form, not only reflects national differences but also differences within our time. It reflects the life we live. It is a happening of our day. New techniques and new designs call for new flower forms or for traditional flowers to be used in new ways.

Today, cut flowers are seen and used as pure design forms—pure lines, colors, and textures used to give emotional expression. There is also a three-dimensional aspect to arranging; forms are surrounded by space to create emphasis. And contrast is used to attract attention. Bigness and boldness and unusual combinations are employed. The horizon is unlimited.

In traditional flower arrangements, still very much in use, the design usually relates to nature and natural growth. Kinds, colors, and textures are grouped. An easy gradation of size and color values provides a quiet transition through the composition. At times, the material and the setting become so unified that the arrangement goes unnoticed. It fits so well.

Not so today. And as I advance in years, I must admit, some

of the new art forms in all media become a little incomprehensible—like trying to follow the plot in a bowl of alphabet soup. This is normal. They are the expressions of another generation. But when these expressions are depicted in flowers, I find myself learning to enjoy them along with the traditional arrangements, my first love. In doing so, I find my horizons expanding. And I am finding the need to grow new kinds of cut flowers.

Since many of these "new" cut flowers, as well as the traditional ones, may not always be available when you want them, you will have to grow and force them yourself. In doing this, you get double the pleasure—first enjoying the growing of them and then enjoying their graciousness in your home.

When growing for cut flowers, use techniques that will make the flowers last longer in the vase. Growing temperatures that are too high or too low, too much or too little watering, excessive feeding—especially with nitrogen—and careless cutting, all affect the keeping quality. Maintaining proper temperature and good soil conditions of moisture and fertility is the secret for growing flowers that last.

Your facilities may not enable you to grow all the cut flowers that can be forced, but there are a number of wonderful flowers that you can grow in limited space—a small home greenhouse, a sun-room, a basement under lights. A few large pots of your favorites are often sufficient.

Each type of flower will have its own cultural needs to be considered—temperature, moisture, supports. Regardless of the end use, the beginnings will have to conform and harmonize with nature.

ASTER or CHINA ASTER (Callistephus chinensis)

CONTROL: Sowing time. Light. Shade.

Asters are old favorites with growers, floral designers, and home gardeners. They are generally grown outdoors in home gardens, and even commercial growers consider them to be cloth house or outdoor crops.

However, good crops can be grown indoors in almost any of

the twelve months of the year. This is the result of some fairly recent discoveries at Ohio State University. Now growers and florists are finding off-season asters to be a welcome addition to the usual chrysanthemums and snapdragons in the winter cut-flower market. The popularity and demand for flowering potted asters is also increasing.

Asters as pot plants are gems for the home. In addition to their lasting qualities—as long as three weeks in the average home—they offer a variety of different colors, including colors that are not available in pot mums and other pot flowers. You may have asters in pure red and white as well as bright rose pinks and true lavenders.

To grow asters as pot plants or cut flowers, you can control the flowering to the dates you want through day length and a schedule of sowing dates. Here is a typical sowing and pot-shift schedule:

Flowering Date	Sow Seed	Shift to Jiffy Pots	Shift to Finish Pots
January	July 15	Aug. 10	Sept. 15
February	Aug. 15	Sept. 10	Nov. 1
March	Sept. 10	Oct. 1	Dec. 1
April	Oct. 20	Nov. 15	Jan. 1
May	Dec. 20	Jan. 10	March 1
June	Feb. 1	Feb. 20	April 1
July	March 15	April 1	May 1
August	April 20	May 10	June 15
September	May 20	June 10	July 15
October	June 10	July 1	Aug. 1
November	June 20	July 15	Aug. 20
December	July 10	Aug. 1	Sept. 1

Although asters as cut flowers can be grown to flower every month of the year, there is nothing gained by growing them indoors or under glass when they bloom naturally outdoors.

For growing asters off season as cut flowers, the important requirements are: 50 to 55 degrees night temperature and additional night lighting. The lighting must be supplied continuously from the seedling stage until the plants are 20 to 24 inches tall. The exception is the growing period from May 1 through September 1, when no lighting is required. The night is short enough. For lighting, 60-watt bulbs in reflectors set 5 feet apart and about 5 feet from the ground—as with mums—are suitable. Lights may be turned on from sundown until 10:00 P.M. or for two hours in the middle of the night.

For cut flowers, shift seedlings to Jiffy pots, then transfer to beds. Space plants about 8 by 8 inches apart. Use sterilized soil. Avoid deep planting. Set plants as shallow as possible without exposing roots.

Pinching is not necessary to induce branching. Normally eight to twelve flowering stems will be produced.

Disbud for large flowers—that is, roll off the tiny side buds and leave only the large top bud. If the plants are not disbudded, a number of short-stem flowers will result.

Some excellent cut-flower varieties are the King asters and the Ball varieties—White Ball, Pink Ball, Rose Ball, and others. They are large-flowered, fully double, long stemmed, and require a minimum of disbudding. The Super Giants are good and somewhat wilt resistant. The Shaggy types are distinctive, with flat, shaggy, interlaced petals. Try Cregos in this type— wilt resistant, large, double, and available in a wide range of colors.

For pot-plant asters, shift seedlings to 2¼-inch Jiffy pots on schedule and grow until ready for the finishing pots. For single-stemmed plants, finish in 3- or 4-inch pots. For groups, finish in 5- or 6-inch pots. When grouping, select plants of uniform size. Two or three plants or more can be used per pot. Use sterilized soil.

Grow the plants at 60 degrees during the months of October through April. Light—60 watts, 5 feet apart and 2 to 3 feet high—up to the time the terminal buds are about the size of a nickel. The exception is the period between May 5 and August 20, when they need not be lighted.

The whole purpose is to keep the plant's "night" under seven hours. Light as near to the middle of the night as possible. The number of hours to light depends upon the season of the year. In summer, no lights. In fall and spring, light about two hours. In winter, light from three to four hours. The same schedule may be followed as for chrysanthemums.

Plants may be shaded for a twelve- or fourteen-hour night between April 1 and September 15, from the time they are no longer lighted until full bloom. This will lengthen the plant's "night" and bring the lateral buds into flower about the same time as the terminal bud. This procedure makes a nice, full-flowered plant, especially when grown only one plant to a pot.

Asters respond to dwarfing by B-Nine growth retardant. Apply ½ percent solution seven weeks after sowing. Height will be reduced by half, and the plants will be more compact and uniform. Spray on standard-sized plants.

Two of the best dwarf varieties to start with are the Dwarf All Saints, which will flower from seed in five to five and a half months, and Dwarf Queen, which is naturally compact and also wilt resistant.

BACHELORS-BUTTON or CORNFLOWER *(Centaurea Cyanus)*

CONTROL: Timing. Light.

If there is a corner of the home greenhouse available for a few deep flats of cut flowers, bachelors-button may be the flower to grow there.

Grow from seed. Seeds germinate in two to four weeks at 65 to 75 degrees. Transfer to fair garden soil, spacing about 8 by 8 inches. Grow at 50 degrees nights to get them started, then increase temperatures to 55 or 60 degrees if necessary. Otherwise, grow them cool—they prefer it. They also prefer full sun. Water enough to keep the soil from being dry and do not feed. Pinch the seedlings when they are established to encourage branching.

These are long-day plants. They will respond to additional light.

For blooms in February and Valentine's Day, sow seeds in September. In October, transplant to deep flats or raised beds. Space 8 by 8 inches. From time of planting until December—

about two months—light nightly for four hours from 6:00 to 10:00 P.M. or in the middle of the night from 10:00 P.M. to midnight. Forty-watt bulbs, 4 feet apart and 2 feet over the plants, are sufficient.

For blooms from March through spring, do not use lights. Sow seeds from September through January—a flat each month. January sowing will flower in May.

Although Blue Boy is commonly grown, a variety of colors is available in a Carnival mixture. There are also close relatives—Imperialis and Americana—from which to choose. A dwarf centaurea, Snowball, growing only 12 inches tall into a solid mound of flowers, should make as fine a winter pot plant as it does a summer border plant. I have never tried it, but you may want to grow a pot or two as an experiment. Handle as you would for cut flowers.

CALENDULA or POT-MARIGOLD *(Calendula officinalis)*

CONTROL: Timing.

Its bright, attractive colors in the dark of winter help to make calendula a popular cut flower.

Calendulas are grown from seed, usually sown in early fall. The seeds need darkness to germinate. Sow ¼ inch deep, water, and cover with cardboard or black plastic. Seeds germinate in two to three weeks at 65 to 75 degrees. The seed flat may be held in the cold frame. Unless the seed medium gets excessively dry, it may not be necessary to water it again.

Calendulas are usually grown in friable soil in a raised bed or in deep flats. Add ½ cup of superphosphate to each bushel of the soil. Space plants about 12 by 12 inches. They like full sun but cool temperatures, so grow at 40 to 50 degrees. They will fare poorly if they are started and grown through a prolonged warm spell.

Water freely, except on dark days. Give plants a good circulation of air. Pinch terminal shoots to encourage side branches. Pinching will cause the plant to grow about 8 flowering stalks. When buds are starting to set, you face a decision.

You can disbud to get a single large flower or let them alone and get a spray of smaller ones. Try both ways to see which you prefer.

For Christmas blooms, sow no earlier than August 15—September 1 in the south. For January, February, and March flowering schedules—allow four months from seeding to bloom.

After flowering, plants may be cut back, and they will flower again in two months.

Some varieties to try are Pacific Creamy White, Ball Improved Long Orange, Ball Gold, and Ball Lemon Queen. A new dwarf, Sunny Boy, makes a compact 6-inch mound of gold, and is reported to be excellent as a winter pot plant.

CANDYTUFT *(Iberis sp.)*

CONTROL: Timing.

Candytuft with its attractive, hyacinthlike flowers is pretty much a commercial cut flower. It is rarely, if ever, grown in the home or in the home greenhouse, although it can be successfully forced without undue difficulty.

Candytuft is grown from seed that germinates readily in one to three weeks at 65 to 75 degrees. Transplant when first true leaves appear. Grow in deep flats or in a raised bed at 50 degrees. Use a rich soil and peat mixture. Space 5 by 5 inches with single plants. Or you can grow the plants in clusters of four set about 1 inch apart. Space the clusters about 6 by 8 inches. Water to keep the soil moist but not wet. Increase the frequency in spring. Feed with balanced fertilizer—4–12–4. Give the plants support as they grow, and let them have full sun.

For February bloom, sow seeds in October. For Easter and April, sow seeds in November and December. For May and Memorial Day, sow seeds around January 15.

There are several types of annual and perennial candytuft grown. The hyacinth-flowered annual type is most common, and Ball Giant White, Empress, and Super Iceberg are among the best. An *Iberis umbellata,* Red Flash, has a striking red color, but the plants tend to be dwarf.

Iberis umbellata varieties can be grown as pot plants. Magic Carpet and Fairy mixtures grow into compact mounds 10 inches wide and 10 inches tall. Sow directly into 4-inch pots. Thin to four or five plants. Grow in full sun. Plants will flower spectacularly in sixty days.

COLUMBINE *(Aquilegia sp.)*

CONTROL: Dormancy. Timing.

Columbines are among the most colorful and easily grown perennials. They thrive in sun or shade and in all types of soils. They are dependably hardy almost everywhere with a minimum of protection. Grown in the garden, they make excellent summer cut flowers.

It is not generally known, but columbines also can be easily forced as indoor cut flowers or pot plants. For combination pots, they are superior to fuchsias and less costly.

For forcing columbines, use plants grown outdoors at least one season. This means that you will need an outdoor supply. About February 1, sow seeds in a flat of sand-soil-peat. Seeds will germinate in sunny window in three to four weeks at temperatures between 65 and 75 degrees. Transplant outdoors after danger of frost is past. Or you may buy your flats already grown at the garden center in spring.

Columbines sown early in spring will flower only sparsely in the first season, but they will flower freely in subsequent seasons.

For forcing stock, transfer some first-year plants into pots. Store in a cold frame, garage, garden house, or cool location until about February 1. Then, bring them out of dormancy by gradually increasing the temperature to 50 degrees. For greenhouse cut flowers, they can be transferred to a raised bed. For combination pots, they can be grown in appropriate pots. Once started, they are virtually trouble-free. A semishaded location outdoors or a north window indoors suits them fine.

Columbines are available in unusual assortments of rich colors. Some strains are delightfully fragrant. Two popular mixtures are Longissima mixture and McKana's mixture. For one-color flowers, try Coerulea for blue, Copper Queen and Rose Queen for red, and Snow Queen for white.

DELPHINIUM *(Delphinium elatum* and *D. cheilanthum)*

CONTROL: Timing. Temperature.

The stately delphinium, one of nature's finest creations, has been made even better through hybridization. Members of delphinium societies and professional growers have improved its culture, its forms, its vigor, its colors, and its majestic beauty. It is one of the most popular flowers we have—a fitting rival to the rose and the chrysanthemum.

Delphiniums are also called larkspur. But larkspurs are annuals. Delphiniums are perennials according to the official definition of the Delphinium Society.

Commercially, as a cut flower, it is grown outdoors more often than it is forced into bloom under glass. It grows well where the climate is moderate but prefers the cooler temperatures and performs better in Ontario than in Florida.

For indoor forcing, to give you flowers on Mother's Day and on into summer, sow seeds in late July or early August. Set the seed flats in the coolest spot you can find, where night temperatures do not exceed 60 degrees. Fifty degrees is even better. Seeds will not germinate well at warm temperatures. Germination takes from three weeks to a month.

Transplant seedlings into a cold frame and let them harden there until late November. Then transplant to a bench or bed in a cold house—around 40 degrees. Space plants about 6 by 6 inches or 6 by 8 inches. Plants do better in moderately heavy loam than they do in sandy soil.

In February, start increasing the night temperature to 45 degrees and then to 50 degrees. Fertilize sparingly with a balanced fertilizer.

This schedule will force delphiniums to produce flowers for cutting from mid-May to mid-July.

Some growers move year-old plants from the garden into the cold frame for later forcing. But the loss to rot is tremendous, and therefore this is not a recommended practice.

There are over 250 species of delphiniums. The delphiniums commonly grown are Giant Pacifics *(D. elatum)* and Belladonnas *(D. cheilanthum).* All like bright sunshine.

The Giant Pacifics are vigorous, long-stemmed, strong growers that are also mildew resistant. A wide range of fine color shades are available. For blue, try Summer Skies; for lavender, try King Arthur; and for white, use Galahad.

The Belladonnas are more delicate plants than the Giant Pacifics, but are more free-flowering. Most of these delphiniums have a conspicuous center, or "bee," which adds to the attractiveness of the flowers. Sapphire is a bright blue with a golden "bee."

Two other species are sometimes grown and are gorgeous outdoors. They are the red larkspur *(D. nudicaule)* and the scarlet larkspur *(D. cardinale),* which despite their names are perennials.

FEVERFEW *(Chrysanthemum Parthenium)*

CONTROL: Light. Timing.

As a cut flower, feverfew is a March through May filler for florists. As a pot plant, it grows into a mound of everblooming flowers. Feverfew is easy to grow from seeds or cuttings.

The seeds are small. Sow on top of seeding medium, water with mist, and cover with glass or plastic to conserve moisture. Seeds germinate in two to three weeks at 65 to 75 degrees in a light area. Transplant to flats and later to 4-inch pots, to raised or ground beds, or to flats for the small grower. Use friable garden soil. Space about 10 inches apart and grow at about 50 to 55 degrees night temperature. Feverfew likes full sun. Feed and water regularly, but don't overdo. Spray for red spider mites.

For Easter and mid-April flowering, sow seed in mid-October. Transplant to pots or beds late in January. Light for three or four hours each night from February 5 until buds show—using 60-watt lights spaced 4 feet apart and 3 feet over bench.

For earlier or later flowering, sow seeds earlier or later and start lighting about three months after seeds have germinated.

For June flowering outdoors, sow in late October or November and transplant to garden or window box after danger of hard frost is over. No lighting is necessary.

For cut flowers, use a tall variety, such as Ultra Double White. For pots and window boxes, try White Stars, Gold Stars, or Golden Ball.

With a few pots of feverfew, a reading lamp, and a timer you can stand back and wait for compliments.

LARKSPUR *(Delphinium Ajacis)*

CONTROL: Timing. Light.

Although larkspurs and delphiniums *(D. elatum)* are near relatives, there are important differences. For one, larkspur is an annual while delphinium is a perennial. (This is a designation made by the Delphinium Society.)

Larkspur is an important commercial cut flower grown under glass and outdoors. In the home garden, a larkspur is a thing of beauty. Plant hybridizers have been hard at work with larkspur, and their creations are just short of miraculous. We have long stems, stronger stems, fully double flowers, graceful spikes, and gorgeous color shades.

However, larkspur is a finicky crop. You can expect trouble if you sidestep cleanliness. The growing area must be light, airy, and clean—sterilized-clean.

Before sowing, soak larkspur seeds in hot water—120 to 130 degrees—for about ten minutes. Sow in flats using a sterile medium. Then keep them cool. If you have a cool basement or fruit cellar, move them in there, or anywhere with temperatures around 50 to 60 degrees. In this temperature range, it may take the seeds from three weeks to a month to germinate. Transplant seedlings to a 3-inch pot—either peat or clay—using a rich, friable soil mixture. Then move them to a well-ventilated location with temperatures around 50 degrees.

An alternate procedure for a September sowing is to sow directly into 3-inch pots set in a cold frame. Seedlings are brought in when space is available, and they are transferred to beds—either raised or on the ground. Raised beds are preferred for drainage and air movement. Plant the seedlings about 10 by 10 inches apart and grow at a maximum night temperature of 50 degrees.

The major problem that growers encounter with larkspur is rot. A damp, unventilated greenhouse will spread rot like a prairie fire. The best prevention is cleanliness. In a greenhouse, water only on bright days when the vents can be opened. And let the soil get a little on the dry side before watering—then water thoroughly and less frequently. Grow in full sun.

A September sowing should give you cut flowers through late spring and early summer, months ahead of the outdoor blooms. For earlier blooms, larkspur, being a long day plant, responds to light. Use 60-watt incandescent bulbs 3 feet high and 4 feet apart and light for two hours at midnight.

Larkspur is available in a wide range of colors, spikes, and flowers. Any of the Supremes, Regals, and Giant Imperials are excellent.

Because of their 5-foot height, larkspurs make poor pot plants.

LUPINE *(Lupinus sp.)*

CONTROL: Timing.

Lupines, with their spectacular stately spires in a variety of rich colors, rank among our most beautiful flowers. The long-stemmed varieties are excellent as cut flowers for arrangements. The dwarf hybrids—only 15 to 18 inches tall—can be grown as enchanting pot plants.

Lupines are easy plants to grow, indoors or out. For forcing indoors, they favor cool growing conditions. In fact, they require cool temperatures to produce stately stemmed flowers. For this reason, they are grown as a winter plant. They like a sunny location.

For flowers in February, March, and April, sow seeds from mid-October to January. Allow about three and a half months from seed to flower.

Lupine seeds are large and are usually started directly in 4-inch pots. They resent transplanting. It helps seeds to germinate if you soak them for a few hours before planting. Sow three seeds in each pot and then thin to the strongest plant. Germination takes from two to three weeks at 65 to 75 degrees.

For cut flowers, sow seeds and finish in deep flats or benches. Space about 8 inches apart. Use a good friable soil—a sandy loam is fine. Keep soil and air slightly on the dry side to prevent rotting. Start growing at 45 degrees night temperature, and then increase to 50 or 55 degrees as center growth lengthens. Remove laterals on main stem for a fine cut flower.

Cut this first flower so that you leave four breaks, or nodes, on the lower part of the plant stem. These nodes will produce a second crop, each break developing into another flower.

For pot plants, grow the seedling in its original 4-inch pot. Keep in a cool, well-ventilated location. Hold night temperatures around 50 degrees. To speed up plants, the temperature can be increased, but the best flowers are grown at the cooler temperatures.

The Russell's hybrids—3 feet tall with 1-foot-long flower spikes—make excellent cut flowers. For pot flowers, Little Lulu and Minarette are delightful.

NEMESIA *(Nemesia sp.)*

CONTROL: Timing.

This showy plant could stand more popularity. The grandiflora strains make excellent cut flowers, growing from 1 to 2 feet in height. The *compacta* type is dwarf in habit, about 6 inches tall, and is excellent for pots and combinations.

For February cut flowers, sow in late August.

For January pot flowers, sow seeds in September and grow in 4-inch pots.

Seeds germinate in one to two weeks at 65 to 75 degrees. For cut flowers, transplant to a raised bed or flat and space about 8 by 8 inches. For pot plants, move to 3-inch clay or peat pots for combinations, or to 4-inch clay pots as an unusual house-plant. Use medium heavy neutral soil.

Grow in sun and at about 45 to 50 degrees night tempera-ture. Nemesia likes a cool house but will tolerate warmth.

Seeds are available in pure colors—blue, white, orange, and red—or in mixtures. For cut flowers, try Giant Strumosa. For pots, use Carnival.

POPPY *(Papaver orientale; P. nudicaule; and P. Rhoeas)*

CONTROL: Timing.

Of the fifty or more species of *Papaver*, we use only three. These are the Oriental *(P. orientale)*, the Iceland *(P. nudicaule)*, and the Shirley *(P. Rhoeas)*.

Most familiar in home gardens are the gaudy, scarlet blooms of the Oriental poppy. They are not the best cut flowers or in-door pot plants, because they do not last long. But they make up for their shortcomings by bringing unmatched brilliance into the home or garden.

The cultural requirements of the other two are pretty much the same. Even though the Icelands are perennials and the Shirleys are annuals, we treat them both as annuals.

The Shirley poppy is a native of Europe. The most famous is "the poppy of Flander's Field." There are some brilliant scar-lets in this species not found in Icelands. Another possible ad-vantage may be that the Shirley's stem is covered with foliage. In the Icelands, the foliage clusters near the ground.

I have grown and forced Icelands and feel that you may find a "something different" kind of plant here. The Icelands are natives of arctic regions. They are giant in size and very showy. Because of their native habitat, they like cool tempera-tures.

For spring bloom, sow poppy seeds in January. For cut flow-ers, sow directly in the beds or flats where they will be grown. For pots, start directly in 4-inch pots and thin after germina-tion. The seeds germinate in seven to ten days at 65 to 75 degrees. Use ordinary garden soil. Grow at around 50 to 55 degrees night temperature.

For February and March blooms, sow in November and light

in January. Shirley poppy is a long-day plant. It responds to two hours of light around midnight.

When cutting flowers, do not cut either when fully opened or during the day. The petals will drop in an hour. Cut in early morning at bud stage, and immediately sear the cut ends. Treated in this way, the cut poppy will last several days.

A popular seed mixture for cut flowers is Gartford's Giants. For pots, use the F_1 hybrid Champagne Bubbles.

STEVIA *(Piqueria trinervia)*

CONTROL: Timing. Temperature. Shade.

Fine fragrant white flowers produced on long stems. Used for cut flowers throughout the winter.

Stevia plants are not grown from seed but are propagated by cuttings. Take cuttings in January from a stock plant you own or from a plant that someone else has. Treat cuttings with rooting hormone. Root in sand and peat in a cool 55- to 60-degree area.

After roots are formed, transplant to 2½-inch pots of friable garden soil. Grow in a cool area at 40 to 45 degrees. Shift to 4-inch pots, and when danger of frost is past, move to a cold frame. Pinch to start branching. Summer in a cool spot until September. Shift to 6-inch pots with some superphosphate added to the potting soil. Bring plants indoors and grow at around 50 degrees. Plants will flower for Christmas.

For November 5 flowering, shade with black cloth for 30 days starting September 1.

For November 15 flowering, shade from September 1 to September 25.

For November 30 flowering, shade from September 1 to September 20.

For December 15 flowering, shade from September 1 to September 15.

For January and February flowering, grow plants at 40 to 50 degrees with no shade.

With practice, you can schedule a long season of blooms by giving separate groups of pots different growing temperatures and different shading periods.

SWEET PEA *(Lathyrus odoratus)*

CONTROL: Timing. Temperature.

Years ago, nearly every floral greenhouse grew sweet peas as winter cut flowers. Although this is no longer the case, sweet peas still are an important winter crop. They can be forced into bloom when other flowers are scarce—in December, January, and February.

For growing in the home or in the home greenhouse, since they require cool temperatures and a trellis of support, they may not be as suitable as other plants. However, if they are particular favorites and you can overcome these drawbacks, they can be grown rather easily in a deep flat on a bench.

For flowers starting in early November and lasting through February, sow seeds in mid-July.

For flowers from Christmas through March, sow in mid-August.

For flowers March 1 through Mother's Day, sow on October 1.

For flowers in April and at Easter and then on through May, sow on November 1.

To grow sweet peas, use a normal loam that has been sterilized to prevent root rot. Water well and then let it alone until it loses its tendency to be mud—the point at which it is neither soppy wet nor crumbly dry.

Soak seeds for a few hours before sowing and then sow in two rows, setting the seeds 1 inch apart and the rows 6 inches apart. Plant about 1 to 1½ inches deep. Then lay a slat or narrow board over each row.

For extensive planting, keep these double rows 2 to 3 feet apart. For sowing in a deep flat—as you would for a home greenhouse—try two of these double rows the length of the flat. In any case, keep in mind that you are going to have a lot of vine to contend with.

After sowing and covering with slats, you should not have to water until seeds have sprouted. This should be within two weeks at a temperature around 65 to 70 degrees.

Remove the board, moisten the soil, and then thin to one plant every 2 inches in the rows.

Temperature is important for flowering fine sweet peas.

They like cool growing temperatures. About 50 degrees at night is a good average in which to carry them along. Day temperatures, when cloudy, may run between 55 and 60 degrees. On sunny days, 60 to 65 degrees. Keep roots cool. This is a compromise temperature range, and you may get some bud drop. But the end result should be earlier and more abundant flowering.

Sweet peas require a great deal of water and full sun. Maintain soil fertility with biweekly feeding of liquid fertilizer.

Sweet peas need support. Build a wire frame over your flat. For ground beds, from posts at the two ends of each double row stretch two wires the length of the bed, one near the ground and the other about 5 feet above it. Tie a series of strings between the two wires about 3 inches apart. When the sweet pea vines have grown to 10 or 12 inches, start training them to climb the strings.

For winter blooms, there are some excellent multiflora and floribunda types available in lavenders, roses, corals, and whites. But avoid the Cuthbertson class for winter blooms. Save them for May flowering—sowing in December—because they seem to withstand the heat of May better than the other sweet peas.

Cut flowers when dry, usually in early afternoon. A stem should have three flowers—two fully developed and the third nearly full. Sweet peas are packed with twenty-five flowers in a bunch.

Because of difficulty holding a cool temperature and bud drop, sweet peas are not commonly grown as pot plants. But if you feel adventuresome, you might try a few plants in a hanging pot in a cool sun-room.

ZINNIA (Zinnia sp.)

CONTROL: Timing.

Zinnias are excellent winter cut flowers. They come in a great variety of flower forms and colors. Yet they are not as popular as you would expect. It may be because they are so easy to grow. Outdoors in the garden they are practically foolproof.

For winter cut flowers, sales, or home use, they are usually grown in deep flats in a greenhouse. To force into bloom in late April and May, sow February 15. Sow February 1 if you want to make Easter.

The factor for success in sowing zinnia seed indoors is warmth. Seed flats must be kept at 65 to 75 degrees night temperature until the seedlings show above ground. I cover the flats with glass to conserve moisture and place the flats on shelves over steam pipes. Seeds germinate in about one week.

After seedlings are up, flats may be moved to a cooler location—even 50 degrees. Although zinnias do well at warmer temperatures, it seems the plants are sturdier when grown cooler.

Transplant to a growing flat of ordinary garden soil with some peat and humus added. Space about 4 by 4 inches. Grow single-stem—no pinch. Disbud to one flower per plant. The extra side buds are easy to snap off with your finger.

Generally two types of zinnias are grown—dahlia-flowered and cactus-flowered. Both are strikingly beautiful.

Among the dahlia-flowered are the Giants, the Lilliputs, and the Cupids. The Giants have flowers that are about 5 inches across, while the Lilliputs and Cupids produce flowers just over 1 inch in diameter on miniature plants. Wind Witch, Envy, State Fair, and Color Bash are some unusual Giants.

In the cactus-flowered class, the flowers resemble chrysanthemums. The stiffness is gone. The petals curve gracefully. The flowers are large. The colors are rich. For cut flowers, Treasure Island is outstanding.

Merry Go Round, Thumbelina, and little Red Riding Hood are tiny compact zinnias. As an experiment, you could try growing these as pot plants. I haven't tried it, but they should do well in a warm home. And the flowers are extremely attractive.

10
Forcing . . . Mostly Pot Flowers

He has no yard behind his house,
No garden green to till,
And so he works the hothouse plan
Upon his window sill.

Old English Song

In forcing flowering pot plants, the home grower has a bonanza of material. It is an exciting area of growing that is open to everyone. It matters not whether your facilities are large or small. A single geranium on a sunny windowsill adds immeasurably to the warmth, charm, and hominess of a modest kitchen.

There are many and diverse control mechanisms you can use with pot plants, either to force them into bloom or to hold them from blooming. For example, only ten minutes of light at night will upset the blooming schedules of poinsettias and often prevent them from flowering. The combined use of dark cloth shade and extra day length by artificial light, makes it possible to pinpoint the blooming of many plants.

Temperature is an important factor. To meet temperature requirements, grow compatible plants together. Generally speaking, those plants that require warm growing conditions will not do well in the cold, and vice versa. Your kitchen may serve as a warm place and your sun-room as a cool one.

Plants requiring bright sunlight and those requiring shade do not mix well either. And just any soil won't do. To grow plants with the least difficulty, provide a soil that fits the requirements of the plants.

Organic soils are muck, leaf mold, humus, and peat. *Loam* is clay or sand mixed with a generous amount of organic matter. *Clay soils* without organic matter are heavy and wet. *Sandy soils* also need the addition of organic matter.

Soils should be sterilized. For a few potfuls, fill a large pot and pour boiling water over it until the water runs out the drain hole in the bottom.

Most pot plants will do well in a soil with a pH of 6.5. Azaleas, gardenias, camellias, and blue hydrangeas are exceptions and require a pH of 5.0.

Most pot plants need regular applications of fertilizer to replace the nutrients in the soil. Different plants have different requirements, but a good average formulation is a 15–30–15 liquid fertilizer. Do not fertilize seedlings or rooted cuttings in 2½-inch pots until they have become established. When plants are shifted to larger pots, add a 3-inch potful of superphosphate to a bushel of potting soil.

When shifting, set the plant at the same surface level as it was in the smaller pot—except for cyclamen, which should be raised slightly. Firm the soil in the pots by pressing the surface with your thumbs and at the same time revolving the pot. Poor contact between the soil particles and the roots causes slow growth.

Immediately after potting, the plant should be watered generously to supply moisture to the soil and to establish contact between the roots and the soil. While growing, keep soil moist but never soggy.

These generalizations will apply in most cases, but they serve as a guide only. As with all generalizations, there are exceptions. Get to know the specific needs of the plants you grow. Most plants are quite appreciative of this understanding and will repay you a hundredfold.

AGERATUM or FLOSSFLOWER *(Ageratum Houstonianum)*

CONTROL: Timing.

The ageratum is a common outdoor edging plant that is also beautiful as a pot plant or in a combination pot with other plants. It is easy to grow and maintain. Simply give it sunshine and keep it watered.

Commercially, ageratum in pots has excellent sales for Mother's Day and Memorial Day, and in flats as summer bedding and border plants.

For outdoor garden use, where it will bloom all summer, grow in flats and transplant to the garden in late spring. For pot plants or combination use, start in flats and finish in pots.

Ageratums may be started from seed or propagated from cuttings. Cuttings root readily in a sand-soil-peat or a vermiculite-soil-peat medium. Simply cut the tops off existing stock plants and insert in the soil. Mist leaves with a fine spray from time to time to maintain humidity. Or insert the entire flat into a large plastic bag with openings to allow for air circulation. Or cover a deep flat with glass, raised slightly on one side for air.

For uniformity in plant and color, Riverside is a good variety to use for cuttings.

There are a number of excellent dwarf varieties that can be grown from seed. For pots and combinations, I find it better to use seed-grown plants. They are more vigorous and "perky." Seeds of Blue Bedder, Blue Ball, and Blue Mink will produce attractive blue-flowered dwarf plants. I use Blue Bedder for outdoor bedding plants and Blue Ball and Blue Mist, because of the larger flowers, for pots and combinations. But all are suitable for pot use.

For pink flowers in beds, pots, and combinations, try Fairy Pink. And for white flowers, use Imperial Dwarf White or Snow Carpet.

Ageratum seeds are small and should be sown on top of the seeding medium without a soil covering. To keep the seeding medium from drying out, cover flat with glass until seeds sprout, usually in three weeks at 65 to 75 degrees.

For early spring pots and combinations, sow in late January.

For bedding, a sowing around March 1 and March 15 will produce blooming plants for spring sales or home garden use.

BEGONIA *(Begonia sp.)*

CONTROL: Timing.

There are three broadly defined groups of begonias—tuberous-rooted, the Rex foliage group, and the fibrous-rooted or *semperflorens*. Included among these groups, but not fitting specifically into any one of them, are some hybridized tuberous kinds.

While begonias make excellent house and garden plants, they are not commonly used in forcing, except for the petite and beautiful *semperflorens*. The Rex group are grown strictly as foliage plants. The tuberous begonias make fine plants for summer pots and shady summer beds, but are disappointing as winter houseplants. They quickly drop their blooms.

There are some splendid showy flower forms and colors in the tuberous-rooted group, and if you accept their limitations, they can be forced to bloom in winter, especially in the home greenhouse.

You can have a camellia-flowered tuberous begonia blooming in a 4-inch pot in six months, starting from seed. For flowers when you want them, simply start your seed six months prior to that date. Seeds sown in June will produce flowering plants for Christmas; in August, for Valentine's Day. Sow in November for Mother's Day and in December for pot plants all summer long.

Seeds are small. Use sparingly and do not cover them. Sow on top of milled peat that has been premoistened. Cover with plastic to maintain the moisture. Hold temperatures around 67 to 70 degrees.

Tuberous begonias may also be started from leaf cuttings or from already formed tubers. In any case, pot tubers or seedlings in 4-inch pots, using a rich, peaty potting mixture. Grow in a uniformly warm temperature—65 to 70 degrees—under light shade. They need humidity, and misting the air around them often helps.

Tuberous begonias are available as single and double camellia-flowered, rose-form, and Picotee types in pure colors or in mixtures. The Lloydi type, being pendulant, is often used for hanging baskets.

Fibrous-rooted begonias, although smaller in bloom size, are easier to grow and more flexible in use. A profusion of blooms on an attractive plant more than makes up for the smaller flower size. Fibrous-rooted *semperflorens* can be easily propagated from cuttings. They root in water or sand or anything moist. And they are just as easy to grow from seed.

Sow in fall for spring bloom. Use a mixture of fine peat and sand. Sow the small seeds sparingly on top. Mist and place the seeding medium into a plastic bag to preserve moisture. Seeds will germinate in two weeks at 65 to 75 degrees.

When large enough to handle, transfer to flats, spacing about 3 inches apart. Use a friable soil with lots of peat and humus added. Grow at 65 to 70 degrees. When the plants begin to crowd, transfer to 3-inch pots. They will bloom continuously starting in four to six months from seed. They grow well in the shade and will thrive in a north window.

They make excellent spring holiday plants, alone or in combinations. They may later be planted outdoors for all summer bloom.

For the Christmas holidays, full 4- or 5-inch pot plants will result from a June 1 sowing. Sow May 1 for Thanksgiving bloom.

There are many fine *semperflorens* from which to choose. Red Wonder, Melody, Indian Maid, and Carmen make nice bushy pot plants covered with blooms. Jewelite, Blushing Baby, and White Christmas—F_1 hybrids—are vigorous and somewhat taller, and perform well under adverse conditions indoors or out. Then there are Fiesta and Cinderella, outstanding for color and bloom, in deep red with bright yellow centers.

BLEEDING-HEART *(Dicentra spectabilis* and *D. eximia)*

CONTROL: Temperature. Timing.
Bleeding-heart is a not-too-common Easter plant.

It is easily grown from seed if you first freeze seeds over the winter to satisfy its cold requirement.

Start plants in spring, indoors or out. Transplant to a shady spot in your garden and grow over the summer. In the fall, move plants to a pot in a size to accommodate the roots. Store in a cool location where they will not dry out—a cool basement or shed. In February, start bringing the plants gradually into the warmth and light. Water moderately. Avoid any abrupt temperature changes. Slowly increase temperatures to 50 or 55 degrees as the plants develop. By carefully adjusting the temperature upward or holding it you can bring the plant into flower at Eastertime. It is a shade-loving plant and does not do well in the full sun.

The bleeding-heart usually grown is *Dicentra spectabilis. D. eximia* is sometimes grown and is the shorter of the two types.

After flowering, plants can be returned to the garden. They are hardy and will last for years, growing to 3 or 4 feet tall.

BROWALLIA *(Browallia sp.)*

CONTROL: Timing.

This is a fine winter pot plant with bell-like white or blue flowers.

Sow seeds in July or August. The seeds are very fine. Sow on top of the seeding medium and cover with plastic or glass to preserve moisture. Seeds germinate in one to two weeks at 65 to 75 degrees.

Transfer to pans—shallow pots—five or six plants to a pan. Use ordinary friable garden loam. Give good light to start. Grow at 60 degrees, although browallias also like warm temperatures and will do well in a house. When plants are established, pinch the tips of terminal growths to keep plants compact.

Grown in this way, plants should bloom by Christmas. Sow later for later blooms—late September and October for Valentine's Day and Easter. However, your Christmas plants will still be in bloom. Once a browallia starts blooming, it blooms all winter. Grow plants in full sunlight.

Browallia viscosa var. *compacta,* called Sapphire, is a compact dwarf plant that produces a profusion of blue flowers. For larger, violet blue flowers on a slightly larger plant, grow *speciosa major,* or try any of the Bells—Blue, Violet, or Silver.

CALCEOLARIA *(Calceolaria* sp.)

CONTROL: Timing. Lights.

Calceolarias are quite exacting in their demands, but these showy pot plants are worth the extra effort. A little additional care is needed, especially in the southern latitudes.

For Easter and early April plants finished in 5-inch pots, sow seeds around September 1.

The seeds are extremely fine. Do not cover or sow too closely. Use a sand, peat, and soil medium. Soil must be sterilized. Mist and cover with glass or cellophane. Set the flat in a cool—around 65 degrees—and shaded spot. Seeds germinate in two to three weeks. Remove glass or plastic cover immediately.

Seedlings damp-off easily, especially if the soil is too wet or the temperature too high. Keep the soil surface for the seedlings dry and expose them to a circulation of air. As seedlings become more established, increase the tendency to dryness in the soil. Then, when seedlings are large enough to handle, transplant them to 2½-inch pots, using a mixture of sand, soil, and peat. Grow in temperatures around 55 degrees. Shelter from direct sun.

When seedlings are large enough—usually in December or January—move directly to 5- or 6-inch pots using the soil-sand-peat potting mixture. Care must be taken to avoid overwatering, but, on the other hand, plants should not be allowed to wilt. Grow in partial shade. Calceolarias are especially partial to the morning light in an east window. Temperature also becomes important. A night temperature of about 50 degrees is excellent. If night temperatures get above 60 degrees, buds will not form. Feed with a balanced fertilizer. And spray for aphids.

Calceolarias respond to additional light and flower earlier when it is used. Use 60-watt bulbs 2 feet above the plants and

4 feet apart. Light from 5:00 P.M. to 10:00 P.M. With lights, a September 1 sowing should flower in late March—light from January 5 to February 10.

For flowering in early March, sow seeds on August 1 and light from November 15 to December 20.

For attractive 5-inch Valentine's Day pots, sow July 1 and light from November 15 to December 20.

For flowering on Mother's Day or in May—if it is possible to grow under cool conditions at this time of the year—sow seeds around October 1 and do not light.

There are several types of calceolaria in use—*multiflora*, *rugosa*, *grandiflora*, and a shrubby class. The *rugosa* is a stronger plant than the *multiflora*, which tends to be fragile. A cross between the *multiflora* and *rugosa*—Ball Multiflora Nana mixture—offers the best qualities of both. For a solid mass of medium-sized flowers in a full range of colors on compact bushy plants try Extra Early Tigered strain or an F_1 hybrid mixture. For an excellent large-flowered variety, try the *grandiflora* dwarf mixture.

The shrubby varieties may be propagated from cuttings made in August from plants that have been carried over the summer, kept cool, and have not been allowed to flower. This procedure is limited to far northern areas with cool summers. Even in the midsection of the country, few growers have been able to do this successfully. We settle for the fight against damping-off and grow from seed.

CAMPANULA or BELLFLOWER *(Campanula sp.)*

CONTROL: Timing.

This common garden perennial also makes attractive winter pot plants. For something different, give *Campanula carpatica* a try. Because of its compact dwarf growth, it makes a nice plant about 12 inches tall and 12 inches across when finished in 6-inch pots.

For flowering early in the following spring, blooms at Eastertime or in April, sow seeds in March. It takes almost a year to produce a beautiful bellflower plant.

Seeds are fairly fine and should be covered lightly. Use milled peat with a little sand as the seed medium. Mist, and cover flat with glass to conserve moisture. Seeds germinate in two to three weeks at 65 to 75 degrees.

Transfer seedlings to a 2½-inch pot, shifting to a larger pot as necessary. Good garden soil with some humus added makes a satisfactory potting medium. Grow fairly cool—around 55 to 60 degrees. A cold frame works well.

Summer the campanula plants outdoors, burying the pots in the ground. After the first light frost, move them back to the cold frame for continued exposure to cold—but not to freezing.

In November, bring them into cool indoor temperatures gradually, first to 40 or 45 degrees, then to 50 or 55 degrees. Do not go much warmer, as they resent heat. Also avoid intense sunlight—normally not a problem in midwinter. Campanulas do like a partially sunny location.

This procedure should bring the beautiful bells into bloom for Easter. Blue Clips and White Clips are two fine varieties to try.

CELOSIA or COCKSCOMB (*Celosia argentea* var. *cristata* and
C. *argentea* var. *plumosa*)

CONTROL: Timing.

Very showy plants that can be used in various ways. Outdoors, they are popular as garden, bedding, and border plants. Indoors, they can be used for cutting and for winter pots.

There are two forms of celosia in common use—the *cristata* and the *plumosa*. The *cristata* includes the familiar garden cockscomb. The *plumosa* produces silky featherlike plumes. In culture, they are handled alike, and they are both easy to grow. Celosias have two requirements. First, they like heat and must be grown at night temperatures over 65 degrees. And second, they must be kept growing. If their growth is restrained in any way—by being pot bound or by low temperatures—the plants will be damaged. They will be stunted, or they will set small, disappointing blooms prematurely.

You can grow celosias from seeds, which germinate in seven

to ten days at 65 to 75 degrees. For pot plants, move the seedlings to 2½-inch pots, and later to 5- or 6-inch finishing pots. For cut flowers, transplant the seedlings to deep flats or to beds.

Seeds sown in July and August will flower in October and November, when outdoor flowers are getting scarce.

Both celosia forms—*cristata* and *plumosa*—have tall and dwarf varieties. The tall are used for cut flowers, and the dwarf are used for flowering pot plants.

For cut flowers, the tall varieties grow from 2 to 3 feet in height. Red Gold and Maple Gold are outstanding tall *cristata*. Forest Fire and Golden Triumph are exceptional among the tall *plumosa*.

For pot plants, the dwarf varieties make compact plants just under 1 foot tall. In the *cristata* group, Dwarf Empress is available in a number of different colors, Toreador is a brilliant red, and Gladiator is a fine yellow. Among the dwarfs in the *plumosa* group are Fiery Feather and Gold Feather. Crusader is a bright red with attractive bronze leaves.

CHRISTMAS CHERRY or JERUSALEM-CHERRY or CLEVELAND CHERRY (*Solanum Pseudo-Capsicum*)

CONTROL: Timing.

The Christmas cherry lost out to the poinsettia. At one time, the Christmas cherry was quite traditional for the Christmas holiday season. However, some measure of its original popularity still continues.

With the Christmas, Jerusalem-, or Cleveland Cherry— whatever name you wish to call it—the attractive, bright red fruit is what we want and not the flowers. Grow in full sun.

This is a simple pot plant to grow, and it will thrive under almost any condition. Sow seeds in early February. They germinate in three to four weeks at 65 to 75 degrees. Transfer seedlings to 2½-inch pots of fair garden soil, moving to 3- or 4-inch pots by late May or early June. Pinch back the tips of the terminal growths to develop bushy plants. Several pinches may be made. Stop pinching about July 1.

Move pots outside when danger of frost is over. Summer the

plants outdoors by burying the pots into the soil. Some growers transplant them to garden beds for the summer, but I do not recommend it. The plants lose leaves when dug in the fall for repotting. Leaving the plant in the pot will also restrict the growth and give you a better shaped plant.

The fruit is set during the summer. By September, roots will have grown out of the drain hole and over the pot. Repot to 5- or 6-inch pots and move indoors. Grow at 65 degrees in semi-shade. Water but do not feed. By Christmas, these plants will make beautiful specimens.

Jubilee or Red Giant are varieties to try.

CHRISTMAS PEPPER *(Capsicum frutescens)*

CONTROL: Timing.

Christmas peppers make attractive plants for the Christmas holidays. As with Christmas cherries, these plants are grown for their colorful fruit rather than their flowers.

Sow seeds in April for 6-inch finished pots. Sow seeds in May for 5-inch finished pots. Or sow seeds in June for growing in 2½-inch pots. Then, in fall, three or four of these plants can be transferred to a 6-inch pot.

Seeds germinate in three to four weeks at 65 to 75 degrees. Transfer seedlings of April and May sowings to 2½-inch pots and later to 3- or 4-inch pots. Pinch the April and May seedlings at least once, but not those of June.

After danger of frost is over, summer the plants in the pots, burying them into the soil. More compact plants result from the restriction of the pot than is the case with those grown without restriction in a garden bed.

In September, move your plants to 5- or 6-inch pots and grow indoors at 65 degrees in full sun or semi-shade. The fruit will be brightly colored by Christmas.

Fiesta is the variety commonly grown.

CINERARIA *(Senecio cruentus)*

CONTROL: Timing. Temperature.

Cineraria is an old-timer—a beautiful flowering plant for the window—that is not grown very often today. And yet today's varieties are far superior to the large, cabbage-leafed plants of old. They bloom in full clusters of daisylike flowers that are bright, colorful, and attractive. And cinerarias are especially appropriate with the colored eggs of Easter.

For Easter plants, to finish in 5- or 6-inch pots, sow seeds in August or September. For 4- to 5-inch Easter pots, sow about October 1. A December sowing will make nice 3-inch pots. The control is temperature. Grow at 50 degrees and increase the temperature to bring them into flower.

To produce flowering plants in January, sow seeds in June. For flowers in February, sow about July 15. For March blooms, sow September 1. For April flowering, sow October 1.

Seeds are small. Sow in a sand and milled peat mixture and cover lightly if at all. Mist, and cover seed flat with glass or cellophane. Seeds germinate in about 2 weeks at 65 to 75 degrees.

As soon as possible, transplant seedlings to 2½-inch pots to avoid damping-off. Use a light soil. Do not add fertilizer. It is important to keep the soil moist and not to allow it to dry out. However, the soil should not be soggy. Hold a happy medium.

When nicely established, move the plants to the finishing pots—usually 5- or 6-inch azalea pots. Avoid overwatering while the plants are establishing new roots. Then keep the plants moist. They love moisture and on sunny-dry days they wilt easily. In the winter they can take all the sun they can get, but in spring protect them with partial shade. Remove damaged foliage as it appears. Spray for aphids. Feed lightly with balanced fertilizer when buds appear.

Cinerarias are cool-temperature plants. A night temperature of around 50 degrees will keep them in good shape at any stage after the seedlings have become established. A slightly higher temperature may be used to speed them up.

Cinerarias respond to additional light. A 100-watt bulb about 2 feet over the plants for several hours in the early evening will cause them to flower about three weeks sooner. But this procedure is not recommended, because the plants grow spindly and do not finish well.

In choosing a variety, look for small foliage on a compact plant with large heads of flowers. Festival, Hansa, and Siter's Rainbow meet these requirements. You will get excellent plants from any one of them.

Starlet and Erfurt are miniatures. Finish them in 3- or 4-inch pots. They are beauties, with tiny mounds of bright flowers—most attractive flowering plants.

COLEUS *(Coleus Blumei)*

CONTROL: Timing.

Coleus is a foliage plant, grown for its leaves and not for its flowers. However, I include it among flowering plants because it is so often used with them. With its multicolored leaves, it is not only a fine year-round houseplant but also especially popular for use in combination boxes and pots.

Coleus is easily propagated from cuttings, making a nice 2½-inch potted plant in four weeks. Nevertheless, it is usually grown from seed, unless you find an extremely attractive specimen you want to perpetuate.

Seeds germinate in two to three weeks at temperatures between 70 and 80 degrees. Being of tropical origin, coleus will grow freely and easily in a warm home. Normal feed, normal care, normal watering are all that is required. They will do well in a north or east window, or anywhere in semi-shade.

For Easter combinations or 3- and 4-inch Easter pots, sow seeds in January. Grow in night temperatures above 60 degrees.

For Memorial Day combinations or for outdoor bedding plants, sow seeds in mid-March.

For attractive 4-inch pots at Christmastime, root cuttings in mid-September.

Seeds are available in mixtures or in single colors. The Brilliant and Rainbow color group are excellent. The foliage is of medium size and the plants are free-branching and bushy. The

Oriental type does not branch as freely, but the plants produce huge leaves. The dwarf Shades and the oak-leaf Carefree types make bright compact plants for window pots or flower shelves. For outdoor use, especially for shaded areas, the Rainbow strain is superb.

CYCLAMEN *(Cyclamen persicum)*

CONTROL: Timing of pot shift.

The cyclamen may be a challenge. But it is worth the try. It is a beauty on a dull winter day.

A grower I know has no trouble at all with cyclamens. He has a rundown, drafty greenhouse where he winters his plants and a knarled worm-eaten apple tree under which he summers them. He then finishes and stores them in an ice-cold garage. And his plants are beautiful. For me, they tend to act up. They may be a problem for you, too. So, let's work at it together.

First, we must remember that it takes over a year to produce a flowering plant. For December and January blooms, finished in 5- or 6-inch pots, seeds must be sown fifteen months earlier, in September. However, if you will settle for 4-inch pot plants, seeds may be sown as late as January.

Prepare a flat of nonacid peat. Water. Space seeds about 1 inch apart and plant about ½ inch deep. Keep flat at 60- to 65-degree night temperatures until seeds sprout, which usually takes six weeks or longer.

After germination, move the seedlings to a 55-degree area. When they are large enough to be handled easily, transplant the seedlings to 2½-inch pots. Use a mixture of two to three parts nonacid peat, or leaf mold, or well-rotted manure with one part rich, loamy soil. Add superphosphate generously. Keep pH around 6.8.

Grow plants in full sun in winter and spring. Keep cool, with night temperature at 50 degrees. Feed lightly with balanced liquid fertilizer.

When roots begin to show through, shift to an intermediate pot size. If you will finish in 4-inch pots, then shift to 3-inch; if you are going to finish in 5- or 6-inch pots, shift to 4-inch. Moving directly to the finishing size is overpotting and will set plants back.

During each shift, it is important to keep the original soil surface slightly higher than the repotted soil surface. Or, more specifically, the plant's hypocotyl must be kept above the surface of the soil.

After shifting, do not overwater—give the roots a chance to reach out in search for moisture. Keep on the dry side, but not enough to wilt the plant. And do not feed until established. Then apply complete fertilizer every three weeks during the spring, summer, and fall.

Start a weekly spray for mites. Mites are a major pest and can ruin a cyclamen.

As the weather warms up, remember that summers are hard on cyclamens, especially in the southern United States. Cyclamen likes cool, moist conditions.

In summer, move your plants to a cool, shady spot. If you can, bury the pots outdoors up to the rims in peat. A shaded and ventilated cold frame where you can keep cyclamen plants misted and cool on hot days should work out well. Keep the plants under a water spray all afternoon if necessary.

As summer wanes, let them have a little sun—some of the slanting rays of evening. The plants are now ready for the second pot shift.

This is a critical time. This controls the flowering date, because cyclamen plants flower when they are pot-bound. A final shift in mid-August will have the plants in bloom during November and December.

Shifting around September 10 should give you flowering plants for Christmas. To check on the progress for Christmas bloom, roots should show through and the plants be fairly pot-bound by mid-October.

If you make your final shift in October, you should have your plants in flower in January and February.

With fall and the threat of frost, get your cyclamens indoors or provide protection in the cold frame. In October, get night temperatures down to 50 or 55 degrees if possible. Also in October, cut back on watering and stop feeding until the plants are in bud. Heavy watering and feeding encourages leaf growth, not buds. Set plant pots on top of inverted pots for better aeration.

Give them sun during budding and blooming. Hold temperatures around 50 to 55 degrees nights. Start feeding again when buds are formed.

Once started, cyclamens will last for years. Simply keep shifting to larger pots. They seem to do well in a cool sunroom.

There are some excellent cyclamen varieties available in red, white, and rose.

If you have the facility to keep them cool, give cyclamens a try.

FORGET-ME-NOT *(Myosotis sp.)*

CONTROL: Timing.

You should have a few forget-me-nots. They are easy to grow as pot plants or for cutting. Every commercial cut-flower market uses some.

Forget-me-nots can be propagated from cuttings or from seeds. Although seeds are preferred, cuttings can be taken in late March in time to become sufficiently established. When grown from seeds, sow in June, July, or even August. The seeds germinate in two to three weeks at 65 to 75 degree temperatures.

For commercial or home-greenhouse cut flowers, plant in a bench or flats in September and space 10 by 10 inches. Use light soil. Grow at about 50 degrees. Forget-me-nots can be grown in a sunny or semi-shady location. Flowers may be cut from December on. The long-stemmed variety Blue Bird is a good one to use.

For spring sales or garden use, forget-me-nots can be carried over the winter in cold frames. In the north, they are not completely hardy and should be covered with loose straw and the sash. Ventilate and remove sash when the hard freeze is over. Where winters are warmer, grow in covered outdoor beds, as you would pansies.

Good varieties for the garden are Blue Eyes and Royal Blue.

For pot plants and pot combinations, Blue Eyes and Ball's Early are usually used because of their restricted growth habit. They flower in about three months after sowing. A late fall or early winter sowing would produce flowering plants in early spring. A November 1 sowing will make nice plants for Valentine's Day.

FUCHSIA *(Fuchsia sp.)*

CONTROL: Timing.

An excellent plant with trailing varieties for hanging baskets or porch boxes and upright varieties for pot plants and combinations. Fuchsias bloom over a long period—all winter indoors, all summer outdoors.

Fuchsias are sometimes grown from seed sown in the fall, which may take from one to two months to germinate at 65 to 75 degrees. More often, they are grown from cuttings.

Use your last year's plant as a stock plant. Fuchsias have a natural rest period of one month at the end of summer. Let the soil dry. Then, in September, remove the plant from its pot and repot it in fair garden soil mixed with 1 teaspoon of ammonium sulfate. Cut the plant back severely. Water and grow at

55 to 60 degrees night temperature. Fuchsias prefer semi-shade. Keep the plant somewhat on the dry side. By November, you can start making cuttings, and you can continue to do so until March.

Root the cuttings in a sand-peat medium at 65 degrees and give bottom heat if possible. When rooted, pot in 2½-inch pots and grow at 60 degrees. In January, your first cuttings can be moved to 3- or 4-inch pots as single plants, or set three plants into a 6-inch pan or shallow pot. These will make excellent blooming plants for Mother's Day.

Strong spring plants in 3- or 4-inch pots can be grown from the other cuttings propagated to February. The sooner the cuttings are made and rooted, the larger the plants will be in spring.

Some popular varieties are Black Prince, Giant Pink, and Little Beauty.

GARDENIA or CAPE-JASMINE *(Gardenia jasminoides)*

CONTROL: Timing. Shade. Light.

Gardenias are shrublike plants native to China. The waxy-white flowers are very fragrant, and they are popular as cut flowers for use in corsages and arrangements. They also make satisfactory indoor pot plants where the conditions are right. In the south, they are grown outdoors as patio plants.

Gardenias are propagated from cuttings. From November through March, take 3- to 5-inch tip cuttings from the top of stock plants. Cuttings should be made just above a set of leaves on the branch. It is important that no leaves be removed from the cutting, a usual practice with other plants. This eliminates open wounds susceptible to canker infection.

Treat cuttings with a rooting hormone. Insert in sterilized sand, peat, or a mixture of both, in a seed flat or directly in 2½-inch pots. Set the flat, or the pots in a flat, over heat—about 75-degree bottom heat. Cover loosely with plastic to maintain humidity, moisture, and a 70-degree top temperature. Cuttings should root in four to six weeks.

The cuttings in the flat should be potted in 2½-inch pots in a mixture of sandy potting soil and peat. Move all rooted cuttings to a light, humid area and grow at 60 degrees.

All cuttings, including those rooted in pots, are shifted to 4-inch pots once they are well rooted in the small pots. This usually takes from two to two and a half months from the initial cutting. Now move to a light area above 60 degrees.

To maintain soil acidity between pH 5.5 and 6.5, which is

important to gardenia culture, use iron sulfate at the rate of 1 ounce per 2 gallons of water. Apply about once a month.

In May and June, bench the plants. That is, move them to the finishing area. Shift the plants to a slightly larger pot and space about 18 by 18 inches. Or transfer plants to deep flat at about three plants per flat. Use a sterilized potting mixture of equal parts soil, peat, and sand to a depth of 4 inches. Mist with cool water to encourage growth.

During the summer, maintain moisture but do not over-water. Continue misting on dry days. Shade with cheesecloth in June and July. Increase iron sulfate applications if leaves turn yellow. Feed every three weeks with ammonium sulfate or 4–12–4 fertilizer. Do not use superphosphate, lime, or bonemeal.

For Christmas and New Year's flowers, especially where a cool summer night temperature of 60 to 65 degress is not possible, shading is necessary. Starting July 20, and continuing for three weeks, cover plants with a black cloth from 5:00 P.M. to 7:00 A.M. A shorter shading period will not initiate buds. The black cloth must be such that it is totally dark beneath it. And it must be cloth, not black plastic.

The flower buds are short and stubby. Vegetative buds for shoots are long and slender. After the buds are set, ten to fourteen weeks are needed for the flowers to bloom.

Maintain good growing conditions and temperatures around 60 to 65 degrees nights. Continue with applications of ammonium sulfate every three weeks. And always use cool water when watering or misting.

In November, adding lights helps to get the Christmas buds to bloom on time. Use 100-watt lights 2 feet above plants and about 4 feet apart. Light for four hours after sunset. Stop lighting when flowers are sufficiently advanced.

Higher temperatures—up to 80 degrees—can also be used to speed up blooming, but humidity must also be increased, or buds will drop.

Between December 15 and January 1, a single plant should produce a dozen flowers for you to cut. To get flowers on this same plant for Easter, May, and Mother's Day, drop night temperatures to 55 to 60 degrees during January. Cut ammonium sulfate feed to every five weeks. Keep soil acid with iron sulfate. In February, increase night temperatures to 60 to 65 degrees. By the end of May, each plant should have produced twenty-five flowers.

Growing your plants on into the second year will increase that number. Each two-year-old plant can produce a total of seventy beautiful cut flowers.

To continue growth, in late May or early June cut plants back to about 24 to 30 inches and remove all thin wood. Mist to encourage new shoot development. Discard all cankerous plants. From then on, summer culture and forcing procedures are the same as for one-year-olds.

For flowering pot plants, keep the first-year seedling plants in pots instead of transferring them to deep flats in June. Then grow them on in pots as you would for cut flowers. For the second year, in late May cut back, shape, and transfer to larger pots.

Grow your pot gardenia in a cool location—under 70 degrees—keep soil acid, feed with ammonium sulfate once a month, and mist and water with cool water. Gardenias prefer a semi-shady location during the hot summer months.

IMPATIENS *(Impatiens Holstii* and *I. Sultanii)*

Where growing light is poor, Impatiens is the answer. It is one of the few plants that will bloom well in shade, indoors or out.

It is not a true forcing plant. You simply start it when you want it. Snap off a shoot, stick it in water, sand, or vermiculite, and there you have it. It is very easy to root from cuttings. In fact, you can't do anything wrong to this plant.

Impatiens are easy to grow from seed, too. Sow in January for 3-inch pot plants in May. Seeds germinate in two to three weeks at 70 degrees. Transplant to flats and later to pots or beds. They are easy to move and suffer no setbacks. They grow in any loose soil, but we usually mix in a little peat to hold moisture.

Once impatiens start blooming, they keep right on. If they get too tall or leggy, cut them back severely.

For compact 8-inch winter pot plants or combinations, use

any of the dwarf varieties that are available—Dwarf mixture, Pixie, Elfin. For taller plants, growing to 12 or 14 inches, try the Holstii mixture with its wide range of colors, bicolors, and shades.

KALANCHOE *(Kalanchoe Blossfeldiana)*

CONTROL: Shade. Temperature.

These bright red flowers are great for the Christmas season either as potted plants or as cut flowers. Kalanchoes are among the relatively few plants that can be forced into bloom during the late fall and early winter period.

Seeds may be sown anytime from January until July. They are very fine and must be used sparingly. Do not cover. Sow on top of a soil-peat seeding medium in small flats. Slip the flats into a plastic sandwich bag to retain moisture. Seeds germinate in a week or two at 65- to 75-degree temperatures. Kalanchoe is also easily propagated by leaf cuttings rooted in sand or vermiculite. Plants so propagated take several months longer to flower.

Move seedlings or rooted cuttings to 2½-inch pots of light soil and peat and grow in a cool 60-degree area. Feed with alternate applications of ammonium sulfate and complete fertilizer. Alternate one month ammonium sulfate—½ ounce to a gallon of water—with a 4–12–4 fertilizer the next month or two. Kalanchoe does not demand to be fed. It also does not require full sunlight.

Plants may be pinched in June to get greater bushiness.

Depending upon when you want these plants in flower and the size of the plants at that time, finish growing them in 4-, 5-, or 6-inch pots. Make the shift in late August. Seeds planted late or flowers wanted early will be small plants and will require small pots. Seeds planted early or flowers wanted later in the year will take the larger pots. Some growers put three small plants into a 6-inch azalea pot.

Shading controls the flowering date. If not shaded and grown at 60 degrees, the plant will bloom naturally in January.

For Valentine's Day, do not shade. The natural winter night

is long enough. Grow plants at 50 degrees night temperature. But do protect from prolonged room lights in the home at night.

For Christmas, use black cloth shading for five weeks between September 10 and October 15, and grow at 60 degrees.

For mid-October, shade with black cloth August 1 to September 10.

For Thanksgiving, shade August 25 to September 25.

As pot plants, kalanchoes are attractive and long lasting in the home. Use a dwarf variety such as Tom Thumb, Scarlet Gnome, and Vulcan.

For cut flowers with brilliant blooms on 12-inch stems, grow Jingle Bells and Brilliant Star in deep flats or 6-inch pots.

MARIGOLD *(Tagetes sp.)*

CONTROL: Timing. Light.

Too often we overlook the beauty in our ordinary commonplace things. Marigolds suffer from this oversight.

Almost everyone is familiar with marigolds—durable, easy-to-grow plants with many uses. They are excellent in flower beds, as cut flowers, in pots, or in combinations. Youngsters dream of the wealth they will amass by selling seed packets. And not the least of the uses for marigolds is in schools, where kindergarten and first-grade children grow them as science projects or as proud and treasured gifts to be presented to mother on her day. The world would be a sadder place without marigolds.

In recent years, marigolds have been greatly improved. Odorless varieties have been developed. Some brilliant golds and new whites are now available. Marigolds are worth your consideration.

Marigolds are annuals grown from seed. Seeds germinate readily in one to two weeks when sown in flats and kept at 65 to 75 degrees night temperatures.

Even though they are native to warm countries, they enjoy cool night temperatures. Indoors and in the greenhouse, for cut flowers or pots, about 55 degrees is just right.

For greenhouse cut flowers—to flower late-November through February—sow seeds in late August. To flower in April and May, sow in January and February. Space about 4 inches apart and grow single-stem on a raised bench. Do not pinch.

Grow your marigolds in well-watered, rich soil. Then disbud, removing all side buds but one when they are pea sized, to get larger, more attractive flowers. Feed regularly with a balanced liquid fertilizer. This will give you marigolds with strong stems on tall plants.

Some good cut-flower varieties are:

Carnation-flowered—Gold Improved or Gold Galore, carnationlike, odorless

Giant African—all doubles, in bright orange and yellow

Giant/Carnation—Crackerjack or Hawaii, a large-sized mixture of orange, gold and yellow shades

Mum-type—Goldsmith or Glitters, mumlike, incurved petals

Unusual—Fantastic, curly orange petals.

Want pot marigolds for Easter? Sow French marigold seeds in February.

For Memorial Day pots and combinations—and for outdoor hanging baskets and flower beds—sow seeds in March. For January and February winter pots and combinations, sow African marigold seeds around September 15, French marigold in mid-October.

Grow indoor pot plants at 55-degree night temperature—or 5 degrees either way. Marigolds like full sunlight. Do not allow soil to get too wet or too dry. Colder temperatures will retard growth, and warmer temperatures will accelerate growth, which gives you a measure of control. In 40 to 45 degrees, they will be brought to a standstill.

Marigolds are long-day plants. In fall and winter they can be forced to flower earlier with supplemental lighting—about 10 footcandles—either from dusk to 10:00 P.M. or two hours around midnight.

For pots and combinations, use the dwarf varieties. Some varieties that make excellent indoor plants in the dwarf

French double class are the Cupids and the Petites—Spry, Harmony, and Butterball. There are also some fine dwarf singles, such as Marietta and Sunny.

In all classes, new and improved varieties are continually being introduced. Truly marigolds live up to one litle girl's description of them as "happy-golds."

PANSY *(Viola tricolor)* and VIOLA *(V. cornuta)*

CONTROL: Timing. Light.

Pansies and violas make excellent 3-inch pot plants and petite cut flowers, but surprisingly, they are not often used for these purposes. A small, colorful pot of pansies will delight a youngster's heart, and it will add a bright touch to any shut-in's room. For small cut-flower arrangements, pansies and violas are ideal, a welcome relief from some of the large, overpowering groupings.

For all-winter forcing, sow seeds around August 15 to September 1. Seeds are somewhat difficult to germinate at this time, when the weather is still warm. Give them 60- to 65-degree night temperatures, if possible. In any case, keep them on the cool side.

Use a sterile, loose medium, such as a mixture of peat with vermiculite. Seeds are fine. Sow thinly—a little goes a long way—and just barely cover them. Keep moisture constant, misting from time to time and covering with glass. To avoid drying out, do not expose to direct sun. Seeds germinate in about two to three weeks.

When seeds have germinated, drop temperatures even lower—to around 50 degrees at night. Transplant to flats of loose, loamy soil mixed with peat and organic matter. To this mixture add superphosphate—about 1 cup to a bushel of soil. (See Appendix C table of equivalents for aid in working with lesser amounts.) The trick with seedlings, as with seeds, is to keep them moist.

After seedlings have become established, you can move the flat into the light, and you can allow the surface of the soil to become dry between waterings. Established plants can be moved to 3-inch pots, if you are going to grow them as pot plants. For cut flowers, grow them in flats. Space them about 6 by 6 inches apart in the flat, and support them with wires.

Keep as cool as possible—around 50 degrees nights. Many growers move the plants to cold frames, leaving the sash open for air circulation during the day.

With cool temperatures, plants will require less water. You may even allow them to dry to the point of wilting a little before watering.

Feed very lightly during winter, increasing slightly in spring or for finishing winter pot plant blooms. Then, give them a watering of 25–0–25 fertilizer—about 1 teaspoon in a gallon of water.

To keep pansies and violas from getting soft, give them full light and plenty of ventilation when growing them and for the time you are enjoying them in the home.

A few flats of pansies and violas will give you a continual supply of cut flowers. Then, in the spring, they can be transplanted into your outdoor flower beds. For continued blooms, in pots or in flats, it is important to keep the faded flowers picked off. Once a plant is allowed to set seeds, it will stop blooming.

Pansies are long-day plants. You can start them flowering and keep them blooming in winter with additional light. Use 40-watt bulbs 2 feet away for two hours at midnight.

There are many excellent strains and varieties of pansies available. Seeds are generally packaged in mixtures—Ball, Roggli, Steele, and Majestic Giant mixtures—offering a balance of large flowers in all pansy colors. For the home greenhouse and warmer South, the Steele mixture does well. Separate colors are also available.

Although violas have smaller blooms than pansies, they bloom more freely. They can also be grown in flats without supports. They are excellent as pot plants and in the garden. If faded flowers are kept picked off, they will bloom outdoors from spring to fall.

If you have violas in your garden, they can be dug during a thaw in March and potted. Try not to disturb the soil around the roots. Set them in a cool, sunny spot, and they will soon be in bloom. Return them to the garden after flowering.

Violas offer some beautiful pure colors as well as bicolors and tricolors. Toyland is a superb mixture. Firmament is sky blue, Avalanche is pure white, Scottish Yellow is a bright gold, and Arkwright Ruby is a scarlet maroon. And there are others, all sturdy plants with bright-colored "perky" flowers.

PETUNIA *(Petunia hybrida)*

CONTROL: Timing. Temperature.

As beautiful, all-purpose flowering plants, petunias stand alone. They are America's number-one bedding plant. They are available in many types—double-flowered, large and small singles, frilled, fringed, and bell-shaped. They offer many colors—pink, cream, red, rose, purple, blue, and white. They make attractive beds and borders, fine cut flowers, charming hanging baskets, bright porch boxes, and cheerful winter pot flowers.

While not widely used as such, petunias do make excellent indoor pot plants and fillers for a combination of potted plants.

For March and April flowering, start seeds in November, and grow at about 45 to 50 degrees. For Easter, start in December. For May, Mother's Day, and Memorial Day flowers, sow in early January. For spring bedding plants, sow around March 1.

Petunias are easy to grow from seeds, which germinate in one to two weeks at 65 to 75 degrees. Seeds are very fine. Do not sow too thickly. Sow on top and do not cover. Mist rather than water. Place a lath over the seeds to retain moisture, or, if sown in flats, cover with glass or plastic.

After germination, drop temperatures gradually. Go to 60 degrees, then 55, and finally to 50 degrees when seedlings have developed one true leaf. Transfer plants to growing flat. Some growers prefer to move seedlings directly to finishing pots, 2½-, 3-, or 4-inch. Others transplant later from growing flat to 4-inch pots.

Use a rich, loamy soil. Two parts garden soil and one part organic matter or peat makes a fine mixture. Petunias are heavy feeders. Feed regularly with a balanced fertilizer.

Stretching is a problem when growing petunias indoors. Plants tend to get leggy. The solution is to keep them cool and give them plenty of air and light. B-Nine growth retardent at 50 percent, applied seven weeks after seeding, reduces stretch and keeps plants short and compact.

Another thing to watch is the tendency of the plants to send out roots through the drain hole in the bottom of the pot. This is especially true when you have sand or gravel beneath the pots. To discourage this errant rooting, set pots on bare benches or plastic.

Petunias rapidly become pot-bound and require increased feedings of the liquid fertilizer.

There is such a wide variety of petunias to choose from that it is difficult to make any recommendations. You'll get some very fine pot plants from the F_1 All Double petunias and the F_1 California Giants. Some varieties in this group have 5-inch flowers in pure colors and two-tones. Grow in 3- or 4-inch pots. The plants are compact and sturdy. Some of the *grandifloras* have vigorous growth habits and therefore are not suitable for pots. They are excellent as cut flowers. However, you will want to grow several of the dwarf early-blooming types of *grandiflora* as pot plants, because this variety includes all the fancy and unusual types of single petunias, fringed and ruffled. They finish faster, so you can sow later—mid-February for blooming plants in mid-May. Try the Cascades and the Magics in all colors.

The *multiflora* petunias are the traditional bedding class— vigorous F_1 hybrids in all shades and colors, including stars and stripes.

Almost anything you want in a flower form or color, you will find in a petunia.

PRIMROSE *(Primula sp.)*

CONTROL: Timing. Pot size.

An entire book could be written about primroses—the beautiful primulas. There are more than 400 *Primula* species, including a hardy perennial class encompassing hundreds of outstanding types and hybrids. Then there are the popular annuals—Chinese, *malacoides,* and *obconica*—truly remarkable flowers.

Because we cannot do justice to them all, we will concern ourselves chiefly with those primroses that make attractive pot plants.

Some persons, and I stand among them, are as allergic to *P. obconica* as to poison ivy. So I say with reluctance—even though relatively few persons are affected—do not grow *obconica. P. malacoides* and the Chinese primrose *(P. sinensis)* do not cause this poisoning. Nor do any of the other primroses. And the nontoxic types are equally gorgeous.

Malacoides holds up well, blooms over a considerable period of time, and offers a bright variety of colors. It is excellent as an individual plant and great in combination pots.

The Chinese primulas are criticized for being delicate to handle—the petals fall easily—but the range and brilliance of their colors cannot be matched. And they will be treated with more care at home than they are in commercial establishments.

If you want large Chinese primrose plants in 5-inch pots for Christmas, sow seeds in early February. For January, February, and March flowers, sow in March and April. For 5-inch pot plants in early spring, sow in June. For 4-inch pot plants in May, sow in early September.

Primula seed does not germinate easily in warm weather. For the germinating medium, use a mixture of equal parts leaf mold, sand, and soil. The seeds are very fine. Sow on top of the medium and do not cover. Mist, and cover the flat with cellophane or glass. Set the flat in a cool spot, preferably around 65 degrees. A shady spot is better than full sun. If exposed to the sun, protect with frosted glass or paper. The trick to germinating primula seeds is to keep them cool and to keep them shaded.

Germination usually takes three to four weeks. After germination, remove the glass, cellophane, or paper covering. When seedlings are large enough to handle, transplant to 2½-inch pots with a soil-sand-humus mixture. Use a nonacid leaf mold. Do not use acid peat.

To grow fine primroses, keep them going. Do not let them get pot-bound at this time, or they will suffer a setback.

As soon as the plants in the 2½-inch pots are well established with true leaves, move to the 4- or 5-inch pots in which they will be finished. Include some slow-dissolving fertilizer in the potting soil. Plant shallow. Keep crowns above the soil. Watch carefully to see that the soil does not get too wet, or yellowing leaves will result, or crown rot in the Chinese primula.

To carry primulas over the summer, keep them shaded, cool, and give them lots of air. They can be summered in cold frames, covered with a shaded sash but open on all sides. Raising the sash an inch or two above the cold frame will allow ample air circulation. Or you can bury pots in a shaded area outdoors.

In the fall, when primroses are moved indoors, continue to keep them on the cool side. Temperatures from 45 to 50 degrees are ideal. Increase to 55 degrees just before they start to flower. Grow in light shade rather than in direct sunlight.

A seed mixture of Chinese primrose will contain nearly all colors except yellow. The Chinese Star sorts produce fringed flowers.

Even more popular than the brilliant Chinese primulas are the easier-to-grow primrose *malacoides*.

Sowing of *malacoides* seed is confined to the period between June and September. Again, it is difficult to get seeds to germinate in midsummer. Keep them as cool as possible and keep them shaded. Sowing after October 5 will produce blind plants—plants with no flowers.

Fine 5-inch pot plants for Valentine's Day and February will result from sowings made in June. Later sowings will produce 3- or 4-inch pot plants flowering in early spring. These smaller plants are excellent in combination plantings or planted 3 or 4 plants to a large pot.

To grow *malacoides,* follow the same procedure as for Chinese primroses. Keep them as cool as possible. They definitely prefer cool temperatures—40 to 50 degrees night—and they suffer from heat. In transplanting, be careful to set the crowns just above the soil line. It is a happy medium—too high will topple and too low will rot. Do not overwater.

Shade from full sunlight from June through September in the north, and from May through October in the south. Be generous when watering during hot weather, but taper down considerably during the dark months.

When primroses become pot-bound, they start to bloom. This is usually the case by late fall. When pot-bound, they will need to be fertilized every ten days with a complete liquid fertilizer.

The *malacoides* have some beautiful red varieties in Riverside and Brilliancy. White Giant in bloom is a sight to behold. There is a good lilac in Ball Lavender.

Among some of the hardy perennial primroses—which can be grown like *malacoides*—*P. veris* makes an outstanding show as a compact pot plant. *P. veris colossea* gives us some brilliant yellows, as well as apricot, crimson, and red. The Giant Munstead strains bring us various shades of apricot. In the Polyanthus, the Pacific strains feature blue, yellow, crimson, and white.

These hardy primroses are best sown in February. The seeds germinate in three to six weeks at 65 to 75 degrees. Transplant to flats and set about 2 inches apart; later move to 3- or 4-inch pots for spring flowering. Planted outdoors they are quite hardy and will make a colorful showing early in the following spring.

Altogether, the primroses make an interesting group of pot plants for late winter and early spring flowering.

SCHIZANTHUS (*Schizanthus* sp.)

CONTROL; Pot size. Timing. Light.

For something different and unusual in pot plants, try the easy-to-grow schizanthus. It thrives in a north window or in a semi-sunny location. Each plant becomes a solid mass of showy blooms that is a wonder to behold. Be assured, your schizanthus entry will win prizes at the spring flower shows.

Schizanthus plants are grown from seed. When to sow is important. Before you set the date, you have to decide upon the pot size in which you will finish growing them. The pot size is your control. Even the earliest fall sowing will not flower until well into spring *unless the roots are checked by becoming potbound.* For plants to be finished in 7- or 8-inch pots for midwinter or early spring bloom—just in time for the spring exhibitions and holidays—sow early in August. Or for 5- to 6-inch pot finishing, start late in August. For 3- or 4-inch pots to bloom in late spring, you can sow in December, or in January at the latest.

Schizanthus is a long-day plant and responds to light. Given supplemental lighting at night, seeds sown in September will flower from February on. Grow under relatively cool conditions—45 to 50 degrees.

There are dwarf and semidwarf types. Giant-flowered schizanthus is a fine semidwarf all-purpose variety. However, it needs to be topped back when about 6 inches tall and then pinched several times. This keeps it compact and shapes it into a choice exhibition plant.

For the dwarf type, there is a Dwarf mixture available, and it does not need pinching or topping. Because of its restricted growth habit, sow about October 1 and finish in 4- to 5-inch pots. The flowers are smaller than the Giant-flowered, but both types make attractive plants.

Put schizanthus high on your priority list of plants to try. You'll be glad you did.

VERBENA (*Verbena hybrida*)

CONTROL: Timing.

Verbena is an old-fashioned plant with a long flowering season. It makes a nice late winter/early spring pot plant indoors, a flowering pot plant for Memorial Day, and an excellent bedding plant outdoors.

Verbenas are annuals. They are available in many bright

colors, have a delightful fragrance, and bloom all season in a full sun. All in all, they are very satisfactory flowers and plants.

Although verbenas are usually grown from seed, they can be propagated from cuttings. Select a few outstanding plants in your outdoor border and cut them back around September 1. By October 1 you will have a number of clean, new tips showing. Cut, dip in rooting hormone, and insert in a small flat of moist sand. Give bottom heat of about 65 degrees if possible. Within a few weeks the rooted cuttings can be moved to 2½-inch pots of friable potting soil. Grow in a sunny area. These should make nice plants for Easter.

For Memorial Day 4-inch pot plants, verbenas are usually grown from seed started in mid-February. Sow earlier for indoor winter pot plants and later for outdoor bedding plants—as late as April 1. Sow in a small flat of potting soil and keep soil temperature between 65 and 75 degrees for three or four weeks. Germination is slow and only about half of the seeds will sprout. After about four weeks, move the flat to a cooler area and grow the seedlings at about 45 to 50 degrees night temperature.

Plants should be pinched back—nip off the top growth—early. Then, for outdoor bedding plants, continue to grow in flats. Otherwise, move to pots—first 2½ inches, then 3 or 4 inches. This procedure should give you bushy plants with several flower heads.

There are two basic types of verbenas—spreading, and upright or bush. Among these, there are dwarf and tall plants. The tall plants may grow to a little over 1 foot in height. The dwarf, to about half that. You can select a variety that will give you the type of plant you want.

In addition, verbenas are available in a wide range of colors. Here are some suggested varieties: In the dwarf spreading type—an excellent group—there are Delight in pink, Sparkle, Dazzle, or Blaze in red, Crystal in white, Amethyst in blue, and Calypso in a blend. In the tall spreading type, there are Defiance or Torrid in red, Lavender Glory in lavender, Royale or Sutter's Blue in blue, and Ellen Wilmott in salmon. Among the upright types, there are Starlight in blue, Firelight in red,

Snowball in white, and Giant Salmon Queen in salmon. There are also some excellent mixtures available if you like to be surprised at the results.

The taller varieties of verbenas respond to dwarfing by B-Nine growth retardant. Spray with ½ percent solution seven weeks after sowing. Height will be reduced about one-third, and the plants will be more compact. The true dwarfs, of course, need no treatment.

11
Forcing . . . Mostly Just for Fun—Plants to Try

Forcing unique plants, conversation-piece plants, and uncommon plants into bloom is still an open field. The list of plants to try is limitless. I will touch upon a few merely in an attempt to kindle your interest in the many possibilities. There are many others I must leave for you to discover yourself. Among them are euphorbias, exotic orchids, bougainvillea, eranthis, eupatorium, gypsophila, stephanotis, and the little-known *Ursina pulchra*. I could go on.

When you feel adventurous and want to try growing and forcing out-of-the-ordinary plants, do not overlook what you may think to be ordinary common garden plants. By way of example, I will provide instruction for phlox and salvia—but there are many more. Take a look at all the "common" flowers from a new perspective—wintertime.

An art teacher I know sets new students straight about their absolute sureness of color by standing on his head. He invites the students to join him. From an upside-down position, students are asked to describe the color of the wall, the ceiling, the sky outside the window, and other objects that everyone thinks he or she knows. From this experience, young art students are taught to question what they think they see.

Preconceived notions about common garden plants can be limiting, too. Because a plant has not been grown as a houseplant and been forced to bloom out-of-season does not mean it can't be. With such forcing tools as light, shade, and temperature control—and commonsense growing practices—at our disposal, it can be fun to try.

Anytime you are going to try a new plant or want to grow some "unique" plant in a pot indoors or want to experiment with unknown flowering plants, here is a suggestion about how you can handle them: Go back to basics. How did the plant grow in its native environment? What was the environment like?

To get answers, stop at a library and consult Bailey's *Manual of Cultivated Plants* or some good plant encyclopedia. It will tell you something about the growth habits of your special flower in its native habitat.

Suppose you find that your plant is a native of Brazil, growing along the banks of the Amazon. From this single fact, you can be fairly certain that it is nonhardy and will have to be treated as a houseplant for the warm indoors. Growing in deep tropical shade, it will probably do well in the subdued light of a home. But if you find the plant gets leggy, it is reaching for more light, so move it to a brighter location. Growing on the equator, your plant will not be subject to day-length or temperature controls. In fact, controls may not be necessary; it may be everblooming. Any regulation that it may need would be for a wet or dry season—a probable drying-off period. Growing on the banks of the Amazon, it would probably need to be watered generously and would prefer a somewhat humid environment. The soil from the river overflow may be sandy loam. And to feed your plant, start out with a balanced fertilizer.

But suppose your plant is a native of the Swiss Alps. Then, it is undoubtedly hardy. It is also a questionable prospect for a warm home. Give it cool growing conditions. And give it the full sunlight of a bright mountainside. Go easy on the fertilizer and watering, and use ordinary garden soil. If it normally blooms in summer, it is probably a long-day plant. Flowers in the fall may indicate a short-day plant. But also consider temperature as a possible control. Seeds may need cold treatment to germinate.

You get the idea, I'm sure. You play plant detective. You get hold of a few facts and try to build a case with them. You will not always be right, but you will be right most of the time. And to discover something that won't work or isn't true is also an important contribution to advancing knowledge.

So try growing unusual plants once in a while. If for no other reason, you'll enjoy it. It's fun. Work out their cultures for yourself. There are many plants that I'd still like to cultivate. And there are also many plants about which we know almost nothing. Who knows, you may become the world's only living expert on *Tricyrtis*.

Here are some flowering plants you may want to try when you are feeling venturesome—just for fun.

ASTILBE *(Astilbe sp.)*

CONTROL: Potting time.

Astilbe makes a large pot plant growing to 2 feet tall. The Spirea-type—its white, pink, or red flowers resemble those of a spirea—can be grown and forced for Easter.

The seeds are very fine. Sow on top of milled peat and potting soil in spring. Mist and cover flat with glass. Seeds germinate in three to four weeks at 65 to 75 degrees. Thin or transplant to a flat of friable soil. Grow cool, around 55 degrees. Transplant to the garden for the summer.

After the first light frost, lift the plants and pot in 5- or 6-inch pots, using a light, porous soil. For sturdier plants, you can let them grow for another season before lifting, dividing, and potting the clumps in fall. In either case, after potting, store them in a cold frame or a cold area at 35 to 40 degrees.

The flowering date is controlled by the date you start the potted plants into growth. Check your calendar for a date fourteen weeks before Easter if Easter is early, or twelve weeks before Easter if Easter is late. That's the date to bring in the pots and get them started.

For Memorial Day flowering, start forcing on April 1.

Grow in 55- to 60-degree temperatures. Will tolerate shade. Water and fertilize moderately at first. Increase water quantity as plants grow and begin to demand more and especially when flowers begin to develop. At this time, I set the pots in saucers filled with water. Feed with ammonium sulfate every ten days.

A forcing variation used by some growers to get flowering astilbe plants from February through May is a warm-water treatment. Clumps are immersed in tepid 110-degree water for one hour in October. They are potted, then stored at 35 to 40 degrees in the subdued light of a shed or basement until early January. Then bring them into a 55- to 60-degree semi-shaded area. Plants will flower in February, thus speeding up the flowering by 1½ to 2 months.

BELLS OF IRELAND or SHELL-FLOWER (*Molucella laevis*)

CONTROL: Timing.

For unique cut flowers grow bells of Ireland. They are unusual and beautiful. Delicately veined green bells contain a tiny white flower. The tall branches resemble floral spikes with green florets. They can and have been used to create striking floral arrangements.

Flower arrangers like bells of Ireland because they are "spiky" plants that can be fashioned into graceful curves. The green bells are so different that they excite curiosity and attention. The green color complements whatever flowers are used with them. And as cut flowers in water, they hold up for a remarkable length of time, remaining in good condition for weeks.

The plants are grown from seeds, and herein lies a minor problem. The seeds need cold treatment for forcing out of season. Sow them in tiny flats of moist peat and sand. Mist and insert the flat into a plastic sandwich bag. Then store the flat in the fruit keeper of your refrigerator for one to two months. Remove to a cool, sunny area—around 50 degrees nights.

I have also used the cold treatment I give rose seeds with satisfactory results. Place the flat into the refrigerator for twenty days, then remove for ten days, return it to the refrigerator for twenty days, and finally remove it to a 50-degree, well-lighted area for sprouting.

After germination, carefully transplant seedlings to deep flats or large pots. Use friable garden soil. Space about 10 inches apart in flats, or one plant to a pot. Plant shallow. Keep the plants moist until they are established. They do not require full sunlight. Once going, they make few demands and will even tolerate drought. The plants will quickly branch out into a number of stems that will grow to about 2 feet tall. Provide some support even though the plants are fairly sturdy.

Seeds treated to germinate in summer will produce plants that may be cut in winter. As a variation, seeds are planted outdoors or in a cold frame in late summer in the north or in early fall in the south. The stocky little plants are then lifted and brought indoors for winter bloom. In parts of Texas, they are left outdoors all winter and make early summer cuttings. For early fall bloom outdoors, we have planted seeds directly into the cold frame in early spring and then have moved the plants to the garden.

Indoors or out, these translucent green bells—which strictly speaking are not flowers at all but calyxes—have a quaint charm unmatched by many true flowers.

BOUVARDIA *(Bouvardia sp.)*

CONTROL: Pinch. Shade.

Bouvardia can be a repeater, that is, it can be forced into bloom again and again throughout the year. It is a small shrub with white, very fragrant, slender tubelike flowers. It once was much more popular than it is today.

Bouvardia plants are grown as pot plants that are used chiefly for cut flowers. They are propagated from stem cuttings or root cuttings.

For stem cuttings, a plant that has finished flowering is placed in a cold area in fall. When brought into 60 degrees, the plants will develop new shoots. In early spring, make cuttings of these new shoots. They root readily in sand and peat with bottom heat.

For root cuttings, in February or March, cut a root portion into 1-inch pieces. Place these pieces on a sand-peat mixture and cover with a ¼-inch layer of sand and peat. Keep moist. In two months the new plants will be ready for potting in 2½-inch pots.

For bushy plants from stem or root cuttings, transplant two or three cuttings into 2½-inch pots and later shift to 4-inch in May or June.

Use a friable soil, about half humus, with some limestone added. A pH of 7.5 is preferred. Water generously during the flowering period. Feed occasionally with a weak nitrogen fertilizer. Grow at 55 degrees and in full sunlight—except in June, July, and August when plants should be shaded with cheesecloth.

By pinching some of the terminal growth on the same plant at different times, or all of the new leaf growth on another sister plant at a different time, you can extend the blooms over a long period. Plants that normally bloom in June may be kept from blooming by pinching until August. In this way you can have flowers throughout the winter.

Bouvardias respond to day length. You can get them to set flower buds by reducing the day length—shading with a black cloth for thirty days with temperatures at 65 degrees or higher.

They can be made to repeat. After normal June flowering, cut off faded flowers and start shading immediately on July 4. Plants will bloom August 4. Or, after new growth develops in July, shade August 1 for flowers in September. Plants not shaded after June flowering will bloom later in the fall.

The *Bouvardia longiflora* is the most commonly used bouvardia and has pink as well as white flowers.

CHRISTMAS CACTUS *(Zygocactus truncatus)*

CONTROL: Fall dry period.

This is an old favorite, with long-lasting red flowers on a plant that will last for years. The pendant flowers bloom at Christmastime along the edge of the plant's thornless, succulent foliage, which is joined together in segments like green dominos.

It is one of the easiest plants to grow. The flat leaf branches

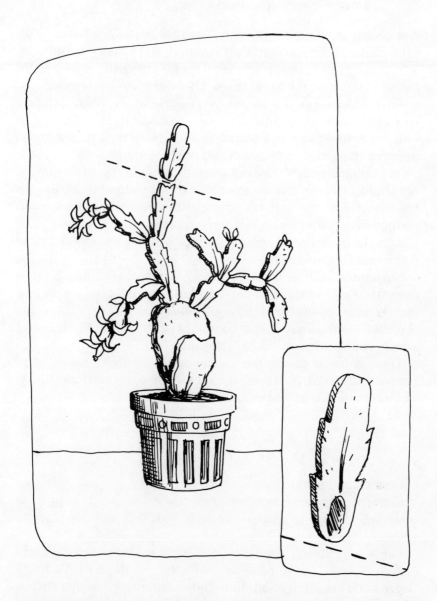

The simplest way to propagate Christmas cactus is by rooting one or more of the stem/leaf segments, which break off the plant easily.

can be cut or snapped off, and they root readily in sand. Keep sand damp but not moist. Cuttings may be started anytime but are usually taken in midwinter. Transplant cuttings to a light, loamy soil mixed with leaf mold. Grow at 55 to 60 degrees.

New plants should be watered generously from January through summer. Plants can be summered in cool shade outdoors. Bring indoors before frost. Grows well under grow-lights or in partial shade such as a north window.

In September or October, start drying the plants—that is, withholding water. Move the plant into subdued light, as in a basement. Let the soil become quite dry for about a month during late fall or early winter, otherwise the plant will not bloom. In mid-November, bring into a light, 55- to 60-degree room and start watering.

Christmas cactus may be grown from seed, but it takes several years before a fair-sized plant results. Sow seeds in a small flat or plan. Use sandy soil and cover seeds with a fine layer of sand about ⅛ inch deep. Mist and set the flat on a warm, sunny windowsill to germinate.

The soil used to pot seedlings should be light, sandy, and porous. Grow at 55 to 60 degrees. When of sufficient size, force into bloom as you would cuttings.

CLARKIA *(Clarkia elegans)*

CONTROL: Timing. Light.

Clarkia, a seldom-grown cut flower, could supply a welcome change to spring arrangements. It is an easy plant to grow.

For early March flowers, sow in late December or early January. Seeds germinate in seven to ten days at 65 to 75 degrees. Transplant to shallow flats containing about 3 inches of garden soil. Space plants about 4 by 4 inches. Plants will branch from base. Prune to two or three stems per plant. Provide string supports for stems to grow on. Stems may grow to be 2 to 3 feet in height.

Do not overwater. From time to time allow the soil to become quite dry to harden the plant stems. Grow in full sun and in warm temperatures—about 60 degrees nights.

Clarkia plants respond to additional light. For February blooms, sow seeds in November and light in mid-December to mid-January.

Give Scarlet Queen a try—or any of the clarkia mixtures that are available.

DIDISCUS or BLUE LACE-FLOWER *(Trachymene caerulea)*

CONTROL: Timing. Light.

As a cultivated flower, didiscus suffers from its resemblance to a flower we consider a weed—Queen Anne's Lace. But if you have room somewhere to grow a different winter cut flower, give didiscus a try. The rounded clusters of lacy blue flowers crown 2-foot-long stems and are especially useful in modern arrangements.

Didiscus responds to extra light at night, which makes it easy to control its date of bloom. Plants from seeds sown in August will bloom in late February if given extra light at midnight from late November to mid-January. Without lights, these plants will bloom in early April.

Seeds sown in June will produce plants that will flower in November when they are given additional light in October. Without lights, these plants will flower for Christmas.

Seeds will germinate in two to three weeks at 65 to 75 degrees. Since they germinate better in darkness, seed flats should be covered. Transfer seedlings to shallow flats, or to 5-inch pots of light, fertile soil. Space about 7 by 7 inches in a flat, or one plant to a pot. Do not overwater, especially when plants are getting started. A soggy soil could set the plants back and cause stunting. Grow in a 50-degree night temperature. Give the plants full sunlight.

ENGLISH DAISY *(Bellis perennis)*

CONTROL: Timing.

This plant is better known in England than in America. In appearance, it is like an aster. In usefulness, it is very much like a pansy or viola. It helps fill out a combination pot or add a different accent to small cut-flower arrangements. In individual pots, it is everblooming.

English daisy plants can be handled as you would pansies. They do not need much room, and a few plants in pots or flats will provide you with an ample supply of cut flowers.

They like cool, humid conditions and do their best during our cool spring months. Their preference to coolness makes it extremely difficult to carry them over our summers, and so they seldom are. Except in areas where summers are cool and relatively moist, it is much easier to start them anew from seeds.

Sow seeds around September 1. They germinate in one to two weeks. Keep temperatures around 60 to 65 degrees. Use a mixture of peat, vermiculite, and potting soil as a seeding medium. Sow on top and mist to work the seeds into the medium. Place the seed flat in a plastic bag to keep moist, but as soon as seeds have germinated, give the seedlings air.

When large enough, transplant to pots or flats of rich, loose loam. Space 8 by 8 inches. Carry them in a cool greenhouse or cold frame at 50 degrees. Give them lots of light and plenty of air to keep them from growing soft.

Plants from seeds sown in late August and grown at 50 degrees should flower from December to late spring.

Because seeds are difficult to germinate and the plants dislike hot weather, southern growers usually buy fully grown plants and then carry them as cool as possible.

The Monstrosa strains are favorites, but there are also other excellent varieties available. The F₁ Pink Fairy Carpet is a beauty.

This is a great little plant to try.

LANTANA *(Lantana sp.)*

CONTROL: Temperature.

Lantanas, which come in bright, jewellike colors, make fine everblooming pot plants.

For winter plants indoors, take cuttings from outdoor plants in September. Select plants with the colors and growing habits you want. Cuttings root easily in vermiculite and peat, perlite, or sand.

You can grow lantana from seed, but when you do, you take potluck. There is no uniformity in the plants or flowers.

Seeds need bottom heat to germinate. Place your flats over heat pipes and keep the soil moist. Seeds take about two months to germinate. Keep temperature around 70 degrees.

Transplant seedlings or cuttings to pots—up to 4 inches, depending upon the plant size. Use a loamy garden soil. Give normal feeding. Lantanas like heat, so grow them in a warm house, about 65 degrees. To hold them back, move pots to a 55-degree temperature. To bring them along faster, increase the temperature. Give them full sun.

This procedure should give you some unusually attractive late winter and spring plants. Nana Compacta—dwarf, mixed colors—is the one to try. *L. Camara* hybrids can be used for cut flowers as well as pot plants.

LOBELIA *(Lobelia Erinus)*

CONTROL: Timing.

Lobelias are dainty little plants for pots, combination pots, and baskets. They are easy plants to grow and to force and do well in warm locations—inside and out.

For flowering plants in April and May, sow seeds in December or early January. For Memorial Day blooms, sow seeds in late January.

Seeds are very fine. Use sifted soil and peat in a small flat and sow on top. Do not cover seeds. After watering with a mister, cover the flat with a sheet of glass or plastic. Seeds germinate in about three weeks at 65 to 75 degrees.

Transfer seedlings to flats or pots of ordinary garden soil with a little peat added. Grow at night temperatures of around 50 degrees for sturdy plants. To move the plants along faster, you can increase the night temperature slightly. In spring, they prefer partial shade to direct sunlight.

Use dwarf annuals for indoor culture. These make compact 6-inch plants. Among these lobelias are some excellent whites, clear blues, and some blues and reds with white eyes. For the best blue, try Bluestone.

For hanging baskets and porch and window boxes, there is a trailing type of lobelia called Pendula that is not often available but is well worth searching for. Try the Cascades in blue and red.

NASTURTIUM (Tropaeolum majus)

CONTROL: Timing.

This popular garden plant can provide a striking gold color to winter cut-flower arrangements. Try it. There are few flowers easier to grow. And its free-flowering habit makes it possible for you to grow nasturtiums in a small space. A flat or several pots of these plants will give you a plentiful supply of cut flowers.

The seeds are large. Plant them about ¼ inch deep. They need darkness to sprout. They will germinate in about two weeks at 65 to 75 degrees.

Transplant to shallow pots or to flats with about 3 inches of garden soil. Space about 10 by 10 inches in a flat, and try two or three plants in a large pot. Do not use rich soil. The worse the soil, the better nasturtiums flower.

Grow nasturtiums on the dry side. Water sparingly. Do not feed. Give full sun.

For midwinter flowers, sow in August or September. Nasturtiums bloom in about two months after sowing and continue over a long period.

Two of the best long-stem spreading-type nasturtiums for forcing are Golden Gleam and Scarlet Gleam. If shorter stems are not objectionable, the upright varieties—Whirlybird Scarlet and Jewel mixture—are outstanding.

NIEREMBERGIA or CUP-FLOWER (Nierembergia sp.)

CONTROL: Timing.

The cup-flower, or nierembergia, is not used enough. Indoors or out, it is a thing of quiet beauty. As a compact indoor pot plant, it is covered with lavender-blue flowers over a long season. Nierembergia plants, like many other plants, can have their blooming season extended by picking off the spent flowers and thus keeping the plant from going to seed.

Outdoors, used among border plants, nierembergia is a tender perennial that flowers easily and freely the first summer after sowing. It will bloom in partial shade or full sunlight. In warmer climates, it may grow to 16 or 18 inches in its second season. In the northern areas, where it must be protected over the winter, it is a compact, somewhat spreading plant seldom reaching 10 inches.

Because of its extreme tenderness—it is unable to withstand temperatures less than 10 degrees—and its rapid growth and flowering from seed, nierembergia is generally treated as an annual in the northern areas.

Nierembergia may be propagated from seeds, divisions, and cuttings. But I think you'll find seedlings much more vigorous than cuttings, which tend to become hard and woody.

Seeds planted indoors in a small flat germinate in two to three weeks at temperatures between 65 and 75 degrees. The seeds are small and require but a light covering. After germination, transplant to pots of soil and peat. Plants will thrive under grow-lights or in partial shade. You can expect blooms in about two months. Grow in an east or north window, or in subdued sunlight.

For an outstanding plant for your home, try the variety Purple Robe. An early sowing in late winter will make choice spring pot plants, which can then be moved to the garden for all-season bloom.

As pot plants, they respond to the same treatment you would give African-violets.

PERIWINKLE or VINCA (*Vinca rosea*)

CONTROL: Timing.

This is a splendid everblooming plant with attractive, glossy foliage. It is compact in form—about 6 to 8 inches tall, and the flowers are phloxlike and borne in profusion.

It is easily propagated from seed. Sow in flats of soil-vermiculite-peat. Cover seeds. Give bottom heat—65 to 75 degrees. Germination is slow—about three weeks.

When seedlings are large enough to handle, transplant them to 2½-inch pots, or directly to 3-inch, in which they are finished. Use a loose garden soil. Grow in 55 degrees in a good light. Water and feed moderately.

Seeds may be sown at any time. Seeds sown in December will make nice plants for late Easter or Mother's Day. For Memorial Day, seeds may be sown in late January.

Periwinkle will continue blooming into the summer and may be moved outdoors when the weather warms. It is a half-hardy perennial and does not winter over for us. But it will withstand heat and drought.

Plants grown outdoors all summer may be lifted and brought indoors for fall flowering.

Periwinkles are available in white, pink, deep rose, or bicolor. Coquette produces a dense, bushy plant with pink flowers. Little Bright Eye is a white with a deep red center. Blanche is a pure white.

The periwinkle is well worth a try.

PHLOX
(Phlox Drummondii)—ANNUAL
(P. paniculata and others*)*—PERENNIAL

Phlox, as a flowering pot plant for the home or as a greenhouse cut flower, needs more trial and acceptance. It is seldom grown and seldom used as a pot plant or a winter cut flower. However, I have experimented with some plantings with remarkable success.

Of course, as an outdoor plant, phlox is popular and widely grown. A number of unusual species and colorful varieties exist. Their descriptions, uses, and culture alone could fill a book.

There are annual and perennial phlox. We'll quickly take a look at each.

Annual Phlox

Two classes of annual phlox are available—a tall class, called Grandiflora, which grows up to 18 inches; and a dwarf class called Compacta, which seldom exceeds 6 inches in height.

The Grandiflora make excellent cut flowers, indoors and out, and its varieties offer a broad range of bright colors and mixtures. They are usually grown in flats for spring garden sales at nurseries. When making your selection, try those chosen as best in the All-American Selection.

The Compacta, frequently used for bedding plants, make fine flowering pot plants. A number of excellent varieties are available—many prize winners in the All-America Selection. For pot plants, I use Globe and Twinkle. Globe is free-flowering and compact, branching from the base to make a full plant. A good range of colors exist. Twinkle is a star dwarf, covering itself with star-shaped pink or red flowers.

For annual phlox, sow seeds in flats. Cover lightly. Seeds germinate in two to three weeks at 65- to 75-degree temperatures. Transplant to pots or in beds.

For late April flowering plants, sow in January. For May blooms, sow in early February.

Grow at 50 degrees with normal feed and watering.

Perennial Phlox

From this large group, probably two species that we call the "summer phlox" are the most often used. These are *P. paniculata* and *P. maculata*. Among them are many varieties of brilliant reds, salmons, purples, and varicolored flowers.

Summer phlox are usually propagated by division and root cuttings. A hybrid race called *P. decussata* may be grown from seed that is packaged as Decussata mixture. Seeds should be exposed to freezing temperatures for several weeks. After this cold treatment, seeds germinate in darkness in three to four weeks at temperatures between 65 and 75 degrees. Transplant to a rich soil and peat mixture in peat or clay pots. Grow in full sun or dappled shade. Keep moist.

In the garden the normal flowering season for perennial phlox is from mid-July to September. Summer phlox like fairly moist and rich soil. Each clump should have about 2 to 3 feet of growing room. In transferring to the garden, plant the entire peat pot or shift from the clay pot—and space properly.

For forcing into flower in June, lift clumps in October and hold in a cold frame until early January. Then move to a cool 50-degree greenhouse or growing area.

You may find *P. subulata* an interesting pot plant in addition to its principal use in rock gardens. It fits well into indoor miniature arrangements. When the plant is not in bloom, its foliage is an attractive green cover. In bloom, the variety *Nelsonii* makes a brilliant showing, indoors and out. There are also other varieties of *subulata*, with flowers ranging from clear white to striking red.

Because it is easy, *P. subulata* is division-propagated. Divide, pot, and transfer to a cold frame until February or March. Then bring into a fairly cool growing location. Water and grow in full sun. Should flower in April or May.

In forcing phlox, annual or perennial, you are pretty much on your own. But these attractive flowers seem to offer an overlooked potential.

SALPIGLOSSIS *(Salpiglossis sinuata)*

CONTROL: Timing. Shade.

Salpiglossis is a fine cut flower for modern arrangements with big, bright-colored—almost gaudy—flowers that keep for days. The bush is about 2 feet tall, and a little rank in growth habit, needing cool temperatures to keep it within bounds.

Sow seeds in August. Cover them with the seeding medium, and then cover seed flat with cardboard. Seeds germinate better in the dark. Germination takes two to three weeks at 65 to 75 degrees.

Transplant seedlings to 2½-inch pots and then shift to deep flats in October or November, spacing 10 inches apart. Use good garden soil. Give normal watering. Grow in direct sun at 50 degrees.

For flowers in March, light two hours at midnight with 60-watt incandescent lights strung 3 feet high and 4 feet apart, from November 15 to January 15.

For May bloom, sow seeds in early January and do not light.

A wide selection of colors are available, including gold, scarlet, and blue. The hybrid Splash seems to tolerate warm weather. Bolero produces large-sized flowers.

SALVIA or SCARLET SAGE *(Salvia splendens)*

CONTROL: Timing. Temperature. Shade.

Here's a suggestion for a "different" Christmas flower. It's a potted salvia, or scarlet sage. It's out of the ordinary and beautiful. The dwarf variety, Fireball, makes a brilliant red and green Christmas plant that can rival a poinsettia. But since you will not find it very often at your florist, you'll have to grow your own.

Here's what you do. Sow seeds eighty-five days before blooming plants are wanted—October 1 for Christmas. Use a mixture of sand, soil, and peat. Cover seeds lightly or not at all. After sowing, soak flats thoroughly, cover with glass to hold moisture, and place the flats in a warm spot where the temperatures are above 65 degrees. Seeds will not germinate at lower temperatures.

Do not water again until seeds germinate, usually in about two to three weeks.

After seeds have sprouted, move flats to a cooler spot—about 55 degrees—to prevent damping-off. Then, when seedlings are established, transplant to 3-inch pots of garden soil. Fertilize. Grow in 60-degree night temperature all the way. No lighting is needed. Do not pinch.

The growing needs of salvia plants are simple—good garden soil, full sun, and a spray program to control red spider mites. Handled in this way, these plants will bloom for Christmas. Once started, they tend to be everblooming. They can be used as they are, in the 3-inch pots, or after the plants are in bloom, three plants can be combined in a 5-inch azalea pot for a striking effect.

Salvia is a short-day plant, and it may be brought into flower at any time by shading with black cloth.

Other excellent red dwarfs are Flamenco and Scarlet Pygmy. An unusual variety to try for Christmas is the Pink Sundae. It grows about 14 inches tall and sends up many stems that terminate in a cluster of bright pink leaves in the same manner as poinsettias.

Besides their use as a Christmas plant, potted salvias are also excellent in spring and summer combinations or as brilliant pot plants to brighten the dreary days of late winter. Or an early dwarf type of salvia sown in March will make nice 3-inch pots for mid-May and Memorial Day.

Used outdoors, salvia makes an excellent bedding plant. Commercial growers find this to be a profitable market. Sow seeds in late March or April. Many excellent varieties are available.

But once you've tried salvia as a Christmas plant, you'll want to grow it for this holiday year after year.

SCARLET PLUME *(Euphorbia fulgens)*

CONTROL: Shade. Temperature.

Scarlet plume is a shrub native to Mexico that is used for cut flowers or as pot plants. Bright, orange red bracts develop naturally around Christmastime.

After Christmas flowering, cut the plant back, and it will flower again in late February or early March.

For earlier flowering, when other flowers are scarce, shade as for chrysanthemums. For September flowers, shade from July 15. For late October flowers, shade from August 15. For November and Thanksgiving, shade from September 1. For December flowering, shade from September 15. In each case, shade until buds show.

For late January bloom, light from October 1 to November 20.

As a cut flower, the stem must be seared to seal in the plant fluids.

Scarlet plume plants are usually propagated by softwood cuttings made in spring—usually April. Include two or three nodes. Sear end lightly and dip in rooting hormone. Cuttings root easily in equal parts of sand and peat at 60 degrees.

Grow plants in a bench as cut flowers, or in pots, at 60 degrees nights. Give them full sun. Use a heavy loam, or slightly acid soil. In benches, space 8 by 8 inches. Pinching will help produce a bushy pot plant. Do not pinch for cut flowers. Water freely. Drop temperature to 50 or 55 degrees when buds begin to open.

Plants can also be grown from seeds, which germinate in one or two weeks at 65 to 75 degrees. Plants are usually carried one year outside and forced in the next year.

THUNBERGIA *(Thunbergia alata)*

CONTROL: Timing.

For colorful hanging baskets or pots, try thunbergia. The dark-centered orange or yellow daisylike flowers are conversation starters: "Look, black-eyed Susan ivies!"

There are a number of thunbergia species, but *T. alata* is especially trouble-free, easy to grow, and rapid in growth. Once in bloom, it will flower all winter indoors.

For summer pots, sow seeds in February. Used in a window box, it is enchanting. For winter pots, bring the plants indoors in the fall.

Thunbergia has fairly large seeds that germinate in about two weeks at warm night temperatures between 65 and 75 degrees. Grow in a warm, sunny area and give normal care. Give full sun.

Thunbergia alata mixture will furnish you with bright flowers in white, apricot, yellow, and orange. White Wings is a beauty—large pure white flowers in a beautiful butterfly form.

TORENIA or WISHBONE FLOWER *(Torenia Fournieri)*

CONTROL: Timing.

Here is a versatile plant you will be glad you tried. It is no prima donna. It will be completely happy with whatever treatment you give it. And it will cheer your home over a long winter period.

Torenias can be grown at any time and for any time. Simply sow the seeds about four to five months before you want them in full bloom, e.g., August 1 for late November flowers.

Once started, torenias are year-around plants. In mid summer, when showy indoor flowering plants are few and far between and when even African-violets are lethargic—torenia's bright blue blooms are most welcome.

For an all-summer pot plant, sow seeds in February. This same sowing will also give you outdoor bedding plants for June.

Torenias grow rapidly from seed. The seeds are fine. Sow on top of sifted peat and vermiculite in a small flat. Cover to prevent drying. Seeds germinate within two weeks at warm temperature—between 65 and 75 degrees.

Transplant several to a pan or shallow pot. Grow in a warm area—above 55 degrees at night. Any friable loam will do. Torenia will grow in sun or partial shade. Give it normal watering and feeding.

The dwarf variety *compacta* is generally preferred. There is a white form with a golden throat available, which when combined in a pan with other torenias—bicolors or blues—is a joy to behold.

VENIDIUM *(Venidium fastuosum)*

CONTROL: Timing. Light.

Venidium shines in modern arrangements. The flowers call out for attention—2-foot stems with 4-inch daisylike blooms in glowing orange and yellow around a large purple black eye.

Natives of Africa, venidiums like dry, sunny heat. Although they are seldom forced and grown, they are easy to grow, and they bloom over a long period of time.

The seeds are sown in August. Use a soil-peat mix. Seeds germinate in ten days on a warm, sunny window ledge. By

November, transplant the seedlings to growing flats of fairly heavy soil. Space 8 inches apart.

For January flowers, light after the November transplant. Stop lighting when buds form. For April blooms, do not light.

WALLFLOWER *(Erysimum sp.)*

CONTROL: Sowing date.

This easy-to-grow, fragrant annual can be grown for late winter cut flowers.

Wallflowers are grown from seed. Seeds germinate in one or two weeks at 65- to 75-degree temperatures. Transplant to shallow flats, spacing about 3 by 3 inches. Shallow flats are important in growing these plants. Deep flats may result in blind plants—plants that refuse to flower. Use a light soil with some lime added. Grow at 50 to 55 degrees for best results, although wallflowers will tolerate warmer temperatures. Give them a bright window.

For yellow, red, and violet wallflower blooms in February and March, sow seeds in early September. Seeds sown in January will flower in May and June. Sow in spring, and you'll get flowers from July to November. Sow in July and August, and wallflowers will bloom in midwinter. Since they have a long blooming period, you will have cut flowers the year around.

Gold Standard and Allioni are reliable varieties to try. Double Early Wonder features scented double flowers in unusual brown and rust colors as well as bright red.

Appendix A
Forcing Schedules*

Flowering Date	Flower	Date to Sow or Start Cuttings	Pot, Bench, or Force Date	Growing Temp. F.	Remarks
** Sept.	Sweet peas	June 15	June 15	50–55	
Sept. 25	Lily-of-the-valley		Sept. 1	70–75	
** Oct.	Sweet peas	June 15	June 15	50	
Oct. 10	Scarlet plume		July	60	Shade Aug. 15–Sept. 15
Oct. 15	Bouvardia	Mar. (tip cutting)	July	50	Pinch to Aug. 15
Oct. 22	Lily-of-the-valley		Oct. 1	70–75	
Nov.	Bouvardia	Feb. (cutting)	late May	55	Pinch to Sept. 10
Nov.	Calendula	July	Sept.	50	
Nov.	Marigold	Aug. 1	Sept. 15	55	
Nov.	Pansy	July	Oct.	50	Light
** Nov.	Sweet peas	June 15	June 15	50	

*Not included here are schedules for chrysanthemums, carnations, roses, or snapdragons. See the individual discussions for working out schedules for these plants.

Where no date is indicated under the column for when to sow or start cuttings, it is because the plant indicated is either a bulbous, cormous, or tuberous plant that should be started on the forcing date, or because the plant used for forcing bloom will be a mature plant started in a previous season. In each case, for full details see the individual discussions in the text.

**Sweet peas are planted where they are to grow, so the planting date is effectively the same as the bench and force date.

243

Flowering Date	Flower	Date to Sow or Start Cuttings	Pot, Bench, or Force Date	Growing Temp. F.	Remarks
Nov. 20	Scarlet plume		July	60	Shade Sept. 15–Oct. 15
Nov. 22	Lily-of-the-valley		Nov. 1	75	
Nov. 25	Tiger lily		July	55	Store bulbs to July
Dec.	Bouvardia	Feb. (cutting)	late May	55	Pinch to Sept. 10
Dec.	Calendula	July	Sept.	50	
Dec.	Camellia		Sept.	50–55	
Dec.	Christmas cactus		Oct.	60	Dry in Sept.
Dec.	Freesia	Aug.	Aug.	50	
Dec.	Gerbera		Aug.–Sept.	50–60	Grow outdoors to Aug.
Dec.	Marigold	Aug. 1	Sept. 15	55	
Dec.	Pansy	July	Oct.	50	Light
Dec.	Solanum	Jan.	March	55	
Dec.	Stevia	Mar. (cutting)	Sept.	50–55	
Dec.	Stock	July	Aug. 15	50	Early varieties
Dec.	Sweet peas	Aug.	Aug.	50	
Dec. 15	Scarlet plume		July	60	Pinch before Sept. Shade Oct. 1–25
Dec. 20	Azalea		Nov. 1	60	Hold cold to Nov.
Dec. 20	Kalanchoe	Jan.	Aug. Sept.	60–65	Shade from planting to Oct. 10
Dec. 25	Begonia	Aug. 1		60	
Dec. 25	Cineraria	May	July	50	
Dec. 25	Daffodil	Aug.–Sept.	Nov. 25	55–60	Hold cold to Nov.
Dec. 25	Gardenia	Nov. (cutting)	Sept.	60–65	
Dec. 25	Hyacinth	Aug.–Sept.	Nov. 25	55–60	Hold cold to Nov.
Dec. 25	*Lilium speciosum*		July 7	55	
Dec. 25	Poinsettia	June (cutting)	Sept.	60–65	Pinch before Aug. 15
Dec. 25	Schizanthus	Aug.	Oct.	50	Pinch to Oct. 15
Jan.	Azalea		Nov. 20	60	
Jan.	Bouvardia	Mar. (cutting)	June	55	Pinch to Sept. 1
Jan.	Calendula	July	Sept.	45–50	
Jan.	Camellia		Sept.	50	
Jan.	Cineraria	June	Aug.	50	
Jan.	Scarlet plume		July–Aug.	60	Pinch to Sept. 1
Jan.	Gerbera		Aug.–Sept.	55–60	Grow out until Aug.
Jan.	Gardenia	Nov. (cutting)	Sept.	60–65	
Jan.	Iris, Dutch	late Oct.	late Oct.	50	
Jan.	Marigold	Sept. 1	Oct. 15	50–60	

Flowering Date	Flower	Date to Sow or Start Cuttings	Pot, Bench, or Force Date	Growing Temp. F.	Remarks
Jan.	Pansy	July	Oct.	50	Light
Jan.	Sweet pea	Aug.–Sept.	Aug.–Sept.	50	
Feb.	Amaryllis		Oct.	60	
Feb.	Anemone	Sept.	late Sept.	60–70	
Feb.	Astilbe		Nov.	55–60	Cold treat by Nov.
Feb.	Calla lily		Sept.	55	
Feb.	Calceolaria	July 15	Sept.	50–55	Light Nov. 1– Dec. 10
Feb.	Calendula	Sept.	Oct.	45	
Feb.	Camellia		Sept.	50–55	
Feb.	Cineraria	June	Aug.	50	
Feb.	Didiscus	Sept.–Oct.	Nov. 1	50	
Feb.	Feverfew	July	Sept.	50	Light
Feb.	Freesia	Sept.	Sept.	50	
Feb.	Larkspur	Sept.		60	
Feb.	Phlox		Dec.–Jan.	50	Dig, store after frost
Feb.	*Primula malacoides*	Aug.	Oct.	50	
Feb.	Stevia	Mar. (cutting)	Sept.	50	
Feb.	Stock	July	Sept.	50	
Feb.	Sweet pea	Sept.	Sept.	50	
Feb. 14	Azalea		Jan.	60	Hold cool to Jan.
Feb. 14	Begonia	Sept. 15		60	
Feb. 14	Daffodil	Oct.	Jan. 15	60	Store cold to Jan.
Feb. 14	Hyacinth	Oct.	Jan. 1	55–60	Store cold to Jan.
Feb. 14	Tulip	Oct.	Jan. 1–15	55–65	Store cold to Jan.
Feb. 21	Lily-of-the-valley		Feb. 1	65–70	
Mar.	Astilbe		Nov.	55–60	Hold cold to Nov.
Mar.	Anemone	Sept.	late Sept.	50	
Mar.	Aster	Aug.	Oct. 1	50	Light
Mar.	Calla lily		Sept.	55	
Mar.	Calceolaria	July	Sept.	50–55	Light
Mar.	Calendula	Aug.–Sept.	Oct.	50	
Mar.	Camellia		Sept.	50–55	
Mar.	Cineraria	Aug.	Oct.	50–55	
Mar.	Daffodil	Oct. (pot)	Feb.	55–60	Store cold to Feb.
Mar.	Didiscus	Sept.–Oct.	Nov. 1	50	
Mar.	Feverfew	July	Sept.	50	Light
Mar.	Gypsophila	Nov.	Dec. 1	50	Light
Mar.	Hyacinth	Oct. (pot)	Feb.	55–60	Store cold to Feb.
Mar.	Larkspur	Sept.	Nov.	60	
Mar.	Phlox		Dec.–Jan.	50	Dry, store after frost

Flowering Date	Flower	Date to Sow or Start Cuttings	Pot, Bench, or Force Date	Growing Temp. F.	Remarks
Mar.	Primula malacoides	Aug.	Oct.	50	
Mar.	Sweet pea	Oct.	Oct.	50	
Mar.	Tulip	Oct. (pot)	Feb.	55–65	Store cold to Feb.
Apr.	Aster	Dec. 1	Feb. 1	55	Light Dec. 10 to bloom
Apr.	Astilbe		Dec.	55–60	Store cold to Dec.
Apr.	Begonia	Nov. 1		60	
Apr.	Calceolaria	Aug.	Sept.	50	
Apr.	Calendula	Nov. 15–30	Jan. 15	45	
Apr.	Candytuft	Nov. 20		45–50	
Apr.	Centaurea	Dec.	Feb.	55	
Apr.	Cineraria	Sept.–Oct.	Oct.–Nov.	50	6 weeks from shift
Apr.	Clarkia	Jan. 25	Feb.	50	
Apr.	Daffodil	Oct. (pot)	Mar.	65	Store cold to Mar.
Apr.	Didiscus	Sept.	Nov. 15	55	Light
Apr.	Feverfew	Nov.–Dec.	Jan.–Feb.	55	
Apr.	Hydrangea		Jan.	55–70	
Apr.	Larkspur	Nov.	Jan.	55	
Apr.	Lilium candidum		Jan.	55	
Apr.	Lilium giganteum		Dec. 15	60–70	
Apr.	Lilum regale		Jan.	55	
Apr.	Lupine	Aug. 1–15		50	
Apr.	Marigold, French	Feb. 1	late Feb.	60	
Apr.	Primula sinensis	Mar.–Apr.	May	50	
Apr.	Stock	Nov.	Jan.	55	
Apr.	Sweet pea	Jan.	Jan.	55	
Apr.	Tulip	Oct. (pot)	Mar.	65–70	Store cold to Mar.
Apr. 20	Lily-of-the-valley		Apr.	65–70	
May	Aster	Dec. 15	Feb. 1	55	Light Dec. 10 to bloom
May	Calla lily		Sept.	55	
May	Candytuft	Dec. 15	late Jan.	45–50	
May	Clarkia	Dec.	late Jan.	55	
May	Feverfew	Dec.	Feb.	55	
May	Fuchsia	Nov. (cutting)	Dec.	55–60	
May	Geranium	Sept. (cutting)	Sept.	55	
May	Lantana	Sept. (cutting)	Sept.	60	
May	Larkspur	Nov.	Jan.	55	
May	Lilium candidum	Sept. (pot)	Mar. 15–30	55	Cool to Mar.
May	Marigold, African	Jan. 1	late Jan.	55	Disbud

Flowering Date	Flower	Date to Sow or Start Cuttings	Pot, Bench, or Force Date	Growing Temp. F.	Remarks
May	Nemesia	Dec.	late Jan.	55	
May	Salpiglossis	Dec.	Feb.	55	
May	Sweet pea	Jan.	Jan.	55	
May	Zinnia	Apr. 1	mid-Apr.	60	
May 15	Begonia	Dec. 1		60	
May 15	Calceolaria	July–Aug.	Sept.	55	
May 15	Hydrangea		Jan.	55–70	
May 15	Lupine	Jan. 15		50	
May 15	Stock	Dec.	Feb. 1	55	
May 20	Lily-of-the-valley		May 1	65–70	
June	Calla lily		Sept.	55	
June	Candytuft	Dec.	Jan.	55	
June	Feverfew	Dec.	Feb.	55	
June	Lantana	Sept. (cutting)	late Sept.	60	
June	Nemesia	Dec.	Jan.	55	
June	Salpiglossis	Dec.	Feb.	55	
June	Scabiosa	Dec.	Feb.	55	
June	Sweet pea	Feb.	Feb.	55	
June 10	Zinnia	Apr. 15	late Apr.	60	
June 15	Phlox	Mar. (cutting)	Dec. 15	50	
June 15	Stock	Feb.	Apr.	55	
June–July	Aster	Feb. 1	Mar. 10	50–55	(Light Feb. 10 on; use late varieties)
June–July	Aster	late Mar.	**May 15**	50–55	No lights
June–July	Fuchsia	Mar. 1 (cutting)	Apr.	55–60	
June–July	Gypsophila	Apr.	May 15	55	

Appendix B
Approximate (Practical) Conversions to Metric

	Given:	Multiply By:	For:
	inches	2.5	centimeters
Length	feet	30	centimeters
	yards	0.9	meters
	sq. inches	6.5	sq. centimeters
Area	sq. feet	0.1	sq. meters
	acres	0.4	hectares
Weight	ounces	28	grams
	pounds	0.45	kilograms
	fl. ounces	30	milliliters
Volume	pints	0.5	liters
	quarts	0.95 (1)	liters
	gallons	3.8	liters
	teaspoons	5	milliliters
Misc.	tablespoons	15	milliliters
Volumes	cups	0.25	liters
	handfuls (cups)	0.25	liters
	bushels	35	liters
Temperature	Fahrenheit scale	divide by 2 and subtract 16	Celsius scale

Appendix C
Table of Equivalents

DRY VOLUME

1 Bushel is—	32 quarts
	64 pints
1 Quart is—	2 pints
	4 cups
1 Pint is—	2 cups
	30 tablespoons
1 Tablespoon is—	3 teaspoons

DRY WEIGHT

1 Ounce is approximately—	2 tablespoons

LIQUID MEASURE

1 Gallon is—	4 quarts
	8 pints
	16 cups
	128 ounces
1 Quart is—	2 pints
	4 cups
	32 ounces
	64 tablespoons

1 Pint is—

    2 cups
    16 ounces
    32 tablespoons

1 Cup is—

    8 ounces
    16 tablespoons
    48 teaspoons

1 Tablespoon is—

    3 teaspoons
    ½ ounce

Appendix D
About Fertilizers

NITROGEN—needed for vegetative and reproductive growth.
Sources:
Sodium Nitrate—quickest available nitrogen but may cause acidity. Apply 1 oz. to 2 gal. water.
Ammonium Sulfate—most often used source of nitrogen. Especially effective when used with superphosphate. Apply 1 oz. to 2 gal. water.
Urea—an excellent source for nitrogen if used sparingly. Apply 1 oz. to 7 gal. water.
Ammonium Nitrate—a satisfactory source for nitrogen but not often used. Apply 1 oz. to 5 gal. water.

PHOSPHORUS—an essential element involved in all plant functions: cell division and root, flower, tissue growth.
Sources:
Ammonium Phosphate—has a high content of available phosphate, as well as nitrate. Apply 1 oz. to 2 gal. water.
Superphosphate—the most used source of phosphorus. Apply dry, mixed with soil at 2 oz. per bushel.

POTASSIUM—a balancing influence, essential to nitrate changes in the plant; develops roots; adds to general vigor of plant.

Sources:

Potassium Chloride and Potassium Sulfate—both used to supply potassium. Application: when mixed with soil, 1 oz. to a bushel; as liquid, 1 oz. to 2 gal. water.

CALCIUM—corrective for acid soils, and adds sturdiness to plants.

Sources:

Quicklime, hydrated lime, or ground limestone. Application depends upon acidity of soil.

SULFUR—lowers pH of soil.

Sources:

Iron Sulfate—acidifies soil and helps maintain green color in leaves. Use for acid-loving plants. Supplies iron for azaleas, camellias, and gardenias. Apply 1 oz. to 2 gal. water.

Aluminum Sulfate—used to acidify soil and to add blue color to hydrangeas. Use 3 oz. to one gal. water and apply about 5 times during forcing period.

COMPLETE FERTILIZER and BALANCED FERTILIZER

A complete fertilizer is a commercial fertilizer already mixed to supply nitrogen, phosphorus, and potassium—abbreviated N-K-P. It is usually a 20–20–20 (20 percent nitrogen, 20 percent phosphorus, 20 percent potassium)—which is an excellent fertilizer when in doubt about what to use.

A complete fertilizer may also be a balanced fertilizer—made up to a balanced formulation. In general, it is a multiple of a 1–2–1 or 1–3–1 ratio—such as a 5–10–5 or a 15–30–15. One of the finest balanced formulations is 4–12–4, and many trademarked fertilizers offer this percentage of available nitrogen, phosphorus, and potassium.

In addition to the three essential elements, most complete fertilizers also incorporate trace elements such as boron and magnesium.

The application rate for complete and balanced fertilizers is usually given on the package.

WHICH FERTILIZER SHOULD YOU USE?

For most flowers to be forced into bloom, a complete balanced fertilizer such as 4–12–4 should be used. The exceptions are:

Azalea—use ammonium sulfate and iron sulfate once a month; a complete fertilizer twice a year.

Calendula—use superphosphate at planting; ammonium sulfate at three-week intervals.

Chrysanthemum—use superphosphate at planting; alternate ammonium sulfate with 20–20–20 fertilizer every two weeks.

Euphorbia—use superphosphate at planting; later give two feedings of ammonium sulfate.

Geranium—use a 2-inch pot of superphosphate and a 2-inch pot of dry 2–10–10 per bushel at planting.

Gerbera—use superphosphate at planting. Urea weekly during spring. Apply hydrated lime in spring and fall.

Kalanchoe—fertilizer not necessary. Optional at infrequent periods; then use ammonium sulfate or balanced fertilizer.

Poinsettia—use superphosphate at planting. Apply 25–10–10 every two weeks after bracts form.

Rose—use superphosphate at planting. Alternate ammonium sulfate with 10–6–4 fertilizer at three-week intervals.

Snapdragon—use superphosphate at planting. Apply ammonium sulfate every month for second crop.

Yellow calla—ammonium sulfate every two weeks.

Glossary

Some Growers' Terms

Bench. To bench is to move plants to a growing area for final active growth; to plant seedlings or rooted cuttings in their final growing medium; to bring pots in from storage for active growth. Opposite of to hold, or carry. Benching is often carried out on a raised table or "bench" to eliminate the need to bend when you tend to the plants.

    Raised bench. Growing plants off the ground. Also, the bench itself, which is a table with enclosed or built-up sides to hold the growing medium, or to keep the pots from falling off. It resembles a large flat on legs. The opposite of a ground bed.

    Ground bed. Growing plants on the ground. A ground bed usually has boards set around the perimeter so that the soil can be raised slightly higher than the walk next to it. Helps drainage. Opposite of raised bench.

Blind shoot. A branch that grows only leaves and does not grow flowers.

Breaks. Branch buds at the base of leaves. When terminal or tip growth is pinched, these breaks grow into side branches.

255

Carry. To set plants aside but keep them growing until they are needed for forcing, as when carrying a stock plant over summer.

Establish. To allow a seedling or cutting time to get over the shock of transplanting and start growing actively. Getting a plant to start growing actively again after shifting or transplanting.

Fertilizer. Organic or inorganic plant food and soil conditioner. Supplies nitrogen (N), phosphorus (K), potassium (P), and trace elements for plants. Inorganic fertilizers may be used to supply a single element, or be available in complete and balanced mixtures.

> **Balanced fertilizer.** N K P in a 1–2–1- or 1–3–1-ratio formulation, such as 4–12–4 which indicates 4 percent nitrogen, 12 percent phosphorus, and 4 percent potassium in available plant food.

> **Complete fertilizer.** An already mixed, packaged fertilizer marketed under a trade name that may contain a 20–20–20 N K P formulation, the numbers indicating percentage of available nitrogen, phosphorus, and potassium.

> **Dilute Fertilizer.** Fertilizer that is mixed with water or applied to plants at a lower than usual application rate, such as 1 ounce per 5 gallons of water instead of a usual 1 ounce to 2 gallons.

> **Liquid fertilizer.** A fertilizer that is *applied* as a liquid, although it may come packaged as a liquid or powder.

Finishing. The final stages of growing or forcing a plant; bringing the plants into bloom.

Flat. A shallow wooden box without a top. It may be 2 to 6 inches deep and is used to hold soil or a number of small pots to germinate seeds or to grow small plants. A most useful grower's item.

Grow-light. Artificial light, usually fluorescent, in place of or in addition to daylight used to grow plants.

Hold. To restrict active growth. Keeping plants or bulbs at minimum growth or dormant—in cold storage or in a dry condition—until a scheduled time for active growth or forcing.

Jiffy pot. Also called a peat pot. Made of pressed organic material. Used for plants that resent transplanting. The entire pot is planted and, as plant develops, the roots grow through it.

Lift. To dig out a plant from the garden or other growing area.

Light. In forcing plants, light means to supply supplemental light at night—usually with a 60-watt bulb—to keep long-day plants from flowering or to start short-day plants. Illumination may be as low as 10 footcandles.

Misting. A system of spray watering. Water is applied as a fine mist by container or hose. It is also a specialized method used for rooting hard-to-root cuttings—a mist nozzle on a water line keeps a constant spray on the cuttings.

Pinch. To nip off a part of an actively growing branch or plant to cause additional branches to grow.

    Hard pinch. Nipping off the tip and several leaves, usually 3 inches or more.

    Soft pinch. Nipping off only the very tip of the last growth, usually about 1 inch.

Pot bound. The condition in which a plant's root system has completely filled the pot in which it is planted. The roots form a tight, almost solid clump.

Potting. Planting in pots rather than in beds, benches, or flats.

Shade. In forcing plants, a black cloth cover placed over plants to shorten day length or daylight hours; to start a short-day regimen for plants to set buds and flower.

Shading. Also *shade*. In growing plants in a greenhouse or cold frame, a whitewash applied to the glass during the spring and summer in order to cut down the intensity and heat of the sunlight.

Shift. To move a plant from a smaller pot to a larger pot.

Transplanting. Moving a plant, seedling, or cutting from one growing medium or area to another. It covers a broader scope than shifting, benching, potting, and lifting.

Index

259